SECOND-LANGUAGE ACQUISITION IN CHILDHOOD

Second-Language Acquisition in Childhood

BARRY McLAUGHLIN
Adlai Stevenson College
University of California, Santa Cruz

 LAWRENCE ERLBAUM ASSOCIATES, PUBLISHERS
1978   Hillsdale, New Jersey

DISTRIBUTED BY THE HALSTED PRESS DIVISION OF

JOHN WILEY & SONS

New York   Toronto   London   Sydney

Lawrence Erlbaum Associates, Inc., Publishers
62 Maria Drive
Hillsdale, New Jersey 07642

Distributed solely by Halsted Press Division
John Wiley & Sons, Inc., New York

ISBN 0-470-26309-1

Library of Congress Catalog Number: 78-52304

Printed in the United States of America

To Quinn and Christopher,
who provided the inspiration for this book.

Contents

Preface

This book is a comprehensive treatment of the literature on second language acquisition in childhood. There is increasing interest in this area and a number of collections of readings have appeared, dealing with various aspects of the topic. There is, however, no general overview of the field for the interested professional reader. The present book is intended to fill this gap.

Like many people, I became interested in how children acquire a second language through my own children. We lived in Germany for three years when our children were very young, and I was impressed with how they could make sense out of English and German and could produce the two languages in their speech. I began to read the professional literature on bilingualism and second-language acquisition and was struck by the sense of excitement that permeated the field. It seemed to me that the excitement that marked research on first-language acquisition in the 1960s had spread to the field of second-language acquisition. There were important breakthroughs on a number of fronts. New and stimulating ideas were providing researchers with a wide range of hypotheses for empirical scrutiny. Moreover, I found some surprises in the older literature. The problem was that the literature, old and new, was relatively inaccessible to the non-specialist. There was a definite need to make the findings available to educators, psychologists, and psycholinguists.

My first attempt in this direction was an article that appeared in the *Psychological Bulletin* (McLaughlin, 1977) in which I itemized some misconceptions about second-language acquisition that have been perpetuated in popular (and sometimes professional) literature. A more detailed treatment of these issues is presented here. In addition, this book provides a fuller discussion of the literature on second-language acquisition and examines bilingual education and second-language learning programs.

I have attempted in this book to view second-language acquisition in terms of contemporary models of language acquisition. Gone are the behavioristic models of yesterday, and slowly departing from the scene are models based on formal linguistic theory. Psycholinguists today want to account both for what the child acquiring a language *can* do and what the child *does* do. For this reason there is increasing attention given to the development of process models of language. In Chapter 2 I discuss these models and throughout the book I view language acquisition, at least in general terms, from this perspective.

Chapter 3 compares second-language acquisition in children and adults and discusses the critical period notion. Many of the issues treated in my review article are elaborated here. Chapters 4 and 5 are concerned with simultaneous and successive acquisition of a second language. I attempt in these chapters to summarize what is known about the developmental processes involved in simultaneous and successive second-language acquisition, to examine the effect of interference between languages, and to discuss the topic of code switching—or how the bilingual alternates languages.

Chapter 6 deals with second-language programs for children in this country and Canada. No attempt is made to provide an exhaustive survey of the various programs; rather, the issues that confront all programs are discussed and some important recent research is examined. Chapter 7 focuses on the effects of bilingualism and on research dealing with cognitive processes in bilingual individuals. In the final chapter I spell out the limits of our knowledge in the area of second-language acquisition and draw some tentative conclusions suggested by research.

The number of empirical studies on second-language acquisition in children is increasing exponentially. There is so much activity in the field at present that it is difficult to keep abreast of the literature, and I apologize for possible oversights. The research boom has also made the picture less clear than one might desire. This is becoming increasingly the case, and the conclusions reached in Chapter 8 might not long survive the empirical onslaught. The field has swung from extreme to extreme—the truth is no doubt somewhere in between.

I am indebted to the Alexander von Humboldt Foundation for the financial support that made writing this book possible. Dr. Suitbert Ertel of the Institut für Psychologie, Göttingen, provided encouragement and research facilities. John Lamendella made me aware of the importance of distinguishing language acquisition from language learning. Above all, I wish to thank my wife, Sigrid, for translating numerous articles and for critically reading the entire manuscript.

B. Mc Laughlin

ACKNOWLEDGMENTS

The preparation of this book has been aided by the cooperation of a number of sources. The figures and tables used have been made available through the courtesy and permission of their original authors and publishers and are listed below in order of appearance.

For Table 1.1:
    From Macnamara, J. The bilingual's linguistic performance: A psychological overview. *Journal of Social Issues,* 1967, *23,* 58–77, page 59, Figure 1. (Copyright 1967 by the Society for the Psychological Study of Social Issues. Reprinted by permission of author and the Society for the Psychological Study of Social Issues.)

For Table 1.2:
    From Swanson, M. M. Bilingual education: The national perspective. In G. A. Jarvis (Ed.), *Responding to new realities.* Skokie, Ill.: National Textbook Co., 1974, page 82, Table 2. (Reprinted by permission of the author and Dr. Albar Pena, Bilingual Education Department, University of Texas.)

For Figure 3.1:
    From Fromkin, V., Krashen, S., Curtiss, S., Rigler, D., & Rigler, M. The development of language in Genie: A case of language acquisition beyond the critical period. *Brain and Language,* 1974, *1,* 81–107, p. 99, Figure 1. (Copyright 1974 by Academic Press. Reprinted by permission of V. Fromkin and the Academic Press.)

For Table 4.3:
    From Clark, E. V. What's in a word? On the child's acquisition of semantics in his first language. In T. E. Moore (Ed.), *Cognitive development and the acquisition of language.* New York: Academic Press, 1973, p. 87, Table 9. (Copyright 1973 by Academic Press. Reprinted by permission of the author and the Academic Press.)

For Table 5.1:
    From Milon, J. P. The development of negation in English by a second language learner. *TESOL*

Quarterly, 1974, *8*, 137–143, p. 140, Table 4. (Copyright 1974 by Teachers of English to Speakers of Other Languages, Washington, D.C. Reprinted by permission of the author and publisher.)

For Table 5.2:
From Ervin–Tripp, S. Is second language learning like the first? *TESOL Quarterly*, 1974, *8*, 111–127, p. 119, Table 2. (Copyright 1974 by Teachers of English to Speakers of Other Languages, Washington, D.C. Reprinted by permission of the author and publisher.)

For Table 5.4:
From Ervin–Tripp, S. Is second language learning like the first? *TESOL Quarterly*, 1974, *8*, 111–127, p. 116, Table 1. (Copyright 1974 by Teachers of English to Speakers of Other Languages, Washington, D.C. Reprinted by permission of the author and publisher.)

For Table 5.6:
From Dulay, H. C., & Burt, M. K. Goofing: An indication of children's second language learning strategies. *Language Learning*, 1972, *22*, 235–252, pp. 245–246, Tables 1–4. (Copyright 1972 by *Language Learning*. Reprinted by permission of H. Douglas Brown, Editor, *Language Learning*.)

For Table 7.1:
From Ianco–Worrall, A. D. Bilingualism and cognitive development. *Child Development*, 1972, *43*, 1390–1400, p. 1395, Table 1. (Copyright 1972 by the Society for Research in Child Development, Inc. Reprinted by permission of the author and University of Chicago Press.)

For Table 7.2:
From Macnamara, J., & Kushnir, S. L. Linguistic independence of bilinguals: The input switch. *Journal of Verbal Learning and Verbal Behavior*, 1971, *10*, 480–487, p. 483, Table 1. (Copyright 1971 by Academic Press. Reprinted by permission of the publisher and John Macnamara.)

For Table 7.3:
From Lambert, W. E., Ignatow, M., & Krauthammer, M. Bilingual organization in free recall. *Journal of Verbal Learning and Verbal Behavior*, 1968, *7*, 207–214, p. 210, Table 1. (Copyright 1968 by Academic Press. Reprinted by permission of the publisher and W. E. Lambert.)

SECOND-LANGUAGE ACQUISITION IN CHILDHOOD

1

Bilingualism in Society

INTRODUCTION

For most people of the world, linguistic diversity is the norm—not the exception. There are many more people in the world who are bilingual than are monolingual. This is sometimes difficult for Americans to appreciate. We have become accustomed to the notion that the world is becoming more homogeneous, that there is a linguistic convergence, with English gradually becoming the universal language. It is no doubt true that English is used widely as a medium of communication in scientific and technical domains, but this does not mean that English is replacing indigenous languages. If anything, the spread of English as a universal technical language is one reason why an increasing number of people in the world are bi- or multilingual. English (or French or Russian) may be learned as an international language, but national and ethnic languages are maintained in communicating with one's countrymen.

A similar phenomenon seems to occur on the national level. It often happens that central governments attempt to enforce national homogeneity by the imposition of a standard national language. The result is usually an increase in bilingualism, with large segments of the population speaking both the standard tongue and the local language or dialect. When the government attempts to do away with local languages and dialects, it meets with resistance and an upsurge of ethnic feelings on the part of the people affected.

Even in the United States, there is resistance to the imposition of a single standard language. Various ethnic groups strive to maintain their identity by raising their children bilingually. Many American children hear Japanese, Spanish, Italian, or French in the home and, occasionally, in the school as well. The attempt to have urban black children taught in "Black English" is, among other things, an effort by a minority to maintain its identity by linguistic means.

1

Bilingualism as a Social Problem

Bilingualism is a social problem precisely because language is so intimately a part of one's identity. The distrust shown by many people and governments toward bilingual individuals stems largely from the feeling that they are not loyal citizens because they can speak another language. Their loyalties are in question because they hold dual linguistic (and cultural) allegiance. The Basques in Spain and the Ukrainians in the Soviet Union are examples of people who have suffered for this reason.

In spite of the efforts of governments and the distrust of their fellow citizens, there seems to be an increase in feelings of ethnic identity, especially among linguistic minorities in Europe. The Scots, the Bretons, the Basques, and the Catalans, among others, have been striving for increasing autonomy and for the bilingual education of their children. For the most part, these efforts have been resisted by the central government, but this resistance often has served to stimulate ethnic feelings.

The more activist ethnic groups are but a small fraction of the total number of multiethnic and multilinguistic communities in Europe: the Catalans, Basques, and Galicians in Spain; the Bretons and Provençals in France; the Welsh, Scots, and Irish in Great Britain; the Flemings and Walloons in Belgium; the Valoise, Piedmontese, and Germans in Italy; the Frisians in Holland; the Italians, Hungarians, Slovenes, Croatians, Albanians, and Macedonians in Yugoslavia; the Laps in Scandinavia; the Germans, Poles, and Slovaks in Czechoslovakia; the Finns, Estonians, Latvians, Lithuanians, and Ukrainians in the Soviet Union, and so forth. This same linguistic diversity is represented even more dramatically in countries of Africa, Latin America, and Asia. India, for example, has 13 major languages aside from Hindi and a large number of minor languages. Even in the Arab countries, which share a common language, classical Arabic coexists with the vernacular variety spoken by the people of Egypt, Syria, or Iraq (Macnamara, 1967a).

In many countries where two or more languages or dialects are spoken, a second language is necessary to serve as a common medium of communication or instruction. Examples include Russian in the Soviet Union, English or French in many countries of Africa, Bahasa Indonesian in Indonesia, and Pilipino in the Philippines. In some cases, a national language is established from one that has not been spoken for centuries or only by a small group; for example, Hebrew in Israel or Swahili in Tanzania. Some countries have two or more official languages—for example, Canada, Switzerland, Finland, Wales, Belgium, and Sri Lanka.

In the United States monolingualism traditionally has been the norm. Bilingualism was regarded as a social stigma and a liability (Fishman, 1966). Immigrant parents—like American Indians (Casagrande, 1948)—sometimes have attempted to raise their children in English rather than in their native tongue, so that the children would become assimilated into the larger social context as soon as possible. Bilinguals did not fit into the American scene because they were carrying extra linguistic baggage. This made them seem foreign and hence suspect.

Although such ethnic groups as Mexican–Americans and Indians currently are attempting to maintain their native languages as part of their cultural identity, it is difficult for the individual to belong to two communities at once. There are often cultural, religious, and moral differences that lead to strain and identity conflict. To be accepted in two communities means having to shift back and forth in language, behavior, and attitudes. This can be an enormous burden for the individual and can drain one emotionally (Ulibarri, 1972). Bilinguals usually opt for one of their two worlds and risk being rejected in the other (Child, 1943).

The same is often true of bilinguals in other societies. The language minority may be looked down upon by the "standard" majority. There may be stereotyping and even hostility. Bilinguals may find that they are disadvantaged economically when compared to their monolingual counterparts. Even in countries where linguistic diversity is officially tolerated, there may be subtle (or not so subtle) forms of discrimination exercised against members of linguistic minorities.

This hostility toward bilingualism has nothing to do with language as such. The hostility is directed not at language but at culture. The bilingual represents an alien way of thinking and alien values. Often, too, the bilingual is a member of a minority group whose interests threaten the economic interests of the majority. Language becomes a convenient way of separating "them" and "us." But language itself is not the critical factor.

What matters are the attitudes of members of the minority and majority communities. When the attitudes are favorable and relations are friendly, bilingualism need not have negative consequences for the individual or for a group. Some countries, such as Switzerland, seem to have achieved a remarkable degree of harmony between people speaking different languages. In America, on the other hand, the experience of assimilating waves of immigrants led to negative attitudes toward those who speak with an accent. The official school doctrine has been that language diversity is undesirable (Kobrick, 1972). The school has been the means of separating immigrant children from their cultural past and of assimilating them into the dominant culture. This view of the school's purpose seems to be changing, however, at least on the official level. Minority group demands for recognition of their cultural values and the passage in 1967 of the Bilingual Education Act, Title VII of the Elementary and Secondary Education Act, have led to an increasing number of bilingual education programs, especially at the kindergarten and early elementary levels.

It remains to be seen whether such programs will succeed in changing the attitudes of the American people. In the public mind, English is the language of technology and industrial progress; bilingualism is associated with the culture of poverty and academic failure. If, however, bilingual education programs give Indians, Mexican–Americans, Puerto Ricans, and other groups a sense of their historical and cultural roots, these minority group cultures may make a compensatory rehumanizing contribution to our industrial mass culture (Christian & Sharp, 1972).

We are, however, a long way from realizing these objectives. There is still a strong residue of xenophobia and isolationism in this country. Prejudice against the foreign and the alien is still widespread. This need not mean the consequences for the bilingual individual are necessarily negative. As we shall see subsequently, general statements about the effect of bilingualism on the individual are difficult to support empirically. There are important social and individual difference variables. The experience of a poor Chicano who acquires English as a second language is different from that of an upper-class white child who learns French or German in a kindergarten where these languages are spoken. The child's own sense of self-identity and confidence also play an important part in determining the effect of bilingualism on development. These social and individual differences make predictions impossible. One person may suffer throughout life because of a feeling of anomie and a sense of not belonging (Zedlitz, 1963); another may experience no such feelings and may view bilingualism as an asset to personal adjustment and intellectual development (Elwert, 1960).

Bilingualism as a Psycholinguistic Problem

In the past 10 years considerable attention has been given to the question of how language develops. Progress has been made in tracing the stages through which children pass in their language development (Brown, 1973a) and in identifying those processes that operate in the child's language acquisition system (Ervin–Tripp, 1970). Careful observation of children learning to talk has revealed certain sets of semantic relations that are reflected in early one- and two-word utterances (Bloom, 1973; Bowerman, 1973; Brown, 1973a). Some insights have been acquired about how children learn relational concepts and concepts of space and time (E. Clark, 1973; H. Clark, 1970, 1973).

Yet there remains a great deal that is not known about language development in children. In part, this is because it is so difficult to study children. One cannot analyze a child's speech in the way a linguist analyzes an adult's. The linguist can ask adults why they use certain forms and whether specific forms are correct or incorrect. With a child, this is impossible. Furthermore, a child's language is developing and does not remain constant; the child's grammar is continually changing.

The best that can be done is either to observe the child's speech or attempt in various ways to test experimentally the child's use of language. The first technique has been the most widely employed and shall be referred to here as the *case–study method*. Most of the important recent findings about children's language development have come through the use of this method. Investigators have spent many hours with a few children, recording carefully their utterances over an extended period of time. In this way information has been gained about the stages through which children progress in phonological, syntactic, and semantic development. There are difficulties with such observational procedures: observers may see only what they want to see and may tend to record data consistent with their hypothesis more readily than data opposed to it. There is also the problem of interpreting the child's meaning, especially in early utterances. When a child says *Milk,* for example, does that mean that the child wants milk, or that an object seen is white like milk, or that milk is in a bottle, or that the child is hungry, or what? The context helps, but one is never entirely sure that one's interpretation is correct. This becomes a critical issue in attempting to infer knowledge of semantic relations in young children on the basis of their utterances (Brown, 1973a).

Because of the danger of observational bias inherent in the case–study method, this approach has been complemented by the *experimental method.* Of course, it is not easy to conduct experiments on language with children, expecially if they are young. They lack the attentiveness and the ability to concentrate on the task that are the prerequisites of good experimental subjects. Nonetheless, ingenious investigators have succeeded in devising experimental procedures that can be used with young children. For example, Shipley, Smith, and Gleitman (1969) tested the spontaneous responses of children in the one- and two-word stages of language development by giving them commands that varied in structure. They found that children past the one-word stage responded appropriately more often when the command was formulated in adult form (*Throw me the ball*) than when the command was formulated in the form that more closely corresponded to the one the child himself used (*Throw ball*). Starr (1974) tested young children's listening preferences for syntactic and nonsyntactic sentences by means of an apparatus with two levers that the child could pull to activate a tape recorder that played either grammatical or ungrammatical sentences. She found that children from 18 to 30 months could discriminate the grammatical from the nongrammatical sentences. deVilliers and deVilliers (1972) used a procedure that required young children to take the role of a puppet they had seen correcting the utterances of another puppet who sometimes spoke correctly with respect to word order (*Fill the cup*) and sometimes incorrectly (*Cup the fill*). Only children who were quite advanced in their language development were able to make judgments of appropriate word order correctly. A final example of a technique successfully employed with young children is the elicited imitation technique (Slobin & Welsh, 1973). Here the child's task is simply to repeat sentences or strings of words uttered by a model. The technique is especially appropriate for assessing the child's syntactic ability.

For the most part, studies of bilingualism in children have used the case–study method. They suffer, consequently, from the difficulties of all case studies: lack of adequate control, selective sampling procedures, lack of measurement reliability, and observer bias. In addition, many of the early studies tended to be descriptive, almost anecdotal. More recent studies, however, have focused on particular issues of current psycholinguistic concern. There also have been a few experimental studies with bilingual children in recent years. Nonetheless, a great deal remains to be learned about bilingualism in children and about the process of second-language learning in the preschool and early school years.

Here are a few of the questions about bilingualism and second-language learning in children that concern psychologists and educators (Carroll, 1969):

- Should two languages be introduced simultaneously or is it better to establish one first?
- Does a child make better progress through informal contact with children and adults who speak a second language or is formal instruction necessary?
- Is it good to use a second language as a medium of school instruction in topics other than the second language itself?
- Does learning a second language make learning a third language easier?
- Does learning a second language interfere with progress in the first language?
- Is it good to introduce written language from the beginning of instruction in a second language?
- What is the nature of the mistakes made in second-language acquisition?
- What are the comparative roles of imitation and creative usage in instruction?
- Is it better to give children controlled amounts of exposure to a second language or should the immersion ("language bath") technique be used?

From a specifically psycholinguistic point of view, there are at least three critical issues of interest in the study of bilingualism in children. The first of these concerns the *developmental sequence* followed by the child simultaneously acquiring two languages or acquiring a second language once a first language has been established. Does the bilingual child follow the same developmental sequence in acquiring two languages as the monolingual child does? What happens if the developmental sequence for the two languages is not the same? Does the child acquiring a second language once the first has been established progress through the same stages of development as a native speaker of that language? Or does the child recapitulate the stages of her own first language when learning a second language? Or is language development completely different in such cases?

A second issue concerns *interference between languages*. What effect does acquiring two languages simultaneously have on the acquisition of each? Are bilingual children retarded in their language development when compared to monolingual children? What types of mistakes appear in the utterances of children acquiring a second language? What is the evidence for phonological, syntactic, and semantic interference in the speech of children who experience a bilingual presentation or who acquire a second language subsequent to the establishment of their first language?

The third issue concerns *code switching*. Here I refer to the child's ability to move from one linguistic code or language to another. The term also is used to refer to types of speech within a single language: formal versus informal codes, intimate versus public codes, colloquial and vulgar codes. Are special processes involved in the bilingual's ability to switch codes? Under what conditions is code switching difficult? What determines the code to be used in specific situations?

What Is Bilingualism?

At this point it is probably a good idea to attempt to tighten up some concepts bandied about until now. First of all, there is the question of what is meant by *bilingualism*. What degree of proficiency must a person possess in two languages to be considered a bilingual? The answer, of course, depends in part on the age of the individual. A bilingual adult is expected to possess a greater facility with two languages than a bilingual child. But suppose an adult has simply a reading knowledge of a second language. Is this person bilingual?

Some authors regard a person as bilingual who knows some words in another language (whether the individual can say the words or not). At the other extreme is the definition of bilingualism that equates it with native-like control of two languages (Bloomfield, 1935). This, however, begs the question of what is meant by native-like and seems to set too high a standard. The appropriate degree of knowledge of two languages seems to lie somewhere between the criterion set by the maximists and that of the minimists. The easiest way out is probably to lean toward the minimist side and allow the label of *bilingual* to be attached to anyone who possesses a mere smattering of knowledge of a second language in whatever medium. Macnamara (1967a), for example, regarded as a bilingual anyone who possessed, even to a minimal degree, at least one of the language skills listed in the matrix in Table 1.1. Any attempt to set a more definite criterion seems arbitrary.

Nonetheless, throughout this book, *bilingualism* refers to the ability "to produce complete and meaningful utterances in the other language [Haugen, 1956, p. 6]." Arbitrary and unspecific as such a definition is, it does not allow the term *bilingual* to be applied to an individual who knows merely one or two words of a second language. In fact, there is no particular advantage to setting arbitrary limits for a definition of bilingualism, since what matters is the extent of the individual's knowledge of the two languages (Jakobovits, 1970).

It often happens that a child's two languages are limited to different situations. One language may be used with playmates and another with parents. The child may use one in school and a different language at home. As a result, the child may become more fluent in certain areas in one language than in another. It is

TABLE 1.1
Matrix of Language Skills[a]

Encoding		Decoding	
Speaking	Writing	Listening	Reading
Semantics	Semantics	Semantics	Semantics
Syntactics	Syntactics	Syntactics	Syntactics
Lexicon	Lexicon	Lexicon	Lexicon
Phonemes	Graphemes	Phonemes	Graphemes

[a] From Macnamara (1967b).

usually fairly difficult for the child to maintain linguistic *balance*—to attain the same level of fluency in all spheres in both languages.

Some authors have distinguished between different types of bilingualism. The most common distinction is that between *compound* and *coordinate* bilingualism (Ervin & Osgood, 1954; Haugen, 1956; Weinreich, 1953). The distinction refers essentially to the semantic aspect of language. Compound bilinguals are defined as those who attribute identical meanings to corresponding words and expressions in their two languages. This fusion of meaning is thought to result from learning a foreign language through vocabulary training in a school situation (i.e., in terms of meanings established by one's first language) or from acquiring two languages in a home where both are spoken interchangeably by the same people and in the same situations. Coordinate bilinguals are defined as those who derive different or partially different meanings from words in the two languages. The distinction in meaning is thought to arise from learning the two languages in different situations where the languages are rarely interchanged. In spite of the existence of at least 27 tests for measuring compound versus coordinate bilingualism (Jakobovits, 1970), the distinction has not been validated experimentally and is difficult to maintain in practice (Diller, 1970; Kirstein & de Vincenz, 1974). Hence I avoid speaking of bilingualism in these terms.

Nor are cases of *diglossia* treated here, either in Ferguson's (1959) original sense of separate language codes (standard and vernacular) that serve different functions within a single society, or in the sense in which the term is used by other authors (Fishman, 1964, 1970; Gumperz, 1962) to refer to separate dialects, registers, or functionally differentiated language varieties of whatever kind. Although admittedly the distinction between language and dialect is often blurred, I use language in this book to refer to standard language types such as standard English, Spanish, French, and so forth.

The use of the terms *native tongue, mother tongue, foreign language,* and *primary language* are avoided. Instead I speak of *first and second languages*. By first language is meant that language which is chronologically first, even though it may belong to a brief stage of the child's development and subsequently may be forgotten and never used. Thus it can happen that a second language—one that is acquired after a first language—becomes the individual's main and even only language in daily discourse. Although there are drawbacks to the chronological distinction between first and second languages (Halliday, McIntosh, & Strevens, 1964), it seems better to differentiate on this basis rather than on the basis of facility in a language (Lado, 1964), since facility may change with time or place.

Strictly speaking, one cannot use the terms *first* and *second languages* in the case of a child who is exposed from birth to bilingual language presentation. In such cases I speak of *bilingual children* and avoid the distinction between first and second languages. Thus children who hear one language from their mother and another from their father or one language from their parents and another from their nurse or playmates and who acquire both languages to the extent that they speak both are referred to simply as bilingual children. Acquisition of the two languages in such cases is *simultaneous*.

A different situation occurs when one language is established first and a second is learned subsequently. Here the first language–second language distinction is valid, and learning can be said to be *successive*. The question arises, however, of deciding when a first language can be said to be "established." For the present purposes, I arbitrarily set the cutoff point at 3 years. The child who is introduced to a second language before 3 years of age is said to be *simultaneously* acquiring two languages. The child who is introduced to a second language after 3 is said to be *successively* acquiring two languages.

A final distinction is necessary between *second-language acquisition* and *second-language learning*. Second-language acquisition refers to the acquisition of a second language in the natural environment, without formal instructions. Second-language learning, on the other hand, implies a formal learning situation with feedback, error correction, rule learning, and an artificial linguistic environment that introduces one aspect of the grammar at a time. Note, however, that adults can "acquire" a language in the sense of being exposed to it in an untutored way; similarly, children can be given formal instructions in a second language. Thus the distinction does not have to do with the age of the individual but with the nature of the experience with the language. Many people have both types of experience—they can be said to be "acquiring" the language through daily contact with native speakers and "learning" a language through formal instructions. While this book focuses on second-language acquisition in childhood, the remainder of this chapter and Chapter 6 deal with second-language learning.

Historical Overview of Second-Language Learning

The teaching of a second language has been part of the curriculum in many forms of educational institutions for centuries. As early as the 3rd millennium B.C., in what was probably the world's first great civilization, the Sumerians had scribes devoted exclusively to education. When the country was conquered by the Akkadians in the last quarter of the 3rd millenium, these scribes compiled the oldest known bilingual dictionaries. To teach their new lords the Sumerian language, they provided lists of Akkadian words with Sumerian translations. Long continuous passages were translated from Sumerian into Akkadian, line by line. Emphasis appears to have been on sense and not on achieving a strict literal translation (Kramer, 1963). Less is known about the methods used in the royal schools of Babylon and Assyria, although they must have been fairly effective, since students were expected to be proficient in several languages after 3 years (Lewis, 1974).

Like the Akkadians, the Egyptians had scribes who taught them the languages of their conquered subjects. As early as the 18th dynasty (1500 B. C.) multilingual tablets existed. Although little is known about how languages were taught, there is considerable evidence that Egyptian scribes in the Middle and New Kingdoms were familiar with the languages of other countries. In the Ptolemaic period, the upper classes in Egypt received their education in Greek. Similarly, in Asia Minor, the majority of people in Hellenistic times who could read or write could do so only in Greek, their second language. Greek was also used widely among the Jews in Egypt and Asia. Jewish scholars were the first to develop comparative linguistics through the study of Semitic and non-Semitic languages.

Classic, medieval, and renaissance periods.   In the Roman Empire, Hellenistic models of speech and culture were widely adopted. Most well-educated Romans were able to speak Greek, and even the less educated understood enough Greek to cope with Greek phrases and expressions in the works of such popular playwrights as Plautus. Children were educated bilingually, often by Greeks who had come to Rome and served as tutors or opened bilingual schools. Children usually had heard Greek in infancy from a Greek nurse or slave. In the school, pupils followed the parallel courses of study of the Greek *Grammaticos* and the Latin *Ludi Magister*. Later they were tutored by a Greek *rhetor* and by a Latin *orator*.

The Greek language was introduced before children had any formal instruction in their first language, indeed before they had any marked control of Latin. By the time children started formal instructions, they were bilingual in both languages, although some children spoke Latin with a Greek accent. This led to occasional patriotic outcries against the emphasis on Greek in the education of Roman children. Moreover, there was some fear that two languages were too great a burden for many children. Nonetheless, as late as the 4th century A.D. bilingual education was an important part of the curriculum of Roman children, even children of the middle class such as Augustine (Lewis, 1974).

At the beginning of the 3rd century A.D., the Romans developed bilingual manuals called *Hermeneumata Pseudodositheans,* comparable to modern conversational handbooks. They contained a Greek–Latin vocabulary and a series of simple texts of a narrative or conversational character. The narrative consisted of some of Aesop's fables, an elementary book on mythology, or an account of the Trojan War. The conversational material consisted of dialogues in Greek such as the following:

> The *paterfamilias* moves toward his friend and says:
>   "Good morning, Caius," and he embraces him. The latter returns the greeting and says:
>   "Nice to meet you. Would you like to come along?"
>   "Where?"
>   "To see our friend Lucius. We are going to pay him a visit."
>   "What is the matter with him?"
>   "He is sick."
>   "Since when?"
>   "Since a few days ago."
>   "Where does he live?"
>   "Not far from here. If you like we can go there [cited in Titone, 1968]."

As one can see from this example, the attempt was made in the conversation to introduce grammatical features systematically.

In Medieval Europe, Latin was the international language of communication and culture. It was a living language and was taught orally and through reading and composition (Titone, 1968). Every educated man was bilingual, having studied Latin from the time he was a young child. This tradition persisted until well into the Renaissance period. After the Reformation, however, Latin was no longer a living language in large parts of Europe.

Toward the end of the Renaissance, emphasis began to shift from the learning of language as a practical tool to the learning of language as a means to an end—that of developing the mind. Latin and Greek were taught because it was thought that the study of grammar was good mental discipline. Since these languages were not living languages, little attention was given to oral communication. Texts were read and translated, and this—together with the study of grammar—became the essence of language training.

In spite of this trend, some textbooks used during the Renaissance period were surprisingly modern in their approach. They encouraged extensive oral practice on the basis of conversation; the first language of the student was to be avoided, and all instruction was to be given in the target language; grammatical forms were to be assimilated through practice in conversation (Titone, 1968). Such texts, however, were relatively rare exceptions to the general rule.

The 19th century. By the 19th century, grammaticalism predominated. Languages were taught via the systematic learning of paradigms, tables, declensions, and conjugations. Modern languages were taught as Latin and Greek were taught—as dead languages whose rules of morphology and syntax were to be memorized. Oral work was reduced to a minimum and conversational drills were abandoned. Students spent their time translating written texts line by line. This tradition continued to prevail in many schools until the middle of the present century.

There were some dissenting voices, however. The American educator, George Ticknor (1833), emphasized the need to learn a language by speaking it, if possible in the country where it is spoken. He argued that no one method was suitable for all learners and that the language teacher must adapt methods to individual needs. Nor should individuals of different ages be taught a language in the same way. The oral approach and the inductive teaching of grammar were more suitable for younger learners, whereas older students generally prefer to learn by analysis of the particular from generals.

Other authors advocated a natural method as opposed to grammar-centered procedures. Heness, Marcel, Sauveur, and Gouin all de-emphasized composition and translation and stressed oral exercises in the target language (Titone, 1968). Gouin encouraged teachers to dramatize sentences in a series of exercises based on actual classroom situations. For him, association, mimicry, and memorization were the pivotal activities of language learning. The text for written and reading exercises was anchored in real-life situations rather than made up of fragments of speech taken out of living context.

The natural method was christened the *direct method* at the end of the 19th century. Its primary advocate in the first half of the 20th century was Maximilian Berlitz, whose schools now exist in all parts of the world. Berlitz argued that the learner must be taught as quickly as possible to think in the second language and for that purpose must use that language constantly without reverting to the first language. Exclusive stress is placed on the oral aspect of the language. Teachers must be native speakers, and classes are small (never more than 10 pupils) so that instruction is as individualized as possible. No grammatical rules are taught; instead, grammar is conveyed to the student by example and by visual demonstration. Reading and writing are skills that one acquires only after the spoken language has been mastered.

Other advocates of the direct method took a similar point of view. The pupil should be "steeped in" the target language and should learn grammar inductively (Jespersen, 1947). Listening, practice, and repetition are the means by which children learn their first language, and these processes should be employed in second-language learning as well (Palmer, 1940). Linguistic principles, especially phonetics, were emphasized in an effort to assure that the speaker's oral pronunciation approximated as closely as possible that of native speakers in the target language.

Recurrent problems.   The reformers of the 19th century and those classic writers concerned with language instruction repeatedly confronted a number of issues that are central to any discussion of second-language learning today (Lewis, 1974). Quintilian and Cicero both expressed concern that the emphasis placed on Greek in the education of young Romans would interfere with their development in the Latin language. The same question of interference between languages appeared again in the writings of Comenius in the 17th century, and he proposed that systematic study be undertaken of the way in which particular languages differ—what today is known as contrastive analysis. The concern for contrasts between languages appeared also in the writings of Henry Sweet (1899), one of the 19th century advocates of the direct method. Sweet felt that effective language teaching required the identification of the similarities and differences between the first and second language so as to foresee and eliminate problems of interference.

The debate over the pedagogic advantages of the oral method has a long history. The classic writers assumed that one should learn to speak the language before reading or writing it, and even in the 17th to 19th centuries such authors as Montaigne, Locke, and Wilhelm Vietor insisted that the spoken, not the written, language be the basis of instruction. Vietor (1905) argued that it is through the ear that the child learns a first language and that it is through the ear that a more mature person must begin the study of a second language. Locke suggested that the best way to instruct a child in Latin was to have a person close to the child who spoke and read nothing else.

There seems to have been general agreement throughout Western history that two languages can and should be taught to children. Some Romans, as we have seen, felt that the acquisition of two languages simultaneously was an intellectual burden for their children and interfered with satisfactory instruction. Nonetheless, bilingual education continued until the decline of the Empire. In the Medieval and Renaissance periods children learned Latin as a second language, although their instruction usually began after their first language was established. The practice of introducing a second language in the schools, once the first language was established, seems to have resulted from practical considerations rather than from any belief that younger children were incapable of learning a second language.

The controversy between cognitive and associationist models of language acquisition goes back to the Middle Ages (Lewis, 1974). Comenius stressed the primacy of the senses in his writings: *"Nihil est in intellectu, quin prius fuerit in sensu"*—"Nothing is a concept of the intellect unless it first has been a sensory percept." Children should be taught by concrete examples and not by the abstract rules of grammar. Locke believed that grammar should be taught only to a person who could already speak the language. He argued that a person who knows a language well does not rely on rules but on memory and on the habit of speaking the language properly. In contrast to the empiricist position, the mentalists believed that it is through the operation of the central processes that languages are acquired. Reliance on habit and association was contrary to the course of nature, and—as William Brooke put it—learning a language in this way "will be long adoeing [cited in Lewis, 1974]." Contemporary empiricists and mentalists continue this debate, although in somewhat different terms, as we shall see in Chapter 6.

Contemporary Approaches to Second-Language Learning

There is no general agreement on the best way to teach languages. Some educators favor contrastive analysis as a means of predicting a learner's difficulties and pattern drills to establish correct habits. A number of Chomsky's followers have advocated transformation exercises, in spite of Chomsky's (1968) own admonition that the insights of linguistics have little practical bearing on language instruction. Other educators use various modifications of the direct method—some favoring total immersion and others a more gradual approach.

In his review of second-language training in primary education Stern (1967) reported that a survey of 45 countries showed that in 32 lands, a second language was part of the primary school education of children younger than 10. In 7 more countries, second-language training is part of the education of older children, and in only 6 countries did there seem to be no second-language training within the primary school system. In 21 countries second-language instruction begins at the age of 7 or younger.

In many countries of Africa and Asia second languages are the language of instruction in schools. This may be a residue of the colonial experience or may simply arise out of necessity in a country with a large number of different languages. Often the vernacular is taught in the primary school with English or French introduced as a second language. A practical issue of some import in such situations is the question of whether it is better to wait until the child can read and write in the first language before introducing the second, or whether the second should be introduced as soon as possible.

Europe.   Williams (1962) has pointed out that only 6 of the more than 3,000 languages of the world are spoken by more than 100 million people. The majority of the world's languages are so restricted in circulation that they must be supported by a second language for cultural, economic, and educational purposes. This is the case, for example, in such European countries as Sweden, Denmark, Finland, the Netherlands, Bulgaria, and Hungary. A similar situation exists in a country such as the Soviet Union where regional or national languages coexist with a common language of intercommunication.

There have been some experimental attempts, especially in the Scandinavian countries and Holland, to introduce second languages in nursery schools and kindergartens. For the most part, however, second languages are introduced in the school when the child is about 10 years of age. Generally, the goal of language instruction in the early grades is to give the child a facility and an experience in the language that will raise the level of language learning in subsequent years. The direct method is typically used with emphasis on oral communication through games, stories, rhymes, and so forth. The child's first language is not excluded, however; it is used to correct mistakes and to help in vocabulary acquisition.

In the Soviet Union, linguistic theory has tended toward the centralist, as opposed to the peripheralist or associationist position (Lewis, 1974). Consciousness of rule-governed processes is the key to second-language education. The student is to be made consciously aware of the theory that ties together the rules and the structure of the language. Adult direction is stressed, rather than personal discovery and habit. Learning depends not so much on repetition as on the student's awareness of the structural significance of what is drilled. Habits are simply the manifestation of a logically prior intellectual awareness. For this reason, second-language training usually begins only when children are able to understand grammatical rules consciously.

There have been, however, experimental attempts in the Soviet Union to teach languages to small children. For example, Ginsberg (1960) reported on a program in Leningrad in which 5- and 6-year-old children were taught German, French, or English in different nursery schools. Teaching was based on play activities, and all grammatical explanations were avoided. When the language was integrated with the activity of the child in role-playing sequences and games, the children did better and were better able to generalize to situations outside the learning experience than was the case in groups where children were taught isolated words and sentence patterns.

In countries where two or more languages are regarded as official languages, both may be taught simultaneously in the schools. Such is the case, for example, in Wales, although here—as in Brittany—the emigration of a large part of the population to industrial areas and the influence of communication media have contributed to the decline of the indigenous language. The revival of nationalist spirit in these countries and in other regions of Europe may help to reverse this trend.

In Wales and in French-speaking Canada a number of programs have been established to start bilingual education in nursery school and kindergarten. In some of these programs the child's second language is used exclusively, and in others the two languages are used on alternate days. As we shall see in Chapter 6, total and partial immersion programs have been remarkably successful in Canada with English-speaking children.

In England, France, and Germany, second-language training is considered a necessary part of education at the secondary school level. In England there has been an increasing number of attempts to begin second languages (especially French) at the primary level. The impact of linguistics is especially noticeable in the British case; applied linguistics is taught in a number of universities and has a definite impact on language teaching in the country. The direct method or variants thereof are preferred, and primary emphasis is placed on the spoken word. The technology of language instruction in English seems to be on a par with that in the United States: audiovisual aids, television, and language laboratories are all in wide use.

In France the attempt to teach second languages to young children seems to be somewhat more limited than in England. There are some experimental schools in Paris where English is taught to young children from the age of 7. The approach used is entirely oral, with emphasis on games, dramatization, and songs. The children also watch simple dialogues between teachers or puppets and attempt to act out the dialogues themselves. The goal of such programs is somwhat limited, however, the principal aim being to prepare young children for the more systematic study of language that occurs at the secondary level.

A more ambitious attempt is that of the Ecole Active Bilingue—Ecole Internationale de Paris, where English is spoken during part of the day in an otherwise French-speaking nursery school. During this part of the day the children receive their instruction in painting, craftwork, dancing, and so forth entirely in English. The nursery school is preparatory to the bilingual experience of the school itself, which continues through the primary school grades. In the primary school, as in the nursery school, a part of each day's instructions is given in English. Emphasis is on oral knowledge of the language, and the reading and writing of English begins only after these skills have been mastered in French.

In Germany the teaching of English usually begins in the fifth grade of the elementary school. There have been some experimental attempts to introduce a second language earlier, but these have not convinced educators that it is more beneficial to begin second-language learning before the age of 11. The most well-known experiment in bilingual education in the German context is that of the John F. Kennedy School in Berlin. Founded in 1960, the school has a student population that is half German and half American. Only a small percentage of these children (less than 10 percent) come from bilingual homes. Training in the second language starts in the kindergarten. Both languages are spoken, and the instructions of the teachers are given in German and English. This program will be discussed in Chapter 6.

United States. In the United States the dominant method of second-language training until World War II was the reading or translation method. There was little interest in teaching languages as media of spoken communication, and little attention was given to languages in primary education. The only exception seems to have been in areas with a large German population where German was taught in the elementary schools. In the 1950s and 1960s interest in language instruction at the primary level increased and a number of programs developed. These usually are grouped under the heading, Foreign Languages in the Elementary Schools (FLES) programs. The main languages of instruction are Spanish, French, and German, although about six other languages are also taught at the elementary level in various parts of the country.

These programs usually employ various modifications of the direct method. Until the late 1950s, there was a shortage of trained instructors, but this situation changed somewhat with the passage of the National Defense Education Act of 1958. Financial considerations have always played a large role, and many programs have been cancelled because of lack of support from local school boards. In addition, many FLES programs suffered because of uncertainty about the best teaching procedures, the mobility of the population of the United States, and inadequate training of language instructors (Stern, 1967).

There is considerable debate about the effectiveness of FLES programs. One problem in making any general assessment of the merits of the programs is that teaching methods vary considerably. In some cases extensive use is made of audiovisual aids, and in other cases the teacher has no aids available. The effectiveness of the program seems to depend greatly on the motivation and social characteristics of the target student group. There is as yet little agreement on the optimal age for beginning FLES or on the optimal method of instruction.

In 1963 the Dade County public schools in Florida established the Coral Way School to meet the special needs of an increasing number of Cuban children enrolling in the school system. This was the first bilingual program in the United States since World War I (Andersson & Boyer, 1970). By 1967 there was enough interest in bilingual education programs to bring about the passage of the Bilingual Education Act, which—as Title VII of the Elementary and Secondary Education Act—allocated funds for bilingual programs.

Bilingual education programs use children's first language to initiate them to the school environment. In this way children are allowed to continue the linguistic development they started in the home and can begin immediately to learn subject-matter concepts without waiting until their second language is developed (Saville & Troike, 1971). The second language is introduced gradually and, once established, is also used in instruction. This seems pedagogically more sound than immediately instructing the child in a second language. There is some evidence, for example, that beginning the school experience in the child's first language assists acquisition of a second language (Seelye & Balasubramonian, 1973). Subsequently, the program ideally fosters skills in both languages with all subjects taught equally in both and language arts classes taught in both.

Bilingual education programs allow children in minority ethnic groups to receive affirmation of their cultural identity at school. The programs attempt to do more than teach English to children who speak other languages. They aim at developing children's positive identity with their cultural heritage (Christian & Sharp, 1972), their self-assurance and confidence, and a legitimate pride in both cultures (Swanson, 1974). Their own language is maintained because it reflects established ways of thinking, feeling, and acting (Pacheco, 1973).

In the early 1970s the number of bilingual education programs in existence increased from less than 30 (Ulibarri, 1972) to between 450 to 500 (Swanson, 1974). About half of the programs are sponsored by Title VII funds and the other half from private funds, special grants, and foundations. The greatest number of Title VII programs are in operation in the state of California, and Spanish is by far the most common language. There are a number of Indian programs; French programs exist in Louisiana, Maine, and New Hampshire; Haitian French in New York, Massachusetts, and Illinois; as well as programs in Portuguese and Chinese. Other languages are sparsely distributed. In Puerto Rico there is a program for English-speaking children returning to the island who know very little Spanish.

Swanson (1974) estimated that there are 5,000,000 ethnic-minority children in the United States who need bilingual education programs. Of this number, 3,100,000 are Mexican–Americans. The number of children in bilingual programs is slightly in excess of 100,000. If the advocates of bilingual education programs are correct in arguing that such programs are the only way of preventing linguistic and ethnic minority children from experiencing educational and psychological setbacks in our schools, the number of programs now in existence is seriously short of the need (Table 1.2).

In practice, bilingual education programs differ greatly in terms of program design and instruction, selection and development of materials, teacher training, and community involvement. Some bilingual educational programs begin at the kindergarten level, but the majority start in the first grade. Some continue throughout the elementary school years, whereas others go only to grades three or four. All programs, however, share the same goals—the development of

TABLE 1.2
Discrepancy Between Need for and
Enrollment in Bilingual Education Programs[a]

Ethnic/language group	Children in need, approximate number	Children enrolled, approximate number	Percent
Mexican–American	3,100,000	71,000	2.3
Puerto Rican	800,000	14,000	1.7
Other Spanish-speaking	380,000	6,000	1.6
French-speaking	350,000	2,000	.6
American Indian (including Eskimo)	180,000	3,000	1.7
Portuguese	60,000	600	1.0
Chinese	40,000	600	1.5
Chamorro	7,500	250	3.3
Other	38,000	3,000	7.9
Total	4,955,500	100,450	2.0

[a] Adapted from Swanson, 1974.

communicative skills in both languages and acceptance and appreciation of the child's cultural heritage and of the value of being bilingual and bicultural.

In Chapter 6 I discuss some different approaches to bilingual education in this country and in Canada. My goal, however, is not to survey early childhood, bilingual education programs. There is so much flux and innovation in this field that any survey is quickly outdated. My intent is principally to understand what can be learned about second-language learning in children through such programs. But the major part of this book deals with the process of second-language acquisition in the natural setting, and so it seems best to look first at what is known about the process of first-language acquisition.

2
First-Language Acquisition

I do not attempt in this chapter the rather Gargantuan task of surveying what is known about the child's acquisition of a first language. The amount of information that has accumulated, especially in the last two decades, is formidable. Furthermore, excellent accounts of first-language acquisition exist elsewhere (especially Brown, 1973a; Dale, 1976). The aim is a more modest one: to provide background and perspective for the discussion that follows in subsequent chapters of the child's acquisition of a second language.

This chapter has three sections. First, I examine different ways of looking at the language acquisition process and at the skills that the child is thought to bring to this task. Then I turn to a consideration of just what it is that the child must accomplish in order to acquire a language. Finally, a brief overview is presented of the developmental stages characteristic of first-language acquisition.

THE CHILD'S LINGUISTIC CAPACITIES

Descriptions of the language development process and of the child's lingustic capabilities differ depending on the epistemological stance one adopts. Usually a distinction is drawn between the rationalist and the empiricist positions. The rationalist regards cognitive abilities as given. Experience does not teach directly; it activates an innate capacity. We know the world as we do, because we are biologically structured to know it in this way. We acquire language as we do, because we are preprogrammed to acquire it in this manner. Indeed, only humans can acquire language, because only the human species is so constituted. Language is a species-specific, innate ability.

The empiricist is skeptical of explanatory attempts that depend on the existence of nonobservable, innate characteristics. It is true that humans are born with a specific biological structure and certain cognitive and linguistic capacities.

These are, however, by no means as general and as predetermining as the rationalist would have it. Innate capacities are few and relatively simple, such as the ability to form associations. The essential characteristic of the human species is plasticity, the capacity to learn from experience. The child has no special ability for language; language acquisition simply reflects a general capacity to learn.

The rationalist does not, of course, deny that the child learns from experience. Obviously, children learn to speak a certain language, because they hear others around them speaking it. On this score the difference between the two positions is one of degree, as it is on the question of the role of innate structures in the learning process. But the two positions differ radically on the question of the child's capacity for language. The rationalists believe in the species specificity and uniformity of language acquisition. The empiricists deny that language acquisition is any different from any other type of learning.

Models of Language Acquisition in Children

In contemporary psycholinguistic theories of language acquisition, the rationalist position usually is advocated by those who follow Noam Chomsky and approach language from a transformational grammar point of view. The empiricist position is associated with B. F. Skinner and other behaviorists for whom language is a response to the stimulus characteristics of the environment. Many workers in the field, however, prefer to side-step this debate entirely. For them, a different model—one that views language in process terms—is superior to that of either behaviorism or transformational grammar. Let us briefly consider each of these three models.

The behaviorist model.   Traditional American, behaviorist psychology has taken a cavalier attitude toward language acquisition. Languages were thought to be learned like anything else. One need not study language learning as such; it was enough to study general principles of behavior. When B. F. Skinner wrote his *magnum opus* on language, *Verbal behavior* (1957), he did not draw on an extended program of research with human subjects performing various linguistic tasks. Instead, his book was an unabashed extrapolation from laboratory research with nonverbal organisms.

In Skinner's system, language is a function of *reinforcement*. The parent teaches the child to talk by reinforcing verbal behavior. The child learns to name things correctly because of reinforcement for doing so. Initially, learning involves a slow and laborious process of successive approximations, but subsequently less tedious procedures for evoking the correct response are possible as the child learns to respond to such generalized reinforcers as signs of approval or praise from parents and other members of the verbal community.

Grammar is acquired like other verbal responses. The child learns a framework within which to place lexical items. When a 2½-year-old girl says, *When you untry to do it,* she does not yet have all of the morphemes in their appropriate order within the grammatical frame. In time she will learn the correct order in the same way as she learns other behavioral patterns. Such learning, like all learning, occurs gradually; eventually most errors will be corrected through selective reinforcement from the verbal community.

Skinner's theory was subjected to rigorous examination by Chomsky (1959), who argued eloquently that the theory was erroneous in its assumptions, untestable, subjective, and cluttered with vague and poorly defined concepts. Reinforcement could not possibly handle the explanatory load Skinner assigned it; grammars could not possibly be learned by fitting words into grammatical frames. How would Skinner, for example, explain why *is* can be substituted for *can be* in the sentence, *Marking papers can be a nuisance* but not in the sentence, *Struggling artists can be a nuisance,* although the two sentences have the same frame? Behaviorist theory, as represented in Skinner's book, was irredeemably naive from a linguistic point of view.

For linguists, other applications of behaviorist principles were equally oversimplified. To attempt to explain language acquisition in terms of such behaviorist concepts as imitation (Miller & Dollard, 1941), sign learning and secondary reinforcement (Mowrer, 1960), or response hierarchies and stimulus control (Staats, 1968) was just whistling in the dark. Chomsky's critique of Skinner was the final nail in the behaviorist coffin. Behaviorist mechanisms did not and could not in principle apply to the acquisition of language.

The difficulty is that the associationistic model assumes that the organism possesses a finite repertoire of behaviors, any one of which may, on occasion, be triggered by specific stimulus parameters. The probability of such an occurrence depends on the organism's history of reinforcement and may be represented by a construct such as habit strength or associative connection. This model runs into trouble when it is applied to language, because in acquiring a language a speaker internalizes a finite set of rules that are, however, sufficient to provide him with a repertoire of infinitely many linguistic responses (Garrett & Fodor, 1968). The stimulus–response, associationistic theory is insufficient because it requires that the speaker select from a pre-existing response repertoire one of a finite number of responses on the basis of some previously established association. Such a model is incapable in principle of accounting for indefinitely diversified responses.

By the time linguists and psycholinguists had finished storming the behaviorist castle, traditional psychological thinking about the nature of language development had been modified appreciably. The older behaviorist models seemed to be definitely inappropriate. Much more sophisticated and complex models were indicated. Some steps in this direction have been made, but the new formulations were attacked as sharply as the old (McLaughlin, 1971). More important, the behaviorist tradition generated relatively little empirical research on the problem of language. This is telling, since the behaviorists had steadfastly maintained that language must be susceptible to empirical scrutiny. Yet over the last two decades, linguistic theory has proved to be a far richer source of hypotheses on language than has behavioral theory.

Furthermore, the language acquisition process did not seem to correspond to the pattern the behaviorists expected. Chomsky seemed to be right about the secondary importance of reinforcement. Careful observation of young children showed that parents rarely corrected errors in pronunciation or grammar. In fact, the grounds on which an utterance is approved or disapproved usually are not linguistic at all (Brown, 1973a). If a young boy says *I ranned faster than him,* his father is more likely to pat him on the back than correct his syntax.

Nor does imitation, another favorite behaviorist mechanism, seem to play a very important role in language acquisition. The child's language is simply too strange. The child has never heard *two foots* or *I comed,* yet such constructions are quite common and persistent. It seems as though the child is going through an active process of testing, discarding, and refining grammatical rule systems. Moreover, this happens even if the child cannot speak at all but simply hears other speaking (Lenneberg, 1962). This seems to exclude any account of language development that gives a central role to imitation.

As more information accumulated about children's language, it became quite apparent that the child's linguistic behavior is much more complex than was supposed. One of the reasons for postulating innate mechanisms was that the speech input to which the child is exposed does not seem to be a rich enough source for induction of the rules of grammar. Furthermore, the facts of grammar are not explicable simply on the basis of surface structure. It seems necessary to postulate some sort of deep structure to account for how we understand ambiguous sentences such as the famous, *They are eating apples.* Transformational grammar seemed to offer a more powerful approach to language than did traditional psychological theory.

The transformational grammar approach.   Chomsky and his followers argued that languages cannot be acquired by application of step-by-step inductive operations. What the child seems to do is formulate a theory of grammar on the basis of limited (and often faulty) data. That all children do this regardless of intelligence, motivation, or emotional state seems to leave little doubt that the human organism is biologically preprogrammed to acquire language. Furthermore, children acquire language in a remarkably short period of time. In a few years they have constructed a grammar on the basis of which they can distinguish sentences from nonsentences. This task is so complex as to suggest the presence of built-in biological structures and genetically programmed maturational processes.

The task of linguistic analysis is to account for how it is that the child produces and understands an indefinite number of new sentences, distinguishes sentences from nonsentences, and interprets ill-formed sentences. According to Chomsky (1957) the grammar of a language can be thought of as a hierarchy—a *deep* or base *structure* component, which produces a set of deep structures; a set of *transformations,* which operates on the deep structure; and a set of *surface structures,* which are the result of the transformations. In addition, there is a semantic component and a phonological component (Figure 2.1). The transformational rules make it possible for the speaker to generate sentences or phrases or clause segments of sentences. No sentences (not even the simple, active, declarative sentences of English) can be generated without the application of at least a limited number of obligatory transformational rules (e.g., rules for subject–verb concord). The meaning of the sentence is a function of the deep structure and the meanings of the individual words (the semantic component of the sentence).

It is possible for two sentences to have different surface structures and the same (or roughly the same) deep structure, as in: *The man threw the ball* and *The ball was thrown by the man*. The difference is that in one case transformational rules have converted the deep structure into an active sentence, and in the other case into a passive sentence. Similarly, it is possible, by applying appropriate transformations to the deep structure, to produce interrogative sentences, negative sentences, and so forth.

Chomsky argued that children cannot help constructing a particular kind of transformational grammar any more than they can control their perception of solid objects or their attention to line and angle. The way children acquire a language reflects not so much experience as the general capacity for knowledge.

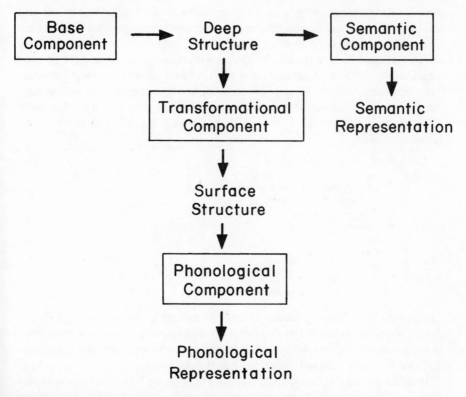

FIG. 2.1   The organization of transformational grammar (the boxes represent systems of rules that determine the structures or representations).

Experience will affect language development, but its ultimate form will be a function of those language universals that exist in the human mind.

The data from which the child works are the utterances of speakers. Language is acquired by developing and *testing hypotheses* about regularities in the corpus to which the child is exposed. Language acquisition is a process of implicit theory construction whereby children formulate hypotheses about the rules governing the linguistic structure of sentences they hear, test these hypotheses against new evidence they acquire, eliminate those hypotheses that are contrary to the evidence, and evaluate those that are not eliminated by a simplicity principle that selects the simplest as the best hypothesis concerning the rules underlying the linguistic corpus (Katz, 1966). The rule system that children develop enables them to generate an infinite variety of sentences, most of which they have never heard from anyone else.

This view of the language acquisition process has been persuasively challenged, however, by Martin Braine (1971a), who pointed out that a hypothesis-testing model is too inefficient to account for the way in which a child acquires a language. Experimental research with concept formation has demonstrated that both positive information and negative information (information as to what is and what is not an instance of what is to be learned) are necessary for efficient learning. This means that children must be able to distinguish what is from what is not a sentence in order to learn which of their hypotheses about the grammar are correct and which are incorrect. Yet, as we have seen, observation of parental interaction with children indicates that parents rarely correct incorrect grammar. They are much more concerned with meaning and truthfulness than with syntax. Furthermore, when children are presented with negative information, they resist using it. Braine cited the following dialogue with his 2½-year-old daughter (Braine, 1971a):

> Child: Want other one spoon, Daddy.
> Father: You mean, you want the other spoon.
> C: Yes, I want other one spoon, please Daddy.
> F: Can you say "the other spoon"?
> C: Other . . . one . . . spoon.
> F: Say "other."
> C: Other.
> F: "Spoon."
> C: Spoon.
> F: "Other . . . spoon."
> C: Other . . . spoon. Now give me other one spoon [pp. 160–161]?

Those who have had experience attempting to correct the grammar of 2- and 3-year-old children can testify that this is the usual outcome. Braine's contention, then, was that children usually do not receive negative information about syntax and that they often do not utilize it when it is given.

In addition, Braine noted experimental research on artificial languages that indicates that learners (both children and adults) are capable of acquiring grammar-like relations merely from exposure to sentences. That is, they learn merely on the basis of exposure to positive instances (even when these positive instances are accompanied, as they are in real-life situations, by unsystematic errors). Braine argued that the evidence suggests that the acquisition process requires a model based not on hypothesis formation but on *discovery procedures*. In his formulation, such a model requires a scanner that receives input sentences and a memory component that accumulates the features of sentences noticed by the scanner. A detailed account of the mode of operation of this model can be found in Braine (1971a); in its essential characteristics the model is similar to computer-based processing models developed for the acquisition and comprehension of natural language (Kelley, 1967; Schank, 1972; Winograd, 1972).

Process models.   This brings us to the third approach to language acquisition—process or strategy analysis. Process models differ from traditional behaviorist models in that they are essentially cognitive models of language. They are mainly concerned not with external, stimulus–response events but with internal, cognitive processes. The model attempts to delineate how language is processed cognitively and how it is manifested behaviorally.

Process models differ from a transformational grammar model in that they are concerned with language behavior occurring in real time; linguistic models, however, such as a transformational grammar approach, are essentially static: emphasis is placed on characterizing what it is that people must know to comprehend and produce grammatical and meaningful utterances. The linguist aims at accounting for the speaker's competence in a language; process models are concerned not only with what it is that people *know* to comprehend and produce sentences but also with what it is that people *do* in such comprehension and production (Clark & Haviland, 1974). This means that attention must be given both to linguistically relevant criteria (such as judgments of grammaticality, paraphrase equivalence, and structural parallelism) and to behaviorally relevant criteria (such as processing time, mistakes in repetition, and mistakes in recall) (Ervin–Tripp, 1970).

Clark and Haviland (1974) have characterized process models as explanatory attempts that accommodate the following information:

- The moment-to-moment changes in the mental state of the speaker or listener.
- The speaker or listener's knowledge of the language, as represented in the rules required for changing from one mental state to another.
- The speaker or listener's processing capacity, as found in the limitations on what rules can be applied, how many can be applied at one time, and how long each rule takes.
- The time required to say or understand an utterance.

Thus such models attempt to accommodate both competence and performance simultaneously.

One reason why process models are becoming increasingly popular among psycholinguists is that they account for language phenomena left unexplained by a static linguistic description. For example, implied requests such as *Could you open the door?* are rarely interpreted as questioning the listener's ability physically to open the door. In most situations, both the speaker and the listener understand that the speaker is conveying a request. One explanation for why this is possible posits that the listener goes through an inferential process, utilizing knowledge of the situation to infer what it is that the speaker means (Gordon & Lakoff, 1971). Since knowledge of the situation changes from moment to moment, a satisfactory account of implied requests requires a dynamic theory that makes reference to the construction of knowledge states, the alteration of such states, and how it is that the speaker or listener is able to consult these knowledge states. And it must be able to do all this in real time (Clark & Haviland, 1974).

A number of other linguistic phenomena require similar situational analyses. The sentence *John says the Dodgers* does not make much sense unless it is seen as occurring in the context of the question *Who won the ball game yesterday?* The study of language is the study of the communicative act and not simply the study of the way in which speakers generate grammatical utterances (although this is an important aspect of language use).

This is the perspective I take to language development throughout this book. I view it in terms of the child's processing capacities and in terms of the strategies the child employs in learning to communicate with others. One advantage of such an approach is that it accentuates the similarities between language acquisition and other types of learning. Children process linguistic data in a manner analogous to the way in which they process sensory information—by registering properties of the input and accumulating them in memory.

At the present time, however, no processing model exists that can account for all relevant linguistic and behavioral phenomena. As Ervin–Tripp (1970) pointed out, filling in the details of such a model will take many years. Present models are usually developed to explain a limited domain in terms of a series of hypothesized mental states, a collection of rules for changing from one mental state to another, and sequentially ordered processes (e.g., Clark & Chase, 1972; Garrod & Trabasso, 1973). More complete models must account for the whole range of tasks that children face as they begin to acquire language, including phonological, semantic, and syntactic processes. Before considering what such models would involve, some comments are in order about children's processing capacities.

Language and Cognitive Development

From the present perspective, the old debate between rationalists and empiricists about innate capacity for language acquisition appears misdirected. Children's cognitive and learning capacities are much more general and predetermining than the empiricists would have it. They are born with certain innate abilities that structure and determine the way they learn. They are not, on the other hand, born with an innate set of ideas, as the rationalists would have it, but with a processing mechanism that enables them to discover linguistic patterns just as they discover perceptual patterns in the world of senses. Both processes are part of general cognitive development. The categories that an individual develops—linguistic and perceptual—are the result of an innate set of cognitive inference procedures.

In Braine's (1971a) model, for example, the scanner is thought to be preset to notice certain features of the input and ignore others. The form of the grammar that the learner is capable of acquiring is therefore predetermined by the range of properties to which the scanner responds. The model allows for the possibility of universal properties of natural languages, not because there are innate linguistic categories, but because language acquisition is governed by a particular sort of processing mechanism.

It follows, then, that what linguists propose to be universals of language are simply products of universal cognitive processes. For example, the noun/verb distinction in language is the result of the cognitive strategy of distinguishing between objects and the relations between objects. Transformations themselves are cognitive operations that are reflected not only in language but in visual perception as well (Bever, 1970).

The priority of general cognitive processes has been stressed by a number of authors (Bates, 1976; Macnamara, 1972; Osgood, 1971; Sinclair–deZwart, 1973; Slobin, 1971). The exact nature of the cognitive prerequisites for language is still debated, although there is general agreement that the language acquisition process involves the assimilation of information into existing cognitive structures and that these cognitive structures set limits on the child's language development.

Processing limitations.   There is evidence, for example, that the length of a child's imitations of an adult model's utterances remains about the same, regardless of the length of the adult model's utterances, and that the length of the imitation is about the same as the length of the child's spontaneous utterances (Brown & Fraser, 1963; Ervin, 1964). There seems to be some processing limitation that restricts the length of utterances children can program. As the child grows older, this limitation is gradually overcome and sentences become longer.

Further evidence for this processing limitation comes from Bloom's (1970) finding that deletions seem to occur in the negative sentences of children. Since negative sentences are usually one word longer than positive sentences, the hypothesis of a length limitation leads one to expect that the addition of a negative element would require that some other constituent of the sentence be dropped. This is what Bloom found. Her daughter said *Daddy like coffee,* immediately followed by *Lois no coffee.* The introduction of the negative *no* seemed to cause the deletion of the verb *like.* Presumably, the child could not process the sentence *Lois no like coffee* at this time.

Why is it that the length of the child's utterances are limited? One answer is that there is a processing restriction imposed by the limitations of operative memory. Brown and Fraser (1963) observed that simple digit-span memory and chronological age are systematically related, with a progressive increase in digit-span memory continuing until adulthood. This pattern replicates the systematic increase in length of utterance (Brown & Fraser, 1963; McCarthy, 1946) and suggests that the two processes are related, utterance length being dependent on the child's memory span.

This conclusion has not gone unchallenged, however. In fact, Martin Braine (1974) denied that there are any length constraints in children's speech. He noted that data from corpora of children's speech consistently have revealed relatively long utterances that break through supposed length constraints. The finding that the length of imitation is independent of the length of the adult model's utterance and about the same length as the child's spontaneous utterance only underscores the fact that the child's imitations are reconstructions generated by the same mechanism that controls spontaneous utterances. The argument for a length constraint based on deletions in negative sentences is contradicted by evidence from Braine's son's speech in which early negative sentences were usually longer than the corresponding affirmative sentences.

Braine argued that children, lacking complete command of the rules of the adult grammar, use a strategy in speech production whereby they single out something pragmatically salient in the situation. Initially, their speech consists of one-word utterances with the single word referring to the one salient feature of the complex they want to communicate. At the two- and three-word stages, the child's utterances still are limited, not because there are performance constraints, but because of the child's use of the salient feature strategy for communicating semantic intentions within the limitations set by syntactic knowledge. Later, as knowledge of the rules of the grammar develops, children can refer to increasingly more features of the complex they want to communicate.

Braine's iconoclastic approach is atypical. Most authors feel that children's speech is limited by performance constraints but disagree as to their source. The memory span hypothesis seems questionable, since as Olson (1973) pointed out, when more appropriate indices of children's memory capacities are used, such as pictorial materials, children do not perform worse on memory tasks than adults (Brown & Scott, 1971). Olson argued that the capacity for immediate memory was ontogenetically invariant and that the performance deficits found in younger children are due to their failure to organize, plan, monitor, and integrate their information processing and memory as efficiently as do older children and adults. Indeed there is evidence that when children as young as 3 or 4 years of age are taught to do so, they can employ many of the strategies they will later use routinely in memory tasks (Flavell, 1970). Olson proposed that the child's initial utterances are single-word utterances, because the child finds that with the help of extralinguistic factors a single word can convey a meaning that an adult expresses in a sentence. As children escape from their egocentric world and have to cope with other persons and points of view, they cannot rely on extralinguistic cues in the immediate situation, and so their utterances become longer.

According to this view, cognitive limitations to the child's language development are indeed based on the limitations of operative memory, though not on the
limitations of immediate memory span. Those cognitive abilities that the child
fails to employ in remembering are also not employed in language performance.
Adult performance involves the ability to plan and organize output, the ability to
monitor and assess the state of this planning and the readiness to perform, the
ability to integrate in real time the flow of information through immediate memory and to retrieve information from long-term memory (Olson, 1973). In addition, adults have a conceptual repertoire and previous learning experience at their
disposal. These obvious differences in cognitive abilities mean that the experience of the child learning a language is different from that of an adult. In Chapter
3 I discuss the question of how different these experiences are.

Processing capabilities.   Susan Ervin–Tripp (1970) singled out three kinds
of linguistic performance that provide information about children's language
processing capabilities. The first of these is *imitation*. When children are given
the task of imitating the sentences of an adult model,they must, at a minimum, be
capable of perceiving the model's speech, storing it in immediate memory, and
organizing output. They must also be capable of performing the appropriate
motor behavior to make the necessary speech sounds.

A second type of performance is comprehension or *interpretation*. What is
involved here is revealed through such tasks as answering and acting upon
sentences and paraphrasing their meaning. The processing capacities involved in
imitation are needed here as well: speech perception, storage in short-term memory, and organization of output. In addition, long-term storage may occur, although many characteristics of surface structure are apparently not stored
(Bransford & Franks, 1972). Furthermore, lexical and syntactic processing at
some minimal level are necessary for the child to perform the interpretative task.

The third type of performance is the *production* of meaningful utterances. All
of the processing capacities involved in interpretation seem to be necessary here,
as well as the organization and motor output processes of imitation. Yet production seems to involve different processing than either interpretation or imitation.
Studies of children's language development indicate that production usually lags
behind comprehension, most likely because the child must learn to organize
sentence output, especially in terms of word order and syntax. Similarly, expert
linguists can mimic greetings and common expressions in other languages without being able to understand or produce more complicated intelligible utterances
in those languages, which also suggests that production differs from interpretation.

At a minimum, then, the child must possess the following capacities to be able
to perform basic linguistic tasks:

1. Perceptual abilities to organize perceptually a string of sounds.
2. Immediate memory storage capacity.

3. Long-term memory storage capacity.
4. Ability to process phonological, lexical, and syntactic information.
5. Ability to organize output.
6. Appropriate motor behavior skills.

In addition, it seems that the child, like the adult, must possess certain heuristic devices to minimize the amount of effort required to process linguistic information (Ervin–Tripp, 1970). Like the adult, the child learns to listen with minimum attention and to process language with great rapidity.

This outline of the child's linguistic capacities is of course very rudimentary. It leaves out of consideration how it is that the child performs more complicated linguistic tasks. How is it, for example, that the child learns to comprehend implied requests such as his mother's request that he shut the door, expressed in the sentence *Michael, you left the door open.* Such requests are understood by children very early. When a child says *I'm hungry,* she is herself using such a strategy. It would seem that to understand and generate such requests, the child must be able to make inferences about various levels of meaning, literal and implied.

Furthermore, these comments on the child's linguistic capacities are rudimentary because they are based on a consideration of general tasks that the child performs such as imitation, interpretation, and production and not on a consideration of more specific tasks that require more specific linguistic skills.

THE CHILD'S LINGUISTIC TASKS

What are the specific tasks that a child faces in acquiring a language? Some authors, principally Susan Ervin–Tripp, have attempted to spell out these tasks. They relate to the acquisition of a phonological system, a semantic system, and a syntactic system.

Phonological Tasks

As Ervin–Tripp (1970) noted, children *discriminate sounds* by the middle of the 1st year and can imitate sounds a few months later. Speech perception appears to depend on interaction with the environment, since the children of deaf parents are not able to discover sound patterns merely through exposure to television or radio. The recurrence of sound patterns at times of significance to the child such as feeding, being held, and being stimulated visually, appears to mark off particular sounds for attention (Ervin–Tripp, 1973a).

Experimental research indicates that certain sound features are more salient in unanalyzed input and are more likely to be preserved in imitation and recall (Ervin–Tripp, 1970):

  • In English, peak pitch, what is stressed or not stressed, and terminal fall or non-fall.
  • Timing and length of stressed syllables.

- Approximate quality of stressed vowels, especially unrounded vowels.
- Approximate location of marked features such as friction and nasal consonants.

Why such features are more salient can only be hypothesized at present.

During the babbling period (the second 6 months) the infant vocalizes an increasing variety of sounds in increasingly complex combinations. These sounds appear to include a large number that the infant does not use in producing meaningful utterances. Infants select out certain sounds from their corpora and use these in intended vocalizations (Jakobson, 1941). There seems to be considerable uniformity among infants exposed to different languages in the first sounds they produce: the front consonants, *p* or *m,* and the back vowel, *a,* preceding the back consonants, *k* and *g,* and the front vowels, *i* and *u* (even though the reverse development occurs during the babbling period).

In addition to the phonemic structure of the language—its sound units—the child must learn its phonological structure—the *rules for combining sounds* into pronounceable sequences in the language and for relating such sequences to the surface structure of sentences. Somehow the child must come to realize that although *trown* is not a word in English, it could be; whereas *lrown* is not and could not be an English word. The reason for this is that there is a phonological rule in English that allows the *tr* combination but not the *lr* combination.

Other phonological rules relate to the stress words receive in sentences. In English, for example, the main stress falls on *black* when the speaker is referring to a *blackboard.* When referring to a board that is black, however, the speaker is more likely to say *the black board,* stressing *board.* The rule in such cases is that the main stress falls on the first vowel of a noun but elsewhere in constituents of other kinds, such as noun phrases (Chomsky & Halle, 1968). It seems that such rules are only gradually mastered by children, but little is known of their developmental course.

Aside from distinguishing sound units and learning phonological rules, the child must learn to *attach sounds to their referents.* This, as was noted, requires the co-occurrence of speech with referential events. A child cannot acquire the linguistically important features of speech unless a significant portion of the sounds heard make reference to concrete objects, relations, and events to which the child already attends. Note that attaching sounds to their referents is a more complex process than simply learning the names of things (as behaviorists usually assume in their theories of meaning). The child stores such words as *want, all-gone,* and *more,* which refer not to observable objects but to one's own inner states and relationships between objects and events (Ervin–Tripp, 1973a).

An adequate model of sound processing, then, must account for how the child learns and stores sound discriminations, how sound units are selected out and produced, how phonological rules are learned and stored, and how sound units are related to lexical items. Aside from perceptual, storage, and retrieval processes, the model must be able to provide some account of the rule-acquisition process and of the various heuristics the child uses to discover phonological rules. Attaching sounds to their referents also involves the use of heuristics, about which little is known.

Semantic Tasks

Somehow the child has to develop a *dictionary of meanings*. Perhaps the first entries in this dictionary are whole sentences of one, two, or three words. In time, though, the dictionary becomes a dictionary of words, each of which is given its particular meaning. The word *dog,* for example, has a certain matrix of phonological features, a set of syntactic markers that define it as a common noun, and a collection of semantic features including perhaps (physical object), (living), (small), and (animal).

As children grow older, they modify and elaborate the semantic features attached to the words in the dictionary. There is some disagreement as to how this is done (E. Clark, 1973). One suggestion, for example, is that the child goes from the concrete to the abstract (Anglin, 1970). Initially, there is awareness only of the specific, concrete features of words. As the child's semantic knowledge increases with age, generalizations are made over more abstract categories. At first children know *rose, tulip, oak,* and *elm.* Subsequently, they group the pairs together under *flower* and *tree.* Then they become able to group all words together under *plants* and, ultimately, under *living things.* One problem with this hypothesis is that children do not inevitably acquire such subordinate terms as *oak* or *elm* before they acquire the superordinate one—*tree.* In fact, the reverse is usually the case.

A somewhat different hypothesis is that there are certain universal, primitive features that are common to all languages and that reflect the basic dispositions of the cognitive and perceptual nature of the human organism (Bierwisch, 1967). The child does not have to learn the primitive features but simply the rules for combining primitives into lexical items. Although the primitives are given as part of biological endowment, the rules differ from language to language. This theory is consistent with much recent thinking about the priority of nonlinguistic to linguistic processes; but it suffers from the important defect of being untestable, in that the primitives have not been identified and the rules for combining them into lexical items have not been specified.

A third hypothesis has been called semantic features acquisition (E. Clark, 1973). The assumption here is that when children first begin to use identifiable words, they do not know their full adult meanings. They have only some of the features or components of meaning that are present in the adult's lexicon. As children acquire semantic knowledge, they add more features of meaning to the lexical entry for individual words until the combination of features corresponds to that of the adult. However, since the young child does not yet possess the full combination of features, the child's referential categories will often differ considerably from those of adults for the same word. If, for example, the meaning of *dog* is defined by the features (physical object), (living), (small), and (animal), the child will give this word an extension an adult would not. The child's category *dog* might include cats, mice, guinea pigs, and other small animals. As other features are added to the definition, the child will gradually narrow down this initial, very general meaning.

Finally, there is the argument that what are learned are not features, but prototypes of common categories (Rosch, 1973). According to this view, children define a category by means of concrete "clear cases," rather than in terms of abstract criterial attributes. This helps to account for why children do not categorize words according to the same principles of abstraction used by adults. Children operate instead on the basis of an internal structure of a category determined by what are perceived to be the best examples of the category. At present, however, there is not enough known about semantic development to choose between the prototype and the semantic features hypotheses.

In addition to building up a dictionary of lexical meanings, the child acquires a set of *semantic relations*. Observers of children's language have noted that early sentences seem to be confined to a relatively restricted and universally shared set of semantic relations. These seem to reflect the way in which the human mind processes nonlinguistic experiences common to all children. Brown (1973a) has listed the following basic semantic relations:

- Agent and action: *Car go, Mommy push*
- Action and object: *See sock, Pick glove*
- Agent and object: *Eve lunch, Mommy sandwich*
- Action and location: *Sit chair*
- Entity and location: *Baby table*
- Possessor and possession: *Daddy chair*
- Entity and attribute: *Yellow block, Little dog*
- Demonstrative and entity: *Here truck, Here sock*

Other authors have slightly different lists (Ervin–Tripp, 1973a; Schlesinger, 1971); one problem with codification is that it is not always clear from what the child says which underlying semantic relations are being expressed.

Note that semantic relations are not the same as grammatical relations such as subject, predicate, and direct object. Instead, they refer to a set of semantic intentions that the child attempts to communicate through linguistic means. Initially, the child's communication efforts may be quite simple: utterances such as *Mommy eat, Baby go, Mommy shoe* are understood by family members in spite of their fragmentary nature. As the child comes into contact with more people and attempts to become more intelligible in a wider variety of situations, these semantic relations must be given more adequate expression in well-formed utterances.

In short, there are at least two tasks involved in semantic development. The first of these is building up the lexicon. An adequate model must account for how and why certain features are initially chosen to characterize lexical items, how semantic features are stored, and how they are retrieved. Second, there is the question of semantic relations: how and in what order are they acquired, what is the role of nonlinguistic experiences, and how are semantic relations given normative (i.e., grammatical) expression?

Syntactic Tasks

Possibly the most important cue for the child in learning to express semantic relations grammatically is *word order* (Braine, 1971a). For example, to recognize that an item acted upon normally follows an action word in English, the child must be able to store such specific instances as *Eat your dinner, Mary rolled the ball.* The semantic relationship between action and object is then matched with the order action–object. Such order processing heuristics are an integral part of syntactic development in all languages, although in inflected languages morphological features probably have a greater role.

The child's dependence on order regularities in a noninflected language such as English will lead to misinterpretations of certain types of sentences. For example, the young child will usually understand the sentence *The boy is chased by the dog* to refer to a picture of a boy chasing a dog. In such cases, the child operates on the basis of a rule that specifies that the sequence Noun–Verb–Noun means Agent–Action–Object.

As the child begins to pay more attention to syntactic information, a *grammar* develops based on the rules discovered in the corpus to which the child is exposed. The child's grammar differs from that of an adult, though there is little agreement on its exact form (see Bloom, 1970; Bowerman, 1973; McNeill, 1966). In several cases, fairly detailed developmental analyses have been made of grammatical constructions.

For example, Klima and Bellugi (1966) found that it was possible to distinguish three phases in the child's development of *negative sentences*. First, the negative word occurs outside of the sentence nucleus in such utterances as:

No wipe finger,
Wear mitten no,
No singing song,
Not a teddy bear.

The only negative forms at this stage are the words *no* and *not*. In the second stage, about 2 to 4 months later, more negative forms occur, especially monomorphic verbs such as *can't* and *don't*. The negative may occur before the predicate:

He no bite you,
I can't catch you.

Or it may be outside the sentence nucleus as it is during the first stage:

No pinch me,
Touch the snow no.

In the third stage, which occurs from 2 to 6 months later, the adult pattern appears:

You don't want some supper,
Ask me if I not make mistake,
I not hurt him.

The development of *questions*, like the development of negative constructions, proceeds from the simple to the more complex. Initially rising intonation and the use of *wh*-words are the only interrogative devices:

No ear?
See hole?
What doing?

In the second stage, the child asks such questions as:

Where my mittens?
What me think?
Why you smiling?

This stage seems to be characterized by the prefixing of question words to otherwise complete sentences. In the third stage, the auxiliary system emerges, and the modal *do* is inflected for tense:

Where the other Joe will drive?
What he can ride in?
What did you doed?
Why you caught it?

Note that even in the third stage the child has not learned all the rules characteristic of the adult grammar. The child says *Why he don't know how to pretend?* whereas the adult would say *Why doesn't he know how to pretend?* The child has not yet learned the inversion rule for *wh*-questions, although *yes–no* questions are inverted at this time.

These and other syntactic tasks are possible, because the child is able to retain information and retrieve it in acquiring grammatical rules. In process terms, children can do this because they possess a language acquisition system with storage capacity in short- and long-term memory, selection and organizational capacity, heuristic features allowing short cuts, and perceptual capacities. In addition, some sort of "interpretation template" (Ervin-Tripp, 1973a) seems necessary to provide interpretation of utterances according to their syntactic and semantic properties, so that formal similarities can be discovered. The complete model, then, has the following minimal components:

- Selective retention of features in short-term memory, especially order of acoustical input.
- Phonological and semantic selection and reorganization for retention in long-term memory.
- Interpretation templates for identifying structures according to the formal and semantic features of sequences.
- Successive processing by alternative heuristics, allowing shortcuts for frequent phrases, for instances where non-linguistic determinants are strong, and so on.
- Formal feature generation to identify abstract classes and provide marking of the lexicon [Ervin–Tripp, 1973a, p. 285].

This is by no means a complete list—the system needs devices for organizing and regulating output, for example. But this should give some picture of what a satisfactory process model would look like.

Ideally, such a model is not language-specific. Its components should be defined in terms general enough to apply to all languages. A more difficult question is whether the model is necessarily age-specific. There are three considerations (Ervin–Tripp, 1973a). First, input conditions change with age—one simplifies semantically and syntactically when speaking with a child. Second, knowledge and operative memory change with age—the adult has knowledge of vocabulary and syntax that the child does not possess and has more efficient memory heuristics than the child. Third, the linguistic skills that the learner brings to the task change with age—the young child is more attuned to acoustical input, the adult to semantic input. The question is whether such age differences affect the basic features of a process model of language: is the model that describes adult competence and performance inevitably different from the model that describes the child's competence and performance? There seems to be no compelling reason to think so (Ervin–Tripp, 1973a), but detailed consideration of this issue must wait until the next chapter.

Communicative Competence

In addition to specifically linguistic tasks, an adequate process model must account for how it is that the speaker utilizes nonlinguistic information in speech to achieve full communicative competence. We saw earlier in this chapter that implied requests such as *Could you open the door?* require a knowledge of the situation in order for the listener to be able to infer what it is that the speaker means. Similarly, when the salesman at the door asks the child *Is your mother home?* he intends the child to understand that he would like to speak with her. Somehow, the child must learn how to process such requests. Apparently children do, since they use similar strategies in their own speech (*My glass is empty, My car is broken,* and so forth).

Another important aspect of communicative competence is learning to use various styles or *codes* of speaking to different people under differing circumstances. The child must master the features of various levels of linguistic structure and must learn the rules for switching levels. There are at least three levels that seem present in all societies: formal or polite, colloquial, and slang or vulgar (Hymes, 1964).

The child in American society has to learn a formal code for dealing with teachers, ministers, and other "formidable strangers" (Gleason, 1973). For instance, it seems that many children develop a characteristic style in talking to adult strangers that is marked by pauses between words, careful enunciation, and a flat, affectless tone (Gleason, 1973). Another stylistic variant that children use is the -in versus -ing ending for the present participle. Fischer (1958) reported that his observation of the speech of 24 children revealed that the choice of -in and -ing variants was related to the sex, class, personality (aggressive/cooperative), and mood (tense/relaxed) of the speaker. As children grew more relaxed in an interview, for example, -in forms became more frequent.

The child uses the colloquial and slang codes in interaction with peers and siblings. Gleason (1973) reported that children's peer-group language was different from the language they addressed to adults. It involved a rich use of expressive words, very frequent use of first names, no terms of endearment, and a striking amount of echoing behavior. In American society, the child typically employs the informal code with parents as well, while in other societies this is not necessarily the case (Ervin–Tripp, 1973b; Lambert, 1967).

Observers of children's language have also noted that children switch codes when speaking to younger children. Children as young as 2 years of age demonstrate lexical, phonological, and paralinguistic changes when they speak to infants (Ervin–Tripp, 1973b). This may, however, be a form of stereotyped, role-playing behavior in young children. Gleason (1973) found age differences in ability to use a baby-talk style in her sample of 4- to 8-year-old children. The older children controlled the basic features of baby talk—short, repetitive sentences uttered in a kind of singing style—but the younger children had not learned this particular linguistic code.

Situationally determined linguistic behavior—as represented by such phenomena as implied requests and code switching—clearly involves complex cognitive abilities. To attempt to outline the prerequisite capacities would be presumptuous. Similarly, the abstract process model required to explain adequately such linguistic behavior will be much more complicated than anything presently on the drawing board. Little empirical data have been gathered, for example, about what features of the nonlinguistic environment trigger code switching in specific situations.

THE DEVELOPMENT OF THE CHILD'S LANGUAGE

I have tried to indicate what linguistic capacities the acquisition of language requires and to outline the characteristics of an abstract process model that would satisfactorily account for the child's linguistic knowledge and behavior. Since the discussion to this point has been chronologically loose, I end this chapter with a brief review of the child's linguistic development. Again, not everything can be said; I attempt simply to provide a backdrop for subsequent discussion of second-language development.

The Early Stage

One way of looking at the child's early language development, consistent with the viewpoint adopted in this chapter, is to focus on the strategies employed in acquiring a language. An analysis in these terms has been presented by John Macnamara (1972) in his discussion of the cognitive basis of language acquisition in infants.

Macnamara began with the proposition that infants acquire their language by first determining nonlinguistically the *meaning* a speaker intends to communicate to them. They do this by developing a set of cognitive strategies that function as short cuts in relating acoustical input to a speaker's intention. For example, once they are able to distinguish an object held before them from the rest of the environment, children adopt the strategy of taking the word heard as the name for that object, and not the name for a property or subproperty of the object. Thus when the child sees a red, round object and hears *ball*, she names the object *ball*. This strategy generally works well, although there are occasionally mistakes— for example, when an oven is always referred to as *hot*.

The child learns the names for colors, shapes, and sizes only after having learned the names for many objects. Similarly, the child does not learn the names for states or activities until having firmly grasped the names for at least some entities that exemplify such states and activities. A constant problem at this stage is learning what the semantic features of words are. The child may, for example, regard certain objects as *toys* and certain other objects as a *truck* and a *train*. The truck or train is not a *toy;* nor are the toys assigned the name *truck* or *train*. Somehow, however, hierarchical categories develop, and the child learns to assign words their appropriate semantic features so that overextensions, such as referring to the television repairman as *Daddy,* become less common.

Subsequently, the child—in hearing others speak—adopts the strategy of taking the main lexical items in the sentences heard, determining the referents for these items, and using this knowledge of the referents to decide what the semantic intentions of the speaker are. For example, the child hearing the sentence *Give John the book* relies on the knowledge that books are objects that can be given to people, but that people cannot be given to books. In this way the child uses nonlinguistic knowledge of the referents of lexical items to arrive at the notions of agent–action, of direct and indirect object, and so forth.

In the scheme Macnamara proposed, *syntactic development* always has reference to meaning. Syntax is learned by noting the syntactic devices such as word order, prepositions, number affixes, and the like that correlate with semantic structures. Such a strategy eventually yields all of the main syntactic devices of the language. There are, of course, complications. The child will hear such sentences as *John hit the ball* and *John walked home*. Both have the same surface structure, but the verb in one case is transitive and in the other, intransitive. To resolve this particular problem, the child must come to realize at some cognitive level that the effect of *hit* on *ball* is not the same as that of *walk* on *home*. This is done by recourse to meaning.

But in other cases, syntactic riddles cannot be solved by semantic means. The rule of subject–verb concord, for example, seems to be purely syntactic. When interpreting the sentences *The boys strike the girl* and *The girl is struck by the boys,* the child must be able to conclude that they mean roughly the same thing, although the voice of the verb is different in the two sentences. Macnamara argued that the evidence from such examples indicates that the child is capable of detecting syntactic regularities in language, regardless of whether they are tied in some way to meaning.

Nonetheless, the evidence does strongly support the priority of semantics in the initial stages of speech development. The child's first utterances are single words, expressing a variety of semantic relations. *Milk* means *This is milk, I want milk, I want more milk,* etc. (Bloom, 1973). The child is at this stage syntactically innocent. At the two-word stage, a few syntactic features appear, but for the most part speech continues to depend primarily on semantics (Bloom, 1970).

In time, increasingly more reliance is placed on syntax to convey meaning. Semantics alone does not do the trick. Children have to express what they mean to adults other than their parents and to playmates. Moreover, they discover that they can convey variations in inner states through language. Language then becomes a powerful tool, the subtle nuances of which must be mastered if it is to be used at all effectively.

Once words are combined, the complexity of the child's language increases. Children begin to employ noun phrases, differentiating nouns from their modifiers. At first all modifiers seem to belong to a single class, although they express a variety of semantic relations, including possession and attribution (Brown & Bellugi, 1964). At a later stage, the child produces such sentences as *That's a your pencil* and *That a blue flower*. Speech at this point is marked with articles, which occur before other modifiers, and demonstrative pronouns, which occur before articles and modifiers. As the process of differentiation continues, possessive pronouns form a separate class, because—unlike other modifiers— they do not occur after articles. Such phrases as *a your pencil* drop out of the child's speech.

As we have seen, *word order* is particularly important in the syntactic development of the English-speaking child. At first there are no inflections at all in the child's speech, and the full weight of syntactic structure falls on word order. This seems to be true of some inflected languages such as Russian and German, although evidence from languages with simple inflectional systems and no standard order such as Garo, Hungarian, and Turkish suggests that inflections are learned simultaneously with (or even prior to) word order.

Inflections appear to be learned according to a pattern in which inflectional classes whose referents are concrete develop first. Slobin (1966a) examined studies of Russian inflectional development (which is much richer than English) and concluded that plural inflections of nouns and imperative marking of the verb develop first (about the time when the child passes from the two- to the three-word stage). Then come classes based on relational criteria such as the tense and person markings of the verb. Third, and much later, are conditional markings of verbs, followed by nouns marked for various abstract categories of quality and action. Finally, very late, are gender markings for nouns and adjectives.

Relatively little is known about early *phonemic and phonological development* (Dale, 1976; McNeill, 1970). Case studies of young children (Burling, 1959; Leopold, 1947; Moskowitz, 1970; Velten, 1943) reveal no consistent pattern. This may be because children themselves are not consistent. There does seem to be evidence that phonemic development consists of the acquisition of a set of contrasts or distinctive features (Jakobson, 1941) rather than disparate sounds. There is a small number of contrasts that distinguish all the phonemes in English: the voiceless-voiced contrast (/p/ versus /b/), the alveoloar-labial contrast (/d/ versus /b/), the continuant-stop contrast (/s/ versus /t/), and a number of others. These contrasts seem to develop in a particular order (Velten, 1943), although probably not in the order predicted by Jakobson's theory. Moreover, although the theory predicts that contrasts are added to the phonemic system in a unified fashion, this is rarely reported. The more usual finding is that a contrast appears first in a single pair of phonemes; only after some time does the contrast generalize to other phoneme pairs.

Analysis in terms of distinctive features or contrasts has been helpful, however, in clarifying the developmental course of the phonemic system. The following are some tentative generalizations (from Ervin–Tripp, 1966):

- The vowel consonant contrasts are probably learned earliest.
- The continuant-stop contrast is quite early.
- Affricatives (*ch, j*) and liquids (*l, r*) usually appear later than stops and nasals.
- Contrasts between low and high vowels (/a/ versus /i/) precede contrasts between front and back vowels (/i/ versus /u/).
- Oral vowels precede nasal vowels.
- Consonant clusters or blends are usually late.
- Consonant contrasts usually appear earlier in initial than in medial or final position.

Studies concerned with the development of phonological rules in children (e.g., Ingram, 1974; Menn, 1971; Moskowitz, 1970) have been directed at discovering the systematic nature of this process. Ingram (1974) argued that the child initially develops a phonological system that is a mental representation of the adult system to which the child is exposed, but that does not necessarily bear a simple relationship to the adult system. That is, the child's phonological development involves the application of strategies that the child uses to organize and systematize phonological information. For example:

- Cluster reduction: simplifying consonant clusters into a single sound—as when *screw* is pronounced *gru* or *clock dak*.
- Reduplication: the child compensates for the inability to represent appropriately or produce the second syllable of a word by repeating the first syllable—*dada* for *daddy*.
- Weak syllable deletion: dropping the unstressed initial syllable in two-syllable words—as when *away* is pronounced *way;* or dropping the unstressed syllable in three-syllable words—pronouncing *pyjama dama*.

Such strategies reflect a simplification process whereby the diversity of the sound system is organized according to a limited number of rules, and a generalization process whereby these rules are applied to the child's own speech productions.

Middle Stages

By the age of 3 or so, the child has usually reached the final stage in the development of negatives and questions. Utterances can be relatively complex but still contain syntactic errors. Some examples:

Can't it be a bigger truck?
Did you broke that part?
What you have in you mouth?
Does turtles crawl?

Obviously at this stage children have not yet mastered all of the inflectional rules of the language. An auxiliary system has developed, however; and the child uses it in declaratives, negatives, and questions.

In addition, complex sentence forms, including relative clauses and conjunctions, appear:

I want this doll because she's big.
You have two things that turn around.

The child can also form complex sentences with *wh-* adverbial constructions:

I show you what I got.
I show you where we went.

Moreover, the child has begun to use complement verbs such as *want, think, hope, see,* etc. (Limber, 1973):

I want to go home.
I see you sit down.

The child at this stage is going through the process of *rule discovery*. This is not to imply, of course, that the child can conceptualize and formulate the various grammatical rules acquired. Yet the fact that the speech of the child is characterized by consistent patterns that are extended to new instances is evidence that the child's speech is governed by rules. Children speaking English do not use all possible word orders. By this stage, they have learned to use one word order for declarative sentences and another for questions. Similarly, the child generalizes knowledge of morphological rules to new instances. This is one reason why such utterances as *He comed* and *Two mouses* appear in the child's speech. Children do not simply imitate words or phrases they hear but use rules to generate new words and phrases.

Jean Berko (1958) studied this rule-discovery process in an experiment designed to test children's ability to extend their knowledge of morphological rules to new cases. She gave children nonsense words and pictures that corresponded to these words. The child's task was to form new combinations, using the nonsense words as a starting point. For example, she presented children with the picture of a *tor* and asked them to name a picture with two of these creatures. Young children were generally able to supply the correct ending /-z/. Similarly, the child was shown a picture of a man who is *ricking* and who did the same thing yesterday. When asked what it was that the man did yesterday, most young children were able to answer correctly that he *ricked*. They had more trouble, however, with such nouns as *gutch, kazh,* and *niz* and such verbs as *spow, mot,* and *bod*. Less than 50% of the preschool children in Berko's sample gave the correct plural form or past tense for these nonsense words (Table 2.1). Note that first-grade children were usually not significantly better.

Aside from syntactic and morphological development, it is clear that *semantic development* continues during the period from 3 to 6 years. By 3, most semantic overextensions seem to have disappeared. Children appear to give most of the words in their vocabulary roughly the same set of semantic features that adults do. Of course, there may be occasions when the child overextends words without this being noticed by adults. Moreover, the set of features the child assigns words is not as elaborate as an adult's. The child's features appear to be derived predominantly from perceptual input—from visual, tactile, olfactory, or auditory sources (E. Clark, 1973). Little is known, however, about how features are assigned or how the child's words come to meet adult semantic criteria.

Children from the ages of 3½ to 4 have been found to interpret the relational terms *more* and *less* as being identical in meaning. When presented with cardboard apple trees on which they could hang from one to six apples and asked to hang more/less apples on one tree than on the other, children at this age level usually understood *more* and *less* to mean the same thing. Questions that contained the word *less* were answered exactly the same way as those with *more* (Donaldson & Balfour, 1968). Similar findings were obtained in tasks where children had to distinguish the pairs, *same–different, big–wee (small), long–short, thick–thin, low–high, tall–short,* and *fat–thin* (Donaldson & Wales, 1970). In each case, the child usually took the second word of the pair to mean the same thing as the first.

TABLE 2.1
Percent of Children Supplying
Correct Morphological Forms[a,b]

Plural of:	Percent correct preschool	Percent correct first grade
glass	75	99*
wug	76	97*
lun	68	92*
tor	73	90
cra	58	86*
gutch	28	38
kazh	25	36
niz	14	33
Past of:		
bing	60	85*
gling	63	80
rick	73	73
melt	72	74
spow	36	59
mot	32	33
bod	14	31*
ring	0	25*

[a] From Berko, 1958.
[b] Asterisk (*) signifies difference significant at $\alpha = .05$.

One way of interpreting these findings is to say that the meaning of the first word in the pair was overextended by the child to cover the second word as well, so that the second word is interpreted as being a synonym rather than an antonym of the first (E. Clark, 1973). This seems to be a fairly common phenomenon. Eve Clark (1974) has noted that it applies also to locative terms such as *in–on, in–under,* and *on–under.* Children younger than 3 seem first to interpret all three prepositions as meaning *in,* then *on* is acquired and takes priority to *under,* and finally all three are distinguished. The child seems to be following a strategy of applying the first learned meaning to both members of such pairs. Since *in* is learned prior to *on,* and *on* prior to *under,* the child's mistakes reflect this strategy. Similarly, since positive dimensional adjectives (*big, tall, fat*) are learned before negative ones (*small, short, thin*), the preference for positive members of relational pairs can also be explained in terms of this strategy (Clark, 1974).

Full communicative competence requires, as we have seen, not only mastery of the formal and semantic aspects of language but control of the various styles of speaking that characterize how different people talk to each other under differing circumstances. In role-playing doctor or postman, preschool children seem to be able to modify their speech accordingly. They also can shift codes when addressing authority figures. Relatively little is known, unfortunately, about the developmental aspects of such abilities (Ervin-Tripp, 1972; Gleason, 1973).

Later Stages

In her now classic monograph on *syntactic development* between the years 5 and 10, Carol Chomsky (1969) showed that a number of important syntactic structures are still being acquired during this period. She tested the child's linguistic knowledge by determining ability to interpret correctly sentences with complex syntactic structures where there were no contextual or semantic clues that might influence interpretation. For example, in English there is a rule for sentences of the form "NP$_1$ V NP$_2$ to infinitive verb," that assigns NP$_2$ as subject of the infinitive verb (*John told Bill to leave*). This Chomsky called the minimal distance principle (MDP). The verb *ask* can be used in a form that constitutes an exception to this rule: *John asked Bill what to do,* although this is not always the case: *John asked Bill to leave.* The verb *promise* always violates the MDP rule: *John promised Bill to go.*

Chomsky found, as predicted, that children had trouble interpreting *promise* sentences and even more difficulty with *ask* sentences. In fact, some 10-year-old children still could not correctly interpret the *ask* sentences. For example, in an experiment in which children were to act out sentences with dolls, protocols such as the following were obtained:

Q: Bozo promised Donald to do a somersault. Can you make him do it?
A: (making Donald do a somersault): I promised you you can do a tumblesault.
Q: Would you say that again?
A: I promised you you could do a tumblesault.

Similarly:

Q: Ask Joanne what to feed the doll.
A: The hot dog.
Q: Now I want you to *ask* Joanne something. Ask her what to feed the doll.
A: The piece of bread.
Q: Ask Joanne what *you* should feed the doll.
A: What should I feed the doll?

In another experiment, Chomsky showed children a doll with a blindfold over its eyes and asked them *Is the doll easy or difficult to see?* Up to the age of about 9 the children answered incorrectly with *Difficult.* Apparently, they interpreted the question as if it were asking whether the doll could see rather than whether someone could see the doll. Indeed, it seems that there are a number of reasons why children misinterpret such questions (Cambon & Sinclair, 1974).

Other evidence for syntactic development after the age of 6 comes from studies of the comprehension and production of passives in older children. Research suggests that children of 6 have considerable difficulty understanding passive sentences and even more difficulty producing them (Gaer, 1969). Only at the age of 7 did some children begin to produce passive sentences when describing pictures; but they required an example, and the acted-upon object had to be shown first in the picture (Turner & Rommetveit, 1967).

On the basis of her research, Paula Menyuk (1971) concluded that children from 5 to 7 years of age have not yet mastered the auxiliary *have,* participial completion, iteration, nominalization, pronominalization, and conjunction with *if* and *so.* In addition, other syntactic structures were only partially mastered. The evidence suggests that there is a consolidation of syntax that continues at least until the age of 12 or so. This process is for the most part gradual, but there may be sudden shifts (O'Donnell, Griffin, & Norris, 1967). Berko's (1958) research with the development of morphology also indicated that older children are still in the process of mastering the appropriate rules.

There is also *semantic development* after the age of 6. Obviously, vocabulary is expanded and the semantic features of words are elaborated. There is evidence that elementary school children have substantial sets of words in their vocabularies that have different meanings than they have in the vocabularies of adults (Asch & Nerlove, 1960). Werner and Kaplan (1964) found that younger children listed items in their dictionaries in terms of functional rather than semantic properties. A bottle was to drink out of, to pour out of, to drink milk from, and so on.

Bradshaw and Anderson (1968) studied children's use of adverbial modifiers using a paired-comparison procedure. Each of nine adjectives—*slightly, somewhat, rather, pretty, quite, decidedly, unusually, very,* and *extremely*—was compared with the other eight as modifiers of the word *large.* Reliable developmental differences were obtained, with 7-year-old children considering *slightly* and *somewhat* to be relatively neutral modifiers. *Slightly large,* for example, was thought by these children to be larger than *rather large* or *quite large.* By the age of 10, *slightly* and *somewhat* were at the lower end of the continuum, as they are in the adult's system. Similarly, *very* was considered equivalent to *extremely* by 7-year-old children, but later it shifted to the more neutral position it occupies in the adult scale.

There is also evidence that *phonological development* continues after the age of 6. Snow (1964) analyzed the sound substitutions of 6- to 8-year-old children on an articulation test and reported that a number of sounds have not been mastered by children in this age range. Menyuk (1971) and Carroll (1971) also noted that certain sounds were not mastered until after the child's 8th birthday.

In their review of research on language acquisition after the age of 5, Palermo and Molfese (1972) noted that in spite of the relatively small amount of research on language development in older children, it is clear that the 5-year-old child has some way to go before achieving adult mastery. Language development can by no means be said to be over when the child enters school. If nothing else, the gap between the child's language at this age and that of the adult—in all areas of linguistic knowledge and behavior—indicates that the learning process continues.

In concluding this chapter, there are several points worth emphasizing. First, of the various ways of conceptualizing the language acquisition process, the most satisfactory is one that takes both the linguistic knowledge and behavior of the child into account. Second, the acquisition of language is a dynamic process, reflecting the child's changing experiences with the linguistic and nonlinguistic environment. Third, full competence in the language requires more than mastery of phonology, syntax, and semantics; the child must also acquire competence in those communicative skills that facilitate interaction with others sharing the same linguistic and social environment. Finally, language development is a gradual process, reflecting the gradual expansion and exercise of the child's cognitive capacities.

3
Language Acquisition and Learning in Childhood and Adulthood

The notion that language acquisition is a gradual process is not universally accepted. Indeed, many authors are much more impressed by the speed with which a child acquires a language. This was one of Chomsky's (1959) main arguments against the behaviorist position: the child simply acquires a language too quickly for this to be explained in terms of reinforcement and successive approximation. He cited the example of the immigrant child who has no difficulty acquiring the language of the new country, whereas the child's parents—in spite of their strong desire and motivation to learn the language—struggle ineffectively with it and impose the phonology and syntax of their first language on the new one.

The child's language acquisition feats so impressed Chomsky and the transformational grammar school that they maintained that the only explanation possible was that children are preprogrammed to acquire language at a definite point in their development. The view that the child possesses a capacity for language that the adult has lost is widely shared (e.g., Andersson, 1969; Jakobovits, 1972; Wilkins, 1972) and has been formalized in what is known as the "critical period" hypothesis.

In this chapter I examine the evidence for and against this hypothesis. Then language acquisition and learning in childhood and adulthood are discussed, first by comparing first-language acquisition of the child with second-language learning of the adult and then by comparing second-language acquisition in childhood with second-language learning in adulthood. We shall see that there are differences of opinion as to how similar these processes are.

THE CRITICAL PERIOD HYPOTHESIS

The critical period for language acquisition is usually defined as lasting from about age 2 to puberty. Before the child reaches age 2, language acquisition is impossible because of maturational factors, and after puberty the natural acquisition of language is blocked by a loss of "cerebral plasticity" resulting from the completion of the development of cerebral dominance of lateralization of the language function. In addition to this biological argument, the ability of young children to acquire a language quickly and efficiently and without an accent is regarded as support for the critical period notion.

The Biological Argument

In discussing the acquisition of languages from a physiological point of view, Wilder Penfield (Penfield & Roberts, 1959) noted that there seemed to be considerable anecdotal and impressionistic evidence that children acquire languages with ease before the age of 9. After that, language learning seems to be much more difficult, as though the individual had become stiff and resistant. Penfield argued that this behavioral evidence has a physiological basis. The brain of the child is plastic, that of an adult rigid and set.

Penfield cited the evidence that children are able to relearn language skills after an injury or disease destroys the speech areas in the dominant left hemisphere, whereas this is often impossible for adults, depending on the severity of the illness. There are cases of children transferring speech dominance to the opposite hemisphere if lesions occur in the speech area, but this does not seem to happen with adults.

Penfield concluded that the brain has a plasticity in childhood (before the age of 9) that it subsequently loses. He felt that an adult cannot learn a language as a child does because the adult learns through structures that have lost their flexibility. The child, on the other hand, can acquire one or more languages with ease because the corticothalamic speech mechanism in the child is still in the process of development.

Lateralization of language function.   The critical period argument was most definitively advanced by Eric Lenneberg (1967) in his classic work, *Biological foundations of language.* Lenneberg argued that natural language acquisition by mere exposure can take place only during the critical period, which he set as occurring between the ages of 2 and puberty. The brain has not developed the capacities it needs for language acquisition earlier, and after puberty the brain has lost its cerebral plasticity because of the completion of the process of cerebral dominance, or the lateralization of the language function.

Of course, Lenneberg did not deny that language learning was possible after puberty. A person can learn to communicate in a foreign language at the age of 40; but automatic acquisition from exposure to a second language seems to disappear after puberty, and foreign accents cannot be overcome easily after this age. Lenneberg also noted that "language-learning blocks" rapidly increase after puberty.

Lenneberg reviewed the evidence for the phenomenon of cerebral dominance and concluded that in childhood the left hemisphere is ordinarily more directly involved in speech and language function than the right, though the right hemisphere is not passive with respect to verbal communication. As the child grows older, however, the two hemispheres become increasingly specialized for function, and eventually, with the completion of lateralization, the polarization of function between left and right takes place, displacing language entirely to the left and certain other functions predominantly to the right. If a lesion occurs in either hemisphere during childhood, this polarization cannot take place, and the language function—together with other functions—persists in the unharmed hemisphere.

Lenneberg cited two kinds of evidence in support of his argument that lateralization for language is complete by puberty: data from unilateral brain damage in children and data from hemispherectomies (or the removal of an entire hemisphere). The evidence from the effects of unilateral brain damage in children (Basser, 1962) suggests that injuries to the right hemisphere cause more language disturbance in children than in adults: of the 20 cases of speech disturbance reported by Basser, 7 were from right lesions or 35% (Table 3.1). In adults, right lesions cause speech disturbance in only about 3% of all cases (Russell & Espir, 1961), usually with left-handed patients. Lenneberg saw this as evidence that children are less lateralized than adults and, conversely, that adults are more lateralized than children.

The evidence from hemispherectomies also suggests that children are less lateralized than adults. Basser's (1962) survey of this literature revealed that in no cases of left hemisphere hemispherectomy of children did speech disorders occur, except for three cases in which the children had aphasia before the operation. The children were apparently able to transfer the speech function to the less dominant hemisphere. In adults, however, complete transfer has not been reported after left hemispherectomies. Lenneberg concluded that the transfer of function, whereby

TABLE 3.1
Lesions After Onset of Speech and
Before Age of 10[a]

	After injury speech was:	
Location of lesion	Normal	Disturbed
Left hemisphere	2	13
Right hemisphere	8	7

[a] From Basser, 1962.

language acquisition takes place in the less dominant right hemisphere, can occur only between the ages of 2 and about 13.

Recently, however, some questions have been raised about Lenneberg's account of the process of lateralization. Krashen (1973) reanalyzed Basser's data on unilateral brain damage in children and pointed out that in all cases of injury to the right hemisphere resulting in speech disturbance, the lesion was incurred before the age of 5. There was one exception in Basser's data where the child was injured at 10, but in this case no speech disturbance resulted. Similarly, all cases of left hemispherectomy with no resultant speech disturbance involved children younger than 5. This suggests that the completion of lateralization occurs much earlier than Lenneberg supposed, possibly by the age of 5.

Additional evidence for this position comes from dichotic listening research. In dichotic listening, subjects are presented with competing simultaneous auditory stimuli, one to each ear. Normally the right ear excels for verbal material, reflecting left hemispheric specialization (Figure 3.1). If lateralization is not complete until puberty, right ear superiority should not be established until that time. Tests with children from the ages of 4 to 9 revealed no significant changes

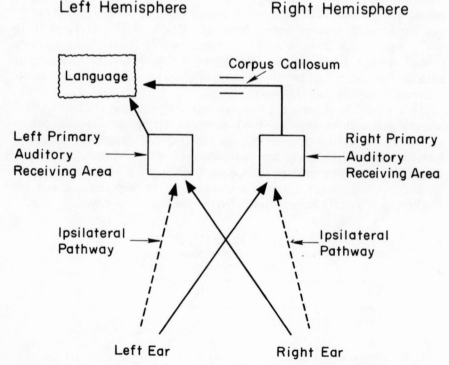

FIG. 3.1   Model of auditory processing in ''normal'' dichotic listening (Fromkin, Krashen, Curtiss, Rigler, & Rigler, 1974).

in degree of lateralization (right ear advantage); nor were the children's scores different from those of adults tested under similar conditions (Berlin, Lowe–Bell, Hughes, & Berlin, 1972; Harshman & Krashen, 1972). This suggests that the development of lateralization may be complete as early as the age of 4.

The evidence, then, appears to call for a revision of the critical period hypothesis as originally put forth. If its biological basis is the lateralization of language function, then the critical period for language development would seem to occur between the ages of 2 and 4 or 5. A great deal of syntax is acquired during this time span but—as we saw in the previous chapter—by no means all syntax. Nor is phonological or semantic development complete by the age of 4 or 5. To assert that the child acquires language during this period of time seems to be too strong a claim.

Certainly the relationship between the presumed critical period and lateralization remains an open question. At present, the data on the developmental course of lateralization are inconsistent; some authors even argue that lateralization is essentially complete at birth (see review by Krashen, 1975). In view of our lack of knowledge about when lateralization is complete, speculations about a critical period based on cerebral dominance seem premature. Furthermore, there are other considerations.

Functional localization.   According to Lenneberg, the development of lateralization in the cerebral cortex brings about specialization for function in the two hemispheres, with verbal functions located exclusively in the dominant hemisphere. Once this development process is over, the brain loses the cerebral plasticity it needs for language acquisition to occur easily and quickly.

Recent research with new methods for monitoring the activity of different brain structures in human subjects has raised questions about the adequacy of a strict localization of function model. Generally speaking, localization of function for higher mental processes in the human cortex is not static and constant but variable during development and at subsequent stages (Luria, 1973). It would be surprising if this interhemispheric plasticity does not apply to at least some language functions as well.

In their studies of split-brain patients (patients whose cerebral commissures had been sectioned to prevent epileptic discharges from spreading from one hemisphere to the other), Sperry and his associates found that certain basic linguistic abilities are reflected equally in both the dominant and nondominant hemispheres. In these studies, (e.g., Gazzaniga, 1970; Sperry & Gazzaniga, 1967; Sperry, Gazzaniga, & Bogen, 1969) split-brain patients were tested for minor-hemisphere speech comprehension by being asked to retrieve unseen objects or carry out commands with the left hand. Since information from the fingers is projected on the contralateral hemisphere, such tests provide information about minor (right) hemispheric functioning. Similarly, a series of words was presented tachistoscopically to the minor hemisphere, and subjects had to indicate with the left hand when the written word matched a spoken word.

Split-brain research of this nature showed that although the verbal abilities of the minor hemisphere were clearly inferior to those of the dominant hemisphere, the minor hemisphere could comprehend spoken and written nouns, some phrases, and very simple sentences. Moreover, the minor hemisphere was aware of the semantic properties of nouns. There is also evidence from reaction-time studies with normal subjects (Moscovitch, 1973) that the minor hemisphere can perform adequately on verbal tasks that are relatively memory-free.

In short, though verbal abilities are functionally localized in the dominant hemisphere because of its greater competence for these behaviors, the evidence does not appear to support a strict lateralization model that would restrict all language functions to the dominant hemisphere. For this reason, Moscovitch (1976) proposed a functional localization model, according to which the minor hemisphere has at least latent verbal skills. These skills are usually not utilized, but they may be when there is damage to the dominant hemisphere or damage to or absence of interhemispheric pathways.

Certainly the question of the extent to which the components of language are functionally and neurologically asymmetrical remains open to debate (Bever, 1971). Research is only beginning on this topic, and it seems certain that the use of new research techniques will refine our knowledge about what is now a relatively murky area. On the basis of what information we possess, however, it seems reasonable to conclude that the brain has more plasticity with respect to language function after childhood than Penfield or Lenneberg were willing to ascribe to it.

Genie.   It follows from a strict reading of the critical period hypothesis that language acquisition ex nihilo is impossible after puberty. If a child has for some reason not acquired a first language during that period, there is little chance that she will do so later. The study of feral children or other children raised in environments of extreme social isolation should throw light on the truth of this contention.

Unfortunately, such studies have rarely provided conclusive evidence for or against the critical period notion. Victor, the wild boy of Aveyron, for example, was 12 when he was found in the woods but was probably abandoned at the age of 4 or 5 (Itard, 1962). If this is so, his speech may have already developed and been effaced from his memory because of his isolation. His subsequent language learning may have been facilitated as a result of this previous experience. Similarly, not enough is known about the background or the extent of language development of other "wolf children" (Singh & Zingg, 1966) to shed light on the validity of the critical period notion. Studies of children reared within institutional settings or of children whose isolation is associated with congenital or acquired sensory loss usually do not bear upon the hypothesis, either because the children were isolated for short periods of time or because they emerged from their isolation at a relatively young age.

The case of Genie (Fromkin, Krashen, Curtiss, Rigler, & Rigler, 1974) is an exception to the general rule. Genie was 13 years and 9 months at the time of her discovery in Los Angeles in 1970; she had suffered physical and social isolation for most of her life. When found, she was unable to stand erect, could not chew solid or semisolid foods, and was incontinent and mute. From the age of 20 months, she had been isolated in a small, closed room. She was physically punished by her father if she made any noise. According to her mother, her father and brother never spoke to Genie, although they barked at her like dogs. The mother was forbidden to spend more than a few minutes with her during feeding. There was no radio or television in the house.

After she was found, Genie was kept in a hospital for almost a year before being given to a foster family. Medical examinations showed no signs of brain damage or neurological disease. Although Genie was functionally severely retarded, she was not autistic or pathologically disturbed. Within 4 weeks of her admission to the hospital, her behavior had changed markedly—she was no longer apathetic and socially unresponsive, but responsive and alert. There was no evidence, then, of anything wrong with Genie other than what resulted from the extreme social and sensory isolation to which she had been subjected.

It was not known for certain whether Genie had spoken prior to her isolation. When she was admitted to the hospital, she could not talk and made few noises of any kind. Tests of linguistic competence have been given to her almost weekly, beginning 11 months after she was found. When testing began, there were some signs of comprehension of individual words, but Genie had little if any comprehension of grammatical structures. Over a period of 2 years, she showed slow but steady development, learning to understand such grammatical structures as singular–plural contrasts, negative–affirmative distinctions, possessive constructions, modification, compound sentences with *and*, comparatives and superlatives, and a number of prepositions including *under, beside, over, next to,* and probably *in* and *on*.

Less progress has been made in speech production than in comprehension, presumably because Genie has not learned the necessary neuromuscular controls over her vocal organs. The sounds she does make show considerable effort, revealing the difficulties she has regulating air flow and volume and controlling her laryngeal mechanisms. Her sound productions are monotonic and have a strange voice quality. Nonetheless, her phonological development does not deviate sharply from that of normal children, and she has recently shown signs of intonation.

Genie has learned to combine words in three- and four-word strings and can produce negative sentences, strings with locative nouns, noun phrases, possessives, and plurals. Her speech is rule-governed, with fixed word orders for sentence elements (SVO) and systematic ways of expressing syntactic and semantic relations. Her language development is slower than normals, but it seems generally to parallel that of normal, English-speaking children. There are differences, however. Genie can deal with written language far more effectively than a child at her stage of language development. She acquired color words and numbers very early, had a 200-word vocabulary at the 2-word stage (compared to the normal child's 50 words), and could comprehend all *wh-* questions equally early (the normal child learns *why, how,* and *when* questions after *who, what,* and *where*). This suggests that Genie's cognitive development exceeds her linguistic development.

In spite of these differences, there is little doubt that Genie has in fact acquired many language skills. What does this mean for the critical period hypothesis? Fromkin and her associates (1974) thought that Genie's development would eventually cease. Dichotic listening tests showed that she was lateralized to the right for both language and nonlanguage functions. Inadequate language stimulation had probably inhibited the language aspects of left hemisphere development, and what success she achieved linguistically seemed to come via the minor hemisphere. Unfortunately, from clinical evidence, the prognosis for continued progress in language learning based on the right hemisphere is not good. Those cases that are known generally show some initial progress, but eventually the patient's language deficit becomes stable.

Nonetheless, regardless of the ultimate outcome, Genie's case does call for a revision of the critical period notion. It suggests that it is necessary for the left hemisphere to be stimulated during a specific period of time for it to participate in normal language development. If such stimulation does not occur during this time, language development must rely on other cortical areas and will proceed less effectively due to the previous specialization of these areas for other functions (Hécain, 1976).

When must the left hemisphere be stimulated? Before lateralization is complete? There is some evidence against this, since lateralization seems to be completed by 4 or 5 years of age, and at least one case of successful language acquisition has been reported after that age. This was the case of a child raised by a mute and totally uneducated aphasic mother until she was 6½ years of age (Mason, 1942). When found, the child was unable to talk, but nonetheless she acquired the complex grammar of English within 22 months so that she could utter such sentences as *Why does the paste come out if one upsets the jar?*

If Genie continues to make progress, her success will provide further evidence against the view that first-language development must take place prior to the completion of lateralization. Indeed, since her comprehension appears much in advance of production, it may be that the deficiencies she shows result from problems in acquiring the motor skills associated with speech. Can it be that there is a critical period for the left hemisphere to be stimulated if successful acquisition of the neuromuscular controls necessary for speech is to be achieved—and that it is only in this respect that a critical period can be said to exist for language development?

Other Arguments for the Critical Period Hypothesis

Associated with the biological argument for the critical period are a number of other arguments based on impressionistic evidence that children acquire language more quickly and with greater ease than adults and that they do so without acquiring the accents that characterize languages learned by adults.

The argument from speed and efficiency of acquisition.   We have seen that Chomsky (1959) used the immigrant child argument in his famous polemic against Skinner and behaviorism. Penfield (Penfield & Roberts, 1959) also noted that the children of immigrant families typically acquire the new language in a brief period of time and can speak it easily and with little accent, regardless of whether they go to school or simply play in the street with other children. The same can rarely be said for their parents, who typically have enormous problems learning the language and usually never learn to speak it without an accent.

It is not clear, however, just why the child acquires a language so much more easily than an adult. Indeed, there is even some question of whether language acquisition is that easy for the child. Close observation of the speech development of children acquiring their first language suggests that the child must expend a great deal of effort, that there are many false starts and mistakes, and that the language acquisition process is by no means automatic (Cukovsky, 1965; Weir, 1962). Even for the 3-year-old child, the process of acquiring a second language requires an enormous amount of exposure and practice (Valette, 1964).

According to the critical period hypothesis, the child capitalizes on maturational processes that make the acquisition of language easy and quick. This is the reason for the speed and efficiency of the child's acquisition as compared to adult learning of second languages. One problem with the speed of acquisition argument, however, is that the child acquiring a first language has much more intensive and continuous exposure to the language than is ever possible for an adult learning a second language (Lee, 1973). Assuming that young children are exposed to a normal linguistic environment for at least 5 hours a day, they will have had, conservatively, 9,000 hours of exposure between the ages of 12 months and 6 years. In contrast, the Army Language School in California regarded 1,300 hours as sufficient for an adult to attain near-native competence in Vietnamese (Burke, 1974). The same argument applies to immigrant children, who typically have much more exposure to the language than do their parents.

The argument based on speed of acquisition may be criticized from another perspective. Many aspects of language do not develop phenomenally fast. Thurstone's analysis of seven primary abilities indicated that verbal comprehension reaches 80% of adult competence only at age 18 and word fluency at age 20. In contrast, number and memory factors reached 80% of adult level at 16, space and reasoning at 19, and perceptual factors at age 12 (Thurstone, 1955). In comparison with other mental capacities, then, language capacity does not seem to develop remarkably quickly.

Returning to the immigrant child example, one can ask just what is responsible for the superiority of children's language acquisition when compared to that of their parents. In addition to the possibility that the child has more exposure to a second language than adults do, it is also very likely that children are more highly motivated to acquire the language than their parents are. For the child, learning to communicate with peers in the classroom or playground is a life-and-death affair. This is often overlooked by those who attribute greater motivation to the parents. Often the parents learn enough of the language to get by in the new environment but—in spite of protestations to the contrary—are not highly motivated to learn much more. They frequently have friends and neighbors who speak the same native language and tend to restrict their social interaction to this circle. Or they may avoid social contact with other adults in the new country, something that the child cannot easily do. Children in the school or neighborhood environment are likely to be forced to interact constantly with peers who speak in their second language.

There are other considerations as well. Less is demanded of the child in achieving linguistic competence—constructions are simple, vocabulary relatively small—when compared with what is necessary for an adult to speak at an adult's level of competence. The child's attitude toward the new language is also likely to be different. It may well be that in the adult, the development of firm ego boundaries and a sense of cultural identity place constraints on language learning that are not found in the child (Schumann, 1975). These psychological and social factors—rather than neurological considerations—may be responsible for any superiority in second-language acquisition on the part of the child.

One inference frequently drawn from the critical period notion is that the younger children are when they begin to learn a second language in the classroom, the better (Andersson, 1973; Montessori, 1959). The young child is thought to learn a second language quickly and without apparent effort; the older the child is, the more fixed language habits become. Some evidence for this view comes from a study by Ramsey and Wright (1974) in which they examined immigrants in Canada and found that the older the child was when introduced to English, the poorer the performance on various tests of English language skill. Children who arrived after the age of 6 tended to have lower scores on tests of language skills as their age of arrival increased. No relationships were found for younger children. There was considerable variance in the scores, however, and correlations were modest.

Furthermore, other research leads to a quite different conclusion from that reached by Ramsey and Wright. Politzer and Weiss (1969), for example, found that in tests of auditory discrimination of French vowel sounds, older English-speaking children performed significantly better than younger children. This was also true for tests of pronunciation and for a recall test for vocabulary items. Politzer and Weiss argued that their results are not necessarily evidence against the critical period hypothesis, since the comparative inability of younger children to identify sounds and to transfer and recall vocabulary in terms of their first language gives them an advantage in learning a second language—without interference from their first language. This conclusion seems somewhat forced, however, and implies that younger children are superior to older children and adults in learning a second language because of their cognitive limitations. This view is at variance with the critical period hypothesis, which stipulates that the young child learns languages with ease because the child's brain is ideally programmed for linguistic input.

Further evidence against the critical period hypothesis comes from a study by Urs Bühler (1972) of Swiss school children learning French as a second language. Bühler reported that research on over 1,500 students who began French either in the fourth or fifth grade showed that the older children performed significantly better on various tests of French language skills on two separate testing occasions. Bühler found these results to be a compelling argument against the proposition that the earlier the child begins to learn a second language, the better.

Of course, it may be that the schools do not utilize the advantage younger children have in developmental psychological terms. Susan Ervin–Tripp (1974) reported, however, that even in a natural milieu where communication was emphasized and where the second language was heard most of the day, older children acquired the language faster than younger children. She found that older children in her sample of 4- to 9-year-old children were superior in their acquisition of morphology and syntax, although they had no more exposure to the second language than did younger children. She attributed this to more efficient memory heuristics and to a superior ability in problem solving and rule learning on the part of older children.

In another study of second-language acquisition—as opposed to formal language learning through instruction—Snow (Snow & Hoefnagel–Höhle, 1975) found that in a sample of American children, adolescents, and adults learning Dutch in Holland, it was the adolescents who acquired the language most readily. This also tells against a critical period notion applied to second-language acquisition.

One final point in this connection: if second languages are easier to learn before puberty, one would expect that after that age people who immigrate to a new country would be less likely to use the new language. Braine (1971a) reported, however, that a study of census data on the language use of immigrants to Israel showed that there was a drop in the use of the new language among those who immigrated after the age of 30; according to Lenneberg's critical period argument, however, the drop should come around the age of 13.

The evidence regarding accents.   In a discussion of second-language acquisition, Scovel (1969) cited Lenneberg's argument that cerebral lateralization is complete at puberty and saw this to be related to evidence that foreign accents appear at this time. He contended that the ability to master a second language without an accent before the age of about 12 was directly associated with the fact that lateralization has not yet become permanent at this time. The adult has lost the cerebral plasticity of the child, and all attempts to eliminate accents in adult speech are, on biological grounds, futile.

One difficulty with this argument is that a single exception constitutes a disproof of the hypothesis. Has there ever been a case of an individual who learned a second language after the critical period and was able to speak it without an accent? Scovel argued that this is biologically impossible. Even Penfield (Penfield & Roberts, 1959) did not go this far, however. He referred to the author Joseph Conrad, who learned English at the age of 15; according to an Englishman who knew him, Conrad spoke the language beautifully and without an accent.

The example is particularly instructive, since Scovel used Conrad as proof that an adult could *not* learn to speak a second language (or a third, since Conrad had learned French and Polish as a child) without an accent. He cited a biographer (Gerald, 1967), who maintained that Conrad had such a strong accent that he was prevented from lecturing in English. Perhaps Penfield's British informant was overly tolerant or perfected Conrad's accent in his memory. Or perhaps Conrad used his nonexistent accent as an excuse for not giving public lectures. At any rate, the example shows the difficulty of relying on subjective and impressionistic judgments of a speaker's accent.

Societies seem to vary considerably with respect to their sensitivity to foreign accents (Hill, 1970); and within a society such as our own, different individuals set different standards for accent-free speech. The linguist is far more likely to perceive an accent than the ordinary person. Must one meet the linguist's criteria or those of the ordinary person? The linguist is probably too precise; for the linguist, almost everyone has an accent, depending on the part of the country one comes from. The ordinary person is probably too imprecise; a foreigner could pass for a native speaker if the foreigner's accent approximated that of some dialect with which the listener was not familiar. Without an adequate definition of what it means to speak with an accent, it seems doubtful whether this question can be resolved.

Nonetheless, there is some empirical evidence that younger children have a biological predisposition that enables them to achieve fidelity in pronunciation. Asher and Garcia (1969) tested 71 Cuban immigrants—most of whom had been in the United States for about 5 years—and found that the younger the children were when they entered the country, the more closely their pronunciation approximated that of native English-speaking children. Oyama (1976) studied 60 Italian male immigrants and also found that the younger the person was when he entered the United States, the better his accent.

Even granting the argument based on accents does not prove the critical period hypothesis to be true. It is quite possible that the motor patterns involved in speech are directly correlated with neurophysiological mechanisms and that once the lateralization of the brain is completed, plasticity in the production of speech sounds is lost. But the critical period hypothesis was applied to all aspects of language acquisition, not simply to the motor aspect.

In conclusion, it seems that the critical period hypothesis remains very much a hypothesis at the present time. The evidence for functional localization based on recent research seems to rule out a strict lateralization model. There appears to be more flexibility with regard to language functions than was believed possible a decade ago. Possibly there is a critical period for the neuromuscular patterns involved in speech, after which time it becomes much more difficult to acquire a new language without an accent. But whether this is the case, whether there are critical periods for other language skills, what the length of the critical period is in each case, and how this relates to the process of lateralization cannot be answered with any certainty. As Hegel said of Schelling's philosophy, this is a night where all cows are black. Fortunately, there is currently a great deal of research on these topics, and some answers may be available in the near future.

FIRST-LANGUAGE ACQUISITION AND SECOND-LANGUAGE LEARNING

In addition to the question of whether children are biologically predisposed to acquire language, there is the question of how children's language acquisition differs from adult language learning. It is this question that I wish to focus on now, first by considering the arguments for and against viewing second-language learning in adults as a qualitatively different process from first-language acquisition in children—then by looking at some experimental research that bears on this issue.

The Debate over Differences in Kind

Does an adult learning a second language with formal instructions learn that language in the same way that a child acquires a first language in the natural environment? There is considerable debate in the literature over this issue, although all authors admit that there are differences between the language learning of an adult and the language acquisition of a child. The focus of debate is whether such differences constitute differences in kind, whether there is a qualitative difference in the two processes, whether the processes are radically different. I consider first the arguments of those who believe that there are qualitative differences between second-language learning in adults and first-language acquisition in children and that these differences require radically different processes. Then I turn to the arguments of those who regard the differences as essentially quantitative and who see no reason for believing that an adult learns a second language in a manner radically different from that in which a child acquires a first language.

The argument for a difference in kind.   Those authors who accept the critical period notion usually favor the view that second-language learning in adults is qualitatively different from first-language acquisition. They hold that the individual is biologically programmed to acquire language before puberty and that optimal grammatical coding is available only to children, not to adults (Halle, 1962; King, 1969; Saporta, 1966; Wilkins, 1972, 1974). The child is thought to process language in a manner different from and superior to the way that an adult processes language (Andersson, 1969; Echeverría, 1974).

According to this view, the language acquisition device of the child is radically different from (and superior to) that of the adult. The child processes language in terms of a preprogrammed linguistic coding ability; the adult processes language in terms of a general coding ability. Thus there are two models (see Figure 3.2) for language acquisition (Echeverría, 1974). This seems to be the view of Noam Chomsky (1968), who at one point suggested that the mind is divided into faculties: whereas first-language acquisition takes place through the faculty of language learning, which atrophies at a certain age, he postulated, languages can still be learned after that age by using such other faculties of the mind as the logical or the mathematical.

One reason given for the qualitative difference between second-language learning in adults and first-language acquisition is that structural changes result from first-language acquisition. If a new language is learned in adulthood, it must be filtered through the learning acquisition system of the individual, modified by the first language (Stern, 1970). The older the individual is, the more the rules and habits of the first language *interfere* with learning a second language;

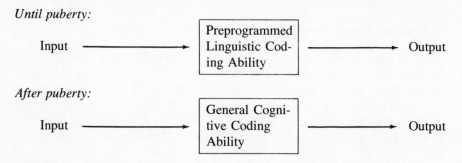

FIG. 3.2   Models of language acquisition before and after puberty (Echeverría, 1974).

once people are in their teens, they can no longer learn a language as they acquired their first language (Politzer, 1965).

The interference argument rests largely on errors made by individuals learning a second language. These errors do not appear in first-language acquisition data; hence the second-learning experience is seen to be qualitatively different. For example, when an English-speaking adult says *Ich warte für ihn* in German, the English prepositional construction in the English equivalent, *I wait for him,* has interfered with and displaced the correct German form, *Ich warte auf ihn.* Children acquiring German as a first language do not make such mistakes; hence the two experiences involve basically different processes.

Another argument is that it is said to be more difficult for speakers of English to learn certain languages—e.g., Chinese—than to learn others—e.g., French, whereas the opposite is true for native Japanese speakers (James, 1971). That is, it is argued that comparison of the second-language learning experiences of speakers of different first languages reveals different degrees of interference due to the different first languages. This again suggests that the learner of a second language must "filter" that language through a language acquisition device that has been modified and restructured by the first language.

Roger Brown (1973b) thought that second-language learning may be responsive to familiar sorts of learning variables whereas first-language acquisition may not. He cited evidence that grammatical morphemes are always learned by the child, although it seems that listeners do not really need them. He noted that adult Japanese learning English as a second language do not seem to learn how to use articles correctly, whereas the child acquiring English as a first language does. Similarly, children acquire tag questions in English without difficulty, whereas adults learning English as a second language often do not learn them at all. Brown was inclined to see first-language acquisition as a unique experience and thought that it may be "profoundly and ineradicably different [p. 104]" from second-language learning in adults.

The argument against a difference in kind.   On the opposite side of the fence are a number of authors who maintain that language acquisition in childhood and second-language learning in adulthood involve essentially the same processes (Cooper, 1970; Corder, 1967; Macnamara, 1973; Newmark & Reibel, 1968; Roberts, 1973). These authors admit that there are differences between the way an adult learns a second language and the way a child acquires a first language, but they argue that these are mostly quantitative differences and do not constitute differences in kind.

The argument from interference is rejected, because it rests on a false assumption about the process of language learning and because it lacks empirical support. The interference notion derives from a learning-theory approach, according to which language learning involves a process of habit formation. Interference results from the fact that old habits have not yet been extinguished. Such an approach leads logically to the untenable position that old habits (the first lan-

guage) must be unlearned or extinguished before new habits (the second language) can be mastered (Dulay & Burt, 1972). Even learning theorists have
expressed dissatisfaction with theoretical formulations relating to interference
phenomena (Tulving & Madigan, 1970). The essential issue is an empirical one:
is there evidence that in learning a second language a person inevitably uses
first-language structures and that errors result from the interference of the first
language?

The argument that differential interference results from two different first
languages when learning a particular second language does not necessarily prove
the qualitative difference position. The fact that an American learns French or
German easier than Chinese and that for a Japanese the reverse is true may
simply be due to the way in which the material is taught (Littlewood, 1973).
With appropriate teaching methods these differences may cancel out. Here again,
the question is an empirical one and must be settled by empirical methods.

Of course it is difficult not to be impressed by the differences in first-language
acquisition and second-language learning. These differences have been commented on repeatedly. Children generalize more between words that sound alike
and confuse the meaning of similar-sounding words (Ervin–Tripp, 1967). Children seem to attend to sounds—to the surface of language—whereas adults
penetrate the surface of the utterance to its meaning (Ervin–Tripp, 1970). Children are also limited, as we have seen in the preceding chapter, by the ineffi-
ciency of their information processing and mnemonic devices. Their language
development is constrained and determined by their cognitive development.

In addition, the way in which children are exposed to their first language
differs markedly from the way in which adults are usually exposed to a second
language. As noted, language acquisition refers to the naturalistic situation,
without any focusing on linguistic form. The child acquires language through
direct experience with events at hand in a natural communication setting. Language learning, in contrast, involves formal instruction and an artificial linguistic
environment. The adult is taught to apply rules consciously, whereas the child
receives no such instruction.

The question is whether such differences in how children and adults are exposed to language mean that different processes are employed in the two cases.
Those who view language learning in processing terms, as a series of strategies
employed by a changing language acquisition system, tend to see no need to posit
a qualitative difference between first-language acquisition and second-language
learning in adults. The basic features of the language acquisition system remain
the same, although input conditions may be different for adults and children
(Ervin–Tripp, 1973a). Memory heuristics improve with age, making it possible
to retain longer input and discover meaning; yet there is a basic similarity of
process. Although the use of written materials and formal instructions increases
efficiency and speed of learning in adults (Braine, 1971b), an adult learning a
second language faces the same task and uses essentially the same strategies as
the child learning a first language.

Thus Taylor (1974) noted that children in the acquisition of their first language do not operate under an imitation and repetition strategy, but rather under a strategy that encourages them to simplify and regularize the syntactic structure of the language they are acquiring. Taylor argued that this strategy of simplifying the target language applies to second-language learning as well. Both adults and children overgeneralize target language rules, reduce grammatical redundancies, and omit those rules that they have not learned, presumably because of their apparent arbitrariness.

Because of their cognitive maturity, second-language learners do not produce the one- and two-word utterances found in the speech of children acquiring the first language. But this does not mean that there is a qualitative difference between first-language acquisition and second-language learning (Ervin–Tripp, 1974):

> Now it is certainly the case that the second language learner makes use of prior knowledge, skills, tactics, but it is also true that the first language learner does this. That is, any learning builds on what has happened before, and it remains a major question just how this occurs. A child learning a language at four, whether a first or second language, has knowledge of the world, knowledge of spatial and object relations, knowledge of causality, which a child of one does not have. A child hearing a sentence he has never heard before, at the age of four, can bring to it knowledge of sound groupings, configurations, which a child of one does not have—whether or not he is listening to a new sentence in his mother tongue or a second language. The fact that the second language builds on prior knowledge is not what differentiates it from first language learning [p. 112].

What differences exist are thought to be quantitative in nature, resulting from the greater cognitive maturity of the second-language learner and from social and affective factors. In processing terms, first-language acquisition and second-language learning are seen to be identical, as evidenced by the kinds of errors observed (Taylor, 1974).

Some Empirical Findings

Unfortunately, there has been very little research directly comparing children acquiring their first language with adults learning a second language. There are obvious problems: comparison is difficult because of different levels of mental functioning, yet methods of testing must be the same for both groups. Nonetheless, there are some data on the important question of whether adults learning a second language go through the same stages of development as children do acquiring that language as their first language. In addition, there have been empirical studies of interference that bear on the question at hand.

Developmental evidence.   Vivian Cook (1973) studied 20 foreign adults learning English and 24 English-speaking children, who ranged in age from 2 years, 11 months to 4 years and 9 months. The adult subjects came from a number of different countries and had been studying English in England for less than a year, though they had exposure to varying amounts of English in their own countries. All subjects were shown a picture and were read a sentence that the picture illustrated. They had to repeat the sentence and in some cases answer a comprehension question. In essence, this was the method of elicited imitation (Slobin & Welsh, 1973), often used to determine linguistic competence.

Both groups performed rather poorly on a series of sentences designed to test various syntactic features of the relative clause in English: *This is the man that drives the bus, The lady the boy is drawing is funny, The hammer that is breaking the cup is big,* and so forth. The children's imitations were correct only 8% of the time and the adults' 26% of the time. Both groups seemed to have approached the task in much the same way, as reflected in the errors they made. Both groups often omitted *that,* even when it was required grammatically; both groups replaced *that* with grammatical alternatives; both groups found the relative clauses following the subject of the sentence easier to imitate than those following the object of the sentence; and both groups recoded syntactic structure to preserve the sentences' meaning. In contrast to the adults, children used more substitutions for the relative (especially *what* for *that*), sometimes shifted the subject of the relative clause to the main clause, and occasionally repeated the last few words of the sentence in giving their answers (... *drives the bus,* ... *is funny,* and so forth).

In general, the trend indicated that adult second-language learners and children made the same kinds of mistakes. Children even made some mistakes that are regarded as typical of foreigners such as omitting the subject of the relative clause or omitting the ''s'' from the third-person singular form of the verb. Both groups did equally poorly on comprehension tests. The differences between the two groups probably reflected differences in the conditions under which they acquired the language; children were allowed to make more grammatically unacceptable substitutions and mistakes than the adults, who were closely monitored in an audio-lingual learning setting. The occasional echoing responses, in which children gave only the last few words of the sentence, probably reflected a strategy of seizing what remains in short-term memory; whereas an adult uses a more complex strategy because his operative memory is more effective.

In a second experiment, Cook tested 66 adults who had averaged 8 months of English instruction in England and 3 years and 8 months of instruction prior to coming to England. They were tested on sentences such as *The wolf is happy to bite* and *The duck is hard to bite.* The subject's task was to tell who was doing the biting in each sentence—the duck or the wolf. Cook found that she could sort her subjects into three types:

- *Primitive rule users,* who consistently regarded the subject of the sentence as the agent of the action.
- *Intermediates,* who gave mixed answers—sometimes following the primitive rule and sometimes giving the correct interpretation.
- *Passers,* who gave completely correct responses to all sentences.

These categories reflected the amount of exposure subjects had to English (Table 3.2) and appeared to represent developmental stages. Apparently, the first

TABLE 3.2
Average Amount of Exposure to English for Groups
Giving Different Types of Responses[a]

Type of response	Amount of instruction in England	Amount of prior instruction
Primitive rule users (7 subjects)	2 months	2 years, 2 months
Intermediates (45 subjects)	7 months	3 years, 5 months
Passers (14 subjects)	12 months	4 years, 8 months

[a] From Cook, 1973.

strategy used developmentally is to regard the subject of the sentence as the agent of the action, then there is a period of uncertainty, and finally the learner is able to interpret the sentence in terms of its deep structure rather than by relying exclusively on surface structure. There is evidence (Cromer, 1970) that children go through a similar process.

Cook pointed out that her results raise some problems for the critical period hypothesis. If adults lose the ability to acquire a language as children do, one would suppose that adults would utilize what knowledge they have to learn a new language. Adults have learned, for example, that sentences can contain sentences embedded in them. One would expect them to use this information and consequently to have less difficulty comprehending embedded relative clauses than a child does. But this did not happen in Cook's first experiment. When presented with sentences such as *The lady the boy's drawing is funny,* adult second-language learners fell into the same trap as children did. The adult's learning seems not to have been facilitated by the first language; as Cook's second experiment suggests, the second-language learner appears to go through essentially the same stages as the child.

Cook also noted that other studies tend to support the notion that children and adults approach language in basically the same way. For example, Palermo and Howe (1970) found that adults, in an analogous experimental learning situation, employed the same strategies as children do when learning regular and irregular past-tense inflections in English. Similarly, Stolz and Tiffany (1972) showed that the characteristic differences between word associations of children and adults could be canceled out by giving adults unfamiliar words.

In a study designed to investigate the acquisition of a set of complex English structures in adult learners of English as a second language, d'Anglejan and Tucker (1975) found results quite similar to Cook's. In their study, d'Anglejan and Tucker tested adult second-language learners of two levels of proficiency—beginners and advanced. The grammatical structures investigated were those complex English structures used by Carol Chomsky (1969) in her study of the acquisition of syntax in children between the ages of 5 and 10. Adult second-language learners were found to process the linguistic data of the target language without relying on the syntax of their first language. The developmental pattern observed for the acquisition of the complex structures paralleled those observed in Chomsky's children. In no case was there evidence of the use of strategies that differed from those used by children acquiring English as a first language.

Thus there seems to be little evidence from studies comparing language acquisition in children and second-language learning in adults that the two groups go through radically different processes. What evidence there is points to the conclusion that the processes involved are basically the same. Of course, this need not be the last word on the topic, and more research is needed directly comparing the adult second-language learner and the child acquiring a first language before any definitive statements are possible.

The evidence from interference.   As we have seen, those who view second-language learning in adulthood as qualitatively different from first-language acquisition in childhood base their argument in part on the evidence for interference in second-language learning. Since one finds adult learners making mistakes that reflect their first language and children making no such mistakes in acquiring their first language, the two experiences must be different in kind. Second-language learning is dependent on habits acquired during the process of first-language acquisition.

This view derives ultimately from traditional interference theory in verbal learning and memory research. As we have seen, however, there is a logical problem with such a theory: old habits must be unlearned or extinguished before new habits can be learned; otherwise they interfere with the new habits. It follows that the learner would have to extinguish (forget) the first language to learn a second language without interference. This is obviously contrary to what actually happens when most people learn a second language.

How then should one think of interference? I shall define *interference* as those errors that occur in the learning of a second language (B) that reflect the acquisition of a previous language (A) and that are not found in the normal development of those who acquire that language (B) as a first language. Such errors must be distinguished from at least three other types of errors (Dulay & Burt, 1972):

- Developmental errors: those errors that do not reflect the learner's first language (A), but are found among those who acquire the second language (B) during childhood as a first language.
- Ambiguous errors: those errors that can be categorized as due either to interference or as developmental errors.
- Unique errors: those errors that cannot be categorized as due either to interference or as developmental errors.

If acquiring a first language brings about structural changes that require subsequent second-language learning to be filtered through a language acquisition system modified by the first language, then one would expect the majority of second-language errors to reflect the interference of first-language structures. Yet the common finding is that the majority of errors are not traceable to first-language structure (Brudhiprabha, 1972; Dulay & Burt, 1972; Ervin–Tripp, 1970; George, 1972; Lance, 1969; Richards, 1971). In most of these studies only about a third of the errors was attributable to first-language structures. Many errors reflect the learner's attempt to generalize and apply the rules of the second language before they are mastered. Others are morphological and syntactic simplifications of first-language learners (Ervin–Tripp, 1969). Others seem to be unique in that they do not reflect first-language structure and are not found in the developmental acquisition data of native speakers of the second language.

This is not, however, to deny that interference errors occur. The argument is to what extent the adult learner of a second language is inhibited by first-language structures. Those who hold that the two types of language learning are qualitatively different are committed to the view that interference from first language is the main source of mistakes in second-language acquisition, since the structures of the first language determine those imposed on the second. The evidence does not seem to warrant such a conclusion. There is some evidence that interference errors predominate in the early stages of second-language learning in adults (Taylor, 1975), but such errors are much less frequent at later stages and by no means constitute the majority of errors.

Indeed, even the minority of errors that are due to interference may not all reflect negative transfer or inhibition. The adult second-language learner may be trying out strategies based on those successfully used in the first language. This intentional use of patterns from the first language to crack the code of the second does not seem to involve interference in the usual sense of the word. Nor does this mean that the second-language learner is necessarily using different processes in learning the language. The child also uses the patterns of the known language to comprehend those that are not known.

SECOND-LANGUAGE ACQUISITION AND LEARNING IN CHILDREN AND ADULTS

Until now, the discussion has focused on the comparison of second-language learning in adults with first-language acquisition in children. Now I will turn briefly to the topics of second-language acquisition and learning in children and adults. Both children and adults can *acquire* a second language in the sense that they may be exposed to it naturalistically, without formal instruction. And both children (at least older children) and adults can *learn* a second language in the sense that they may be exposed to the language through formal instruction in the classroom. What evidence is there that adults and children acquire, or learn, a second language differently?

Second-Language Acquisition

It is often argued that the child has a superior biological predisposition for language acquisition (this applies to second or third languages as well as to first languages). Hence the young child is thought to acquire a second language easily and quickly. The evidence, however, does not support this viewpoint. The few studies that have been conducted suggest that older children and adolescents do better than younger children in acquiring a second language in a natural environment (Ervin–Tripp, 1974; Snow & Hoefnagel–Höhle, 1975).

Nonetheless, direct comparison between young children and adolescents or adults acquiring a second language is difficult because of several factors. First, the criterion for success is vastly different for the child as compared to the adult. Children are considered fluent when they can communicate at a level appropriate for their age. An adult must communicate with other adults about much more complicated issues, where deficiencies in vocabulary and syntax show up more readily. It is also difficult to hold constant such factors as motivation to learn and exposure to the second language across different age groups. Yet there have been some well-conducted studies in this area.

These are the studies by Asher and his associates (Asher, 1965, 1969; Asher, Kusudo, & de le Torre, 1974; Asher & Price, 1967), who attempted to mimic the way in which children acquire languages in the natural setting. Asher argued that one possible reason why children acquire second languages faster than adults (assuming they do) is that their language acquisition is often synchronized to physical responses. The child has to make action responses in play and in response to commands. In contrast, an adult attempts to learn the language quite independently of physical behavior. What would happen, Asher asked, if adults were required to acquire language as children do, by synchronizing their second language with physical responses?

In one of his studies (Asher & Price, 1967) four age groups were compared in their acquisition of Russian: children from second, fourth, and eighth grade classes and a group of college undergraduates. All subjects were English speakers with no knowledge of Russian. They were divided into two groups at each age level. In the first group—called the Act–Act group—subjects were to imitate an adult model who physically responded to Russian commands to stand, sit, walk, stop, turn, squat, and run. Each utterance was presented 10 times in a random sequence. There were retention tests immediately after the training phase, 24 hours later, and 48 hours later. After each retention test new training was conducted with increasingly complex constructions. By the last training session, the subjects heard such commands as *Pick up the pencil and paper and put them on the chair* and *Walk to the door, pick up the pencil, put it on the table, and sit on the chair*.

Training and retention tests were the same for the second group—called the Observe–Act group—except that this group merely saw the model perform the

Russian commands; only during the retention tests were subjects to act out commands. This, however, did not significantly affect their performance relative to the Act–Act group (Figure 3.3). Both groups performed approximately as well at each age level. All groups of children were significantly poorer than adults on measures of retention. Thus, in spite of the fact that the task appears to approximate closely the way in which languages are acquired in the "natural setting," children displayed no superior language acquisition capabilities.

The superiority of the adults in such tasks no doubt reflects cognitive maturation. *In situ,* this may be offset by other factors that favor children. Anecdotal and impressionistic evidence that children are superior in second-language acquisition most likely stems from nonlinguistic and nonbiological factors such as amount of exposure, motivation, lack of inhibition, and other personality variables. When the child is placed in an experimental situation where these factors are controlled or do not operate, performance is inferior to that of an adult.

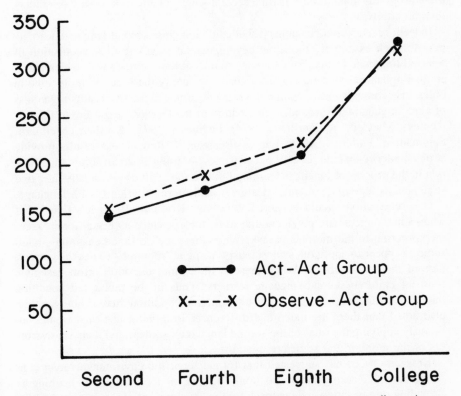

FIG. 3.3   Retention of commands as measured by mean total recall scores on all retention tests (based on Asher & Price, 1967).

Second-Language Learning

If we turn to the more formal learning situation, we find generally the same pattern of results. There is, for example, some experimental research in which adults and children learned a miniature artificial language under controlled conditions. In this research (Braine, 1971a), the learning of adults was superior to that of children. In addition, there is the evidence, cited earlier, that older children perform better than younger children in the classroom, second-language learning situation (Bühler, 1972; Politzer & Weiss, 1969). In a study of third and fourth grade children learning Japanese as a second language, Grider, Otomo, and Toyota (1961) also found that older children performed better on tests of language skills. All of these findings run against the argument that younger children have superior ability in learning a second language.

As we shall see in Chapter 6, large-scale programs in teaching foreign languages to English-speaking children have not attained what was expected on the basis of children's vaunted language learning abilities. There is no evidence from these programs that children learn a second language any more easily or quickly than do adults.

Indeed, recent research suggests that adult and child second-language learners pass through essentially the same developmental stages in their acquisition of selected linguistic forms. For example, studies of the accuracy with which learners of English as a second language correctly supply the required morpheme in obligatory contexts indicates that the same accuracy hierarchy results regardless of age, language background, or the nature of the learner's exposure to English (Bailey, Madden, & Krashen, 1974; Fathman, 1975; Krashen, Sferlazza, Feldman, & Fathman, 1976; Larsen–Freeman, 1976a). These results provide strong evidence that the onset of puberty does not bring about an abrupt modification in the process of language learning but that the adult uses basically the same strategies as the child, in spite of a great deal more experience with language.

One reservation should be noted, however. Krashen (1976) has found that when adult subjects are given enough time, they produce a very different accuracy ordering in the morpheme task. When there are no time constraints, adult subjects appear to apply rules consciously, using a "monitor" to test the correctness of their productions. When there is little time, the adult errors resemble those of children second-language learners. Thus in the monitored condition there is a difference, whereas in the unmonitored condition there is not. Krashen also noted that there are individual differences in monitor use (that is, in consciously applying the rules of the second language): some individuals are overusers of the monitor and some are underusers.

Krashen (1976) has suggested that formal linguistic environments may contribute to both learning and acquisition. The classroom contributes to learning by providing rule isolation and feedback for the development of the monitor. And to the extent that language use is emphasized, the classroom serves simultaneously as a source of simplified input for language acquisition. Furthermore, although Krashen does not make this point, it would seem that in informal, naturalistic settings, older children and adults can consciously learn rules (for example, when they ask native informants to tell them the rules behind particular constructions). If this is the case, the distinction between the processes of learning and acquisition becomes increasingly nebulous and perhaps should be abandoned for a distinction based on the use of the monitor. This, however, is fraught with methodological pitfalls: how is one to determine whether the individual is consciously (or subconsciously) acquiring or using rules? At the present time, it is probably best (though not very satisfying) to maintain the learning–acquisition distinction based on the nature of the setting, while acknowledging that the same processes may be involved in both formal and informal settings.

The switch from a subconscious (unmonitored) to a conscious (monitored) approach to second languages is often thought to occur at puberty. Krashen (1975) suggested that changes in cognitive development that occur around puberty—such as the onset of "formal operations" in Piaget's sense—relate to adult–child differences in second-language development. Though ruling out an explanation based on the development of cerebral dominance, Krashen thought that it was possible that there are neurological events related to the cognitive maturation of the individual that in turn affect the development of a second language.

Other authors (Curran, 1961; Lambert, 1967; Schumann, 1975; Titone, 1973) have stressed affective and social factors to account for adult–child differences. This view was summarized by Taylor (1974), who argued that the psychological learning strategies involved in second-language development are basically the same for children and adults, differing essentially in the degree of cognitive maturity of the learner. Affective variables set limits to what is learned but do not affect the basic process.

In any event, there is considerably more to be known about the biological substratum of language. Certainly biological development affects first-language development, but not enough is known about how and to what extent. While there may be a critical period for some aspects of first-language acquisition, there does not seem to be evidence of biological limits to second-language acquisition or learning. An unqualified "frozen brain" theory does not seem supported by available evidence. Nor is there evidence that children possess special, biologically based language abilities that give them an advantage over adults in language learning. Clearly, however, there is room for more research in this area, especially research in which adults and children are compared in various learning and acquisition contexts.

4
Simultaneous Acquisition of Two Languages in Childhood

This chapter is concerned with the study of children who acquire two languages simultaneously. In such cases, it is inappropriate to speak of first and second languages. Both languages are first languages, although one usually dominates in certain situations or with certain persons. If children hear one language from their parents and another from their playmates, for example, they will tend to speak the parents' language when in contact with them and will restrict the other language to the play situation. If contact with parents is much more extensive than contact with playmates, the language the child speaks with parents is likely to predominate. Perfect linguistic balance across situations seems difficult, if not impossible, to achieve, since amount of exposure across situations is never constant.

Bilingualism admits of degrees, however. This is consistent with the definition adopted in the first chapter: the ability to produce complete and meaningful utterances in two languages. Although bilingual children may be more fluent in one language in certain spheres than in the other language, they can produce complete and meaningful utterances in both. For the most part, the children studied in the research considered in this chapter were able to communicate with ease at a level appropriate for their age in either language. In some cases there were shifts in dominance from time to time as the child moved from a bilingual to a monolingual environment, but usually the child adjusted to the bilingual environment when placed in it again.

One problem in speaking of the simultaneous acquisition of two languages is defining a cutoff point at which one language can be said to have been established. If a 2½-year-old, English-speaking child moves to France and starts to acquire French, is the child simultaneously acquiring two languages; or has English been established already, with French being acquired as a second language? As mentioned in Chapter 1, I have arbitrarily set the cutoff point at 3 years of age. The child who is introduced to a second language before 3 years will be regarded as acquiring the two languages simultaneously; the child introduced to a second language after 3 will be considered to have had one language established and to acquire the second successively, as a second language. I do not mean by this that the first language is fully acquired at the age of 3 years; I do not believe that it can be said to be fully acquired at 6 years. But by the age of 3, it would seem that the child has had a considerable head start in one language; it is no longer a question of acquiring the two simultaneously.

Of course both groups—children who acquire two languages simultaneously and children who acquire them successively—can achieve bilingual competence. The child's ultimate bilingualism is not a function of how early a second language is introduced. Simultaneous acquisition of two languages is not necessarily superior to successive acquisition in assuring retention of both languages. A child brought up in a bilingual environment from birth may lose that bilingualism when contact with one of the original languages is lost. Indeed, the acquisition of a second language after a first language is established may facilitate long-term retention, although there is no empirical evidence on this point.

STUDIES OF BILINGUAL CHILDREN

Most of the studies I discuss here are case studies based on diaries or other records kept by parents whose children were introduced simultaneously to two languages. Usually the parent keeping the record was a professional linguist, although this is not always the case. In some studies linguists or psycholinguists used records made available to them by parents. In other studies linguists reported on their observations of other people's children.

There is considerable variation in the quality of these studies. Some, which I do not consider at any length here, are anecdotal and impressionistic. Those that I do discuss are more objective, although in all studies the issue of reliability looms large. There is ample room for error in observational research (especially if one is observing one's own child). The child may be seen to have abilities he or she does not possess; ill-formed utterances may be transformed into well-formed sentences; mistakes may be overlooked or suppressed (or seen to occur when they do not). The tendency is to see what supports one's hypotheses and to ignore the rest.

Another problem with the case report is that the information provided is not always what could be hoped for. The observer may have been quite meticulous and scrupulous in taking notes on the child's speech but may have overlooked much that is of interest from the perspective of present-day linguistics and psycholinguistics. Observation must be a selective process. The speech of even very young children provides too much data for everything to be recorded. Only in recent years are there studies that deal systematically with particular theoretical issues in bilingual language acquisition. Most of these studies involve children who acquired a second language subsequent to the first language, a topic that concerns us in the following chapter.

Nonetheless, a great deal can be learned from the diary literature pertaining to children who were simultaneously exposed to bilingual language presentation. Most of the studies discussed here are linguistically sophisticated and carefully conducted. In some cases they reflect a Herculean labor of recording and analyzing the child's speech. The landmark study in this respect is Leopold's classic report (1939, 1947, 1949a, 1949b) on the language development of his daughter, Hildegard. This still stands as the single most valuable source of information about bilingualism in the young child. I group the studies around Leopold's, looking first at earlier studies and then, after a discussion of Leopold's findings, examining more recent studies of bilingual language acquisition.

Early Studies

The earliest detailed study of childhood bilingualism is that of the French linguist Jules Ronjat (1913). In the summer of the year 1908, Ronjat, whose wife was German and at that time pregnant with their son, received the following advice concerning bilingual language training from his colleague, Maurice Grammont:

> There is nothing for the child to be taught. It is sufficient simply to speak to him when the occasion to do so arises in one of the languages he is to learn. But here is the crux: *each language must be embodied in a different person.* You, for instance, should always talk French to him and his mother German. *Never switch roles.* In this manner he will begin to speak two languages without noticing it and without having to put forth any special effort in learning them [Ronjat, 1913, p. 3].

This method was strictly enforced by Ronjat and his wife, with considerable success. The child appeared to distinguish the two languages quite early. Before his second birthday he had developed a system of testing new words by using the word with German and with French pronunciation until he was prepared to assign it to "mama's box or papa's box" (*"le casier mama ou le casier papa"*). This testing period (*temps d'essai*) never lasted longer than a week, and after the word was assigned there was never any doubt as to where it belonged.

Ronjat reported that by 3 years and 5 months his son Louis could correctly utter the phonemes of both languages. This represented a slight retardation when compared to the norms available for monolingual-speaking French and German children. The retardation was in the normal range, however, and Ronjat did not regard this as a negative consequence of bilingual presentation.

In his vocabulary development, Louis Ronjat initially tended to favor his "mother" tongue. This imbalance was temporary, however; and before long the child deliberately tried to learn words in both languages simultaneously. If he knew the name for something in one language only, he would ask for its name in the other. There seemed to be no evidence of confusion between languages.

This is clearly the most important aspect of Ronjat's study. The child spoke both languages as a native-speaking child would. Even when he used loan words from one language in the other language, he gave the word its appropriate pronunciation; French loan words in German were given German pronunciation and vice versa. Each language was person-specific—a nurse or servant was identified (after some initial confusion) as French- or German-speaking and thereafter was spoken to only in that language. If his father spoke to him in French with a message for a German-speaking servant, the boy gave the message in German without any apparent effort. It was not as if the boy were translating but, as we would say today, simply shifting registers or language codes.

Although Ronjat spoke only French to the child and his wife only German, there were occasional slips. These did not faze the child; he simply responded in the correct language. At table his parents spoke German to each other; but if the child broke in with something to say to his father, he always did so in French. On one occasion the father used the word *approbation* at dinner in German and with a German pronunciation. The boy did not know the word and asked his father, *Qu'est-ce que c'est, approbation?* with the correct French pronunciation.

The child showed remarkably few signs of interference between languages. Those rare mistakes that his father observed were mainly grammatical and syntactic. There were almost no mistakes due to clang associations—confusion of meaning between similar sounding words. Nor were word order mistakes common. The child, for example, would never say *Wein rot* for *Rotwein* on analogy with *vin rouge*. Thus, although interference errors did occur, they were not very frequent. The predominant impression was that the child kept the two languages independent of each other.

Ronjat reported that his son learned both French and German equally well and that his bilingualism had no deleterious effect on his intellectual development. Ronjat attributed the child's success in not confusing the two languages to the strict observation of the principle *une personne, une langue*. In contrast, Ronjat noted that another bilingual child, whose parents were not as consistent in their behavior, had considerably more difficulty learning the two languages. Ronjat concluded that imbedding each language separately in a specific and constant person greatly facilitates learning.

Apparently the effect was long lasting, since it has been reported that Louis Ronjat had equal fluency in both languages at the age of 15 (Vildomec, 1963). He preferred French for technology and German for literature. There was no evidence that the extreme nationalism and anti-German feeling in France at the time of the First World War had any effect on his bilingualism.

The importance of making the two languages person-specific was also emphasized by the Serbian linguist, Pavlovitch (1920), whose son grew up in France. The family spoke Serbian, but when the child was 1 year and 1 month, a

French friend of the family began to spend a great deal of time with him. Both languages appeared simultaneously, and there was no obvious confusion between them. Corresponding phonemic systems of both languages were mastered at approximately the same time and without confusion. Initially, French vocabulary developed slower than Serbian, and the child seemed to use words with the same reference as synonyms. This continued from the age of 1 year and 9 months to 2 years. At that point, the child seemed to become aware that he was exposed to bilingual presentation, and thereafter confusion between the languages ceased. Both languages were kept consistently independent of each other.

Pavlovitch attributed the child's ability to distinguish the languages to the fact that the use of one or the other language was associated with a particular person. As with Ronjat's child, this sharp differentiation of the two languages appeared to help acquisition and to prevent confusion. Although the child realized that his parents could speak and understand French, he consistently spoke Serbian to them in the family environment. Unfortunately, Pavlovitch's study ends when his child was 2 years of age and leaves important questions unanswered, such as the development of inflections, which is quite different in the two languages.

In another early study of a child exposed to bilingual presentation, Hoyer and Hoyer (1924) carefully observed the babbling of their infant, who heard Russian from his mother and German from his father. The child began to utter comprehensible words at 11 months but reduced his utterances in such a way that whole syllables were dropped (especially unstressed syllables). He seemed to employ only those sound elements that were present at this time in his babbling monologues. Whether these particular sounds resulted from his exposure to the languages in his environment or whether they are universally found in children at this period could not be answered with any assurance; nonetheless, some of the sound elements in the child's babbling did appear to reflect sound combinations to which he had considerable exposure.

Recent research on babbling suggests that the sound features the child produces are universal (McNeill, 1970). This was the conclusion of some early investigators as well (Bühler, 1930; Grégoire, 1937). Ronjat (1913) observed that sounds the infant had never heard appeared in his son's early babbling. Thus the notion that bilingual presentation has an effect on a child's babbling seems unsupported by available evidence.

One of the few if not the only early study of bilingual children by an American was Madorah Smith's (1935) report on the language development of eight children from an English- and Chinese-speaking bilingual family. The children were born in China of missionary parents and lived there, except for 1 year in America, until the youngest child was 20 months old. They heard Chinese from their native nurses, other servants, and practically all Chinese children and adults. All of their non-Chinese acquaintances spoke English. Their parents used both English and Chinese in speaking to the children.

Smith's study was based on data from the mother's diary, kept from the time the oldest child was born until the family returned to America. These data were not ideal, because they were unsystematically gathered; nonetheless, they allowed some comparison across children. They were analyzed for sentence length, number of errors per 10 words, number of inflected forms of English words in proportion to the total number of English words, percentage of mixed sentences with words from both languages, and percentage of Chinese words used. The most interesting information for our purposes was the percent of mixed sentences, since this provides some index of the amount of confusion between the two languages.

Much more mixing was reported by Smith than by Ronjat or Pavlovitch. The two languages were confused until the third birthday of most of the children. The average age of the children at the time of the last recorded mixed sentence was 39 months. This was most likely due to the parents' use of both languages. Even among themselves, the children—though preferring English—also occasionally used Chinese. Apparently, this lack of consistency in presentation caused younger children to confuse the two languages. There was no clear demarcation between Chinese and English. Smith concluded that it is best for young children to receive two languages from different sources, with each adult in the home using one language consistently.

There is some evidence that children are capable of acquiring more than two languages simultaneously. Geissler (1938), a German teacher in Belgrade, reported that some young children he observed were able to master as many as four languages without mixing them. They did this quite naturally without the kind of disciplined presentation characteristic of the training of children such as the sons of Ronjat and Pavlovitch. Geissler's report is highly impressionistic, however; and his comments on language development are vague and based on scanty evidence.

Nonetheless, his study is a paragon of objectivity for German research on bilingualism during the 1930s. At this time, German authors such as Schmidt–Rohr (1933) were inveighing against the dangers of bilingualism: the mother tongue—*die Muttersprache*—must be preserved in its purity, or else the child would be in danger of losing his German nationality and would become an atheist. Bilingualism was harmful to the individual: after all, people were not required to live with two religions . . . (Weisgerber, 1935).

Lenna Emrich (1938) reflected this mentality in her study of a German child (her own?) raised from her 6th week in Bulgaria. The child's parents spoke to her in German, but her nurse spoke only Bulgarian. The child showed the typical bilingual development: she understood both languages with ease, learned the sound systems of both languages, and began to build up her vocabulary in both languages. When she was 1 year and 9 months, however, the family returned to Germany for 3 months. The child had serious problems adjusting to this change but continued to make steady progress in German. Shortly after the girl's second birthday, the family moved to an area where another (unspecified) Slavic language was spoken. The new nurse was bilingual, but the child refused to speak the Slavic language with her. Emrich saw this as an indication that German was now internalized as the child's language—a happy ending since bilingualism had created only problems for her.

We should remember, however, that at this time the attitude of most Americans toward bilingualism was similar to that of their German contemporaries. In the 1920s and 1930s a prime goal of the American school system, as we shall see in Chapter 6, was to eradicate bilingualism, which was thought to be a social evil. Perhaps this is one reason why there was so little interest in bilingualism among American researchers at this time. In 1939, however, this situation changed with the publication of the first volume of Leopold's monumental *Speech development of a bilingual child* (1939, 1947, 1949a, 1949b).

Leopold's Study

Werner Leopold's four-volume magnum opus is a detailed analysis of the language development of his daughter Hildegard, who was spoken to in German by her father and in English by her mother. Except for a short visit to Germany at the end of her 1st year and a longer visit (7 months) when she was 5 years of age, the child was always in an English-speaking social environment. Thus the German language was essentially a private language whereby she communicated with her father. Hildegard obviously did not achieve the amount of balance in her bilingualism that the sons of Ronjat and Pavlovitch achieved. After her second birthday, this imbalance became increasingly noticeable as her father's influence became lessened, relative to the widening circle of English-speaking individuals in the child's environment. German tended to become more and more passive, and English words were increasingly chosen for active employment.

In the first volume of his work (1939), Leopold carefully analyzed his daughter's vocabulary to the age of 2 years. His analysis included a chronological survey of word acquisition, mortality statistics, phonetic accuracy, semantic classification, and bilingual synonyms. Of particular interest is his discussion of how certain words appeared in the child's early speech, only to drop out of active use later. There were 241 words that were actively employed at the age of 1 year and 11 months, out of a total of 377 words that had been used by the child to this point (Table 4.1). Of these active words, 46 (19%) had both English and German prototypes. Note that mortality was large for German words, suggesting that English was beginning to become more dominant, although the loss of English words accounted for about ⅓ of the total loss. Furthermore, many English words were more recent than the German words and therefore had a smaller mortality. Seventy of the 195 English words had been acquired during the last month in this period.

TABLE 4.1
Mortality Statistics Based on Hildegard's Early Speech[a]

	German	German–English	English
Total words (377)	104 (28%)	78 (21%)	195 (52%)
Active words at			
1:11 (241)	43 (18%)	46 (19%)	152 (63%)
Inactive words at			
1:11 (136)	61 (45%)	32 (24%)	43 (32%)

[a] Data from Leopold (1939).

Leopold suggested the following possible reasons for the mortality of words in the child's vocabulary:

- Phonetic form: certain words dropped out because of phonetic difficulty. *Radio* appeared early but apparently proved too difficult for Hildegard to cope with.
- Homonymy: other words may have dropped out because they took the same form in the child's early speech. Hildegard used *mama* to mean food and mother; but its use with the first meaning was discontinued, perhaps because it interfered with its use with the second meaning.
- Acquisition of more specific terms: overextended words (*pretty* to refer to all admired objects) are abandoned in favor of specific names of object.
- Change of interest: the word *Schnee* (*snow*) disappeared from the child's vocabulary when winter passed; the word *measles* was used only during the family epidemic; and so forth.
- Rejection of nonstandard terms: emotional and self-expressive words such as [bu::] for thunder and [k$_x$] for disgust with the taste of food appear sporadically but are not established.
- Struggle with synonyms: some words are abandoned as synonyms took their place. This happened within both languages as overextensions were abandoned for terms with more precise meanings. In addition, there were shifts from a word in one language to its equivalent in the other. This usually involved shifts from the German word to its English equivalent (e.g., *Augenblick* replaced by *wait*), but there were cases where the English gave way to the German (e.g., *mitten* to *Handschuh*).
- Lack of stability: no specific reasons for instability can be found. The use of the word appeared simply to be a passing vogue.

Of particular interest in the present context are shifts in usage from a word in one language to its equivalent in the other. Although some bilingual synonyms were acquired simultaneously in both languages, in other cases a word occurred first in one language and only subsequently did its synonym in the other language appear. For a while, the two words seemed to be in competition with each other and one tended to be preferred. The child seemed to have adopted the strategy of giving things one name only. However, once she realized that there were two languages in her environment, this competition ceased and she managed to use the appropriate words in both languages (although the increasing predominance of English complicated this task).

In Leopold's (1947) second volume he discussed the child's sound system during the first 2 years. His analysis is typically thorough and includes tabulations of Hildegard's representation of standard sounds, an analysis of sound substitutions, and an analysis of her phonetic system. He applied Jakobson's (1941) theory of contrasts to his data and found it to match relatively well, although not in all details. Like Jakobson, Leopold maintained that the sound system develops phonemically rather than phonetically and that sound substitutions reveal method and system rather than randomness.

Like Ronjat (1913) and Pavlovitch (1920), Leopold found little evidence of interference between the two languages on the phonetic level. Even though Hildegard heard two different *l* sounds in the two languages, for example, the effect of bilingual presentation on her speech production was brief. There was no instance where Leopold found unequivocal evidence of a phonetic effect of bilingualism. The simplifications and phonetic substitutions that occurred have also been found in the speech of monolingual children.

In the third volume, Leopold (1949a) discussed questions of syntax and morphology with reference to his daughter's speech during the first 2 years. From 8 months to 1 year and 8 months, one-word utterances prevailed. These Leopold viewed as generally taking the place of what we would call sentences in standard speech. As the speech of the child developed, it changed from a noninflected language to a language with endings comprehended as structural elements. This transformation was not the product of steady growth over time but rather seemed to occur "by leaps and bounds."

Leopold's account of the development of syntax corresponds in many respects to observations made by later investigators of children's language development as described in Chapter 2. He noted the importance of word order, the initial preference for *what* and *where* over *why* questions, the slow development of auxiliary and modal verb constructions, and the relatively late appearance of conjunctions and compound sentences. Hildegard did not achieve subordination of one clause to another in the time studied, and in general her syntactic development was still in a primitive stage at the end of the first 2 years.

Morphological development was also relatively primitive during this time, lagging behind more conspicuous syntactic structures. Hildegard did learn some English plural forms, including the irregular plural *feet;* but German plurals were rare, although the German plural *Füsse* also appeared. German noun inflections did not appear, except for the possessive, which also appeared in English. There were a few instances of adjectival inflections in Hildegard's German, but they seemed to be immediate echoes of her father's speech. Her verbs usually lacked endings in German, probably because she preferred to use the uninflected form.

There was no conclusive evidence that the third-person endings were applied to English or German verbs. In general, Hildegard at this time had taken only the first steps toward learning the morphology of the language.

Leopold (1949a) found no evidence for an effect due to bilingual presentation on the child's syntactic or morphological development. One problematic factor was his daughter's failure to use the *-en* ending in her German infinitives. This could possibly be attributed to English influence, but Leopold was not willing to ascribe this to bilingualism. It was also possible that Hildegard—as a German monolingual—would have favored the pure stem, which is often heard in German imperatives and is also early in monolingual German speech (Preyer, 1882).

Although Leopold found no conclusive evidence for interference between languages in the first 2 years, it should be pointed out that this situation changed later when English became more dominant and German was pushed back to a subsidiary position. German pronunciation was then affected by English habits of articulation; there was a common mixture of English words in German sentences, and hybrid forms appeared. English words generally were given German endings and prefixes (*pouren, practicen, geyawnt,* and *monthe*).

A somewhat similar process was observed in the area of syntactic development. Initially, during the first 2 years, there was a free mixing of English and German within a single utterance. The constructions were primitive and incomplete, and the two languages were not used as separate instruments. Hence it was impossible to find an influence of the constructions of one language on those of the other. Even those cases of puzzling word order that were observed could not be regarded as due to the interference of competing syntactic models. Leopold argued it was more likely that since Hildegard had absorbed neither English nor German syntactic patterns with sufficient assurance at this time, variations in word order were due to psychological factors—e.g., the desire to give the psychological subject (an item of dominating interest) an emphatic position. Later, when English began to predominate, the influence of English on the structure of sentences and on the composition of idiomatic phrases became very noticeable.

Leopold (1949a) also analyzed semantic development during the first 2 years, especially the question of how standard meanings are acquired by the child and how and why certain words are overextended. In Hildegard's speech, for example, *wauwau* was used to refer to all sorts of animals including bedroom slippers with a simulated dog's face on them. Other words also were given similar extension: one ingenuous example was her combination of the word *auto* with her word for bird, *peep–peep*, to signify *airplane*.

The last volume (1949b) is Leopold's diary of Hildegard's speech development from her 2nd to her 12th birthday. In addition, Leopold included a brief section on the development of the speech of his younger daughter, Karla, from her 2nd year to her 10th. Leopold felt that in both of his daughters consciousness of dealing with two languages began early in the 3rd year. Only at the end of the

3rd year did the active separation of the two languages begin. From that point on the two languages developed as separate systems.

Studies of Bilingual Children After Leopold

The tradition of the linguist–parent was continued after Leopold by the social anthropologist, Robbins Burling (1959), whose son Stephen acquired Garo, a language belonging to the Bodo group of Tibeto–Burman. The child heard English exclusively until his arrival in India at the age of 1 year and 4 months. Subsequently, he had more contact with Garo speakers than with English speakers (especially since his mother was hospitalized for part of this time), and the Garo language became predominant.

Burling noted that certain elements in his son's English phonemic system developed later than the corresponding elements in Garo, the Garo phonemes being used initially in place of the English ones. In fact, although at 2 years and 9 months or so, a systematic separation of Garo and English vowel systems seemed to occur, the consonant system never became differentiated; the Garo sounds were simply used as replacements for the English ones.

Morphological development in English remained very primitive during the time studied (to 2 years and 10 months). The child used some plural endings but not with consistency. In contrast, morphological development in Garo was extensive. This language consists of several stretches of syllables set off by characteristic junctures that can be called words (*ba-bi on-a-ha* for *Babi gave it to me*). Before his second birthday, Stephen had learned various verb suffixes to create past, future, imperative, and other constructions. Shortly thereafter, he acquired adverbial affixes, interrogative suffixes, noun endings, and numerals. In spite of the complexity of the system, the child never used an incorrect morpheme order. Nor did he have trouble with word order in English (in contrast to Burling's daughter, a monolingual, English-speaking child).

Burling's son assimilated his English vocabulary into Garo and appended Garo endings on English words without hesitation. His sentences were Garo in morphology and syntax, although some lexical items were English. Later, when English sentences appeared, the same process occurred in reverse, with Garo words given English morphology and syntax. This was not too surprising, since all of the English-speaking adults around the child used Garo words in their English speech. Nonetheless, the child's usage was consistent; there was never any question of which language he was using, since morphology and syntax were either all Garo or all English.

Burling's study was unusual in that it is one of the few case studies of bilingualism involving a child learning a non-European language. The report of the French psychologist, Tabouret–Keller (1962), is also unusual in that it is one of the few studies of a child whose parents were from a working class background. The child's father was a mine worker and her mother came from a poor rural background. The father was bilingual from childhood in French and a German dialect; the mother was raised speaking the German dialect but had learned French in school. Tabouret–Keller observed that both parents mixed both languages in speaking with the child, who heard French roughly ⅔ of the time and the German dialect ⅓ of the time.

By 2 years of age, the child had a larger French than German vocabulary; ¾ of her words were French and ¼ German. Tabouret–Keller was not able to ascertain why certain words were chosen from one language and other words from the other, although she speculated that certain dialect words were preferred because they were more easily inflected than the French equivalents. About 60% of the child's early sentences were mixed in that both French and German words appeared in them. The child's usage could not be predicted from a probabilistic model based on parental input, since such a model predicts—as Tabouret–Keller demonstrated—a far greater proportion of homogeneous French sentences than was actually obtained (20%) and far fewer homogeneous dialect sentences than the child used (also 20%). Tabouret–Keller attributed this lack of correspondence to the influence of the child's playmates on her speech. These children all spoke the German dialect, and this had the effect of increasing her usage of dialect words over what would be predicted by a probabilistic model.

Both Burling and Tabouret–Keller observed considerable mixing in the children they studied. This was also true of Murrell's (1966) study of his daughter, who acquired language in a trilingual environment. For the first 2 years of her life, the child heard Swedish at home and Finnish from a nurse and in kindergarten, with the exception of 2 months (from 1 year and 2 months to 1 year and 4 months) when the family was in England. When the child was 2 years and 1 month old, the family moved to England; and English began to predominate, although the child's mother and occasionally her father continued to speak to her in Swedish.

The child's speech development seemed to be impaired by this experience. She was slow in her morphological development; and there were no word-order regularities in her speech by 2 years and 8 months, although the subject usually appeared before the predicate. There was extreme interference between the languages, and hybrid phrases such as *on bordet* for *on the table* were frequent. There was also sound fusion: for example, the Swedish *bussen* and the English *bus* were combined to form *bas(s)en*. Murrell did not attribute this to morphological fusion (the English *bus* with the Swedish *-en*), since at this point in the child's development the meaning of the affix morphemes was unknown.

Rūķe–Draviņa (1965, 1967) also found sound confusions in the speech of two Swedish–Latvian bilingual children who were learning to speak a language with a rolled apical /r/ (Latvian) together with one possessing the uvular /R/ (Swedish). She found that the uvular /R/ was acquired earlier and tended to intrude and replace the apical /r/ in the other language. Sound borrowings occurred most often in words with the same form in both languages. This same phenomenon was observed by Zaręba (1953) in the speech of his Swedish–Polish bilingual daughter. Both Rūķe–Draviņa and Zaręba found that Swedish word intonations and phraseology intruded in the less dominant Latvian and Polish speech of their children. Rūķe–Draviņa (1967) argued that interference is always present in bilingualism and is more marked, the closer the languages are in their phonological and morphological characteristics.

In contrast, Engel (1965) noted in her case study of her son that confusion of speech sounds rarely occurred. The boy was exposed from birth to English and Italian with Italian predominating. He heard English only from his father, although his parents spoke English to each other. It seemed that the child's ability to keep the sound units distinct, especially sound sequences and intonation, was the means by which he differentiated the two languages.

Engel pointed out that her son's English, though much the weaker of his two languages, developed contemporaneously with his Italian. There were some semantic confusions and hybrid words—Italian endings were often attached to English words without the child being aware of mixing English and Italian morphologically. Yet though there was confusion on this level, there was none with respect to sounds. Engel saw this as an indication that language is not monolithically structured but has two levels: phonetic and morphological–semantic. This distinction seems consistent with my comments in Chapter 3 on the critical period hypothesis. Perhaps the critical period notion as elaborated by Lenneberg applies to the phonetic level of language but not to what Engel called the morphological–semantic level.

Totten (1960), whose children were raised bilingually in Swedish and English, reported that they initially tended to mix both languages. It was only after they distinguished the languages that the problem of interference between the two disappeared. There was no problem learning different sound systems, however, in that the children acquired the accent of the more fluent parent in both languages. The child's plasticity in this regard was also noted by Metraux (1965), who observed that the influence of friends and playmates was extremely effective in counteracting a child's accent. In her comments on French–English bilingual children, Metraux noted that the children would often pretend not to understand another language if it was not the language with which they were accustomed to speaking with a particular person. When parents spoke to children in another language or tested their knowledge in a language they had habitually used with someone else, the children would refuse to answer.

This specificity in the use of linguistic systems was also observed by Oksaar (1970) in a case study of her 3-year-old, Swedish–Estonian-speaking child. This child spoke Swedish with his playmates and Estonian to his parents. The two domains were usually kept apart, but there were cases where both playmates and parents were present. In such cases, the child spoke Swedish, even if he was in the Estonian home environment.

Oksaar recorded her son's utterances on a tape recorder from the 2nd month of his life. Emphasis was placed on collecting data about the child's speech in different contexts—alone, with other children, and with his parents. In addition, recordings were made at certain times twice a month on 3 successive days. It was observed that the child's use of the sound system of Estonian was not influenced by the speech of a Swedish playmate with whom he was in constant contact, although one might expect confusion because of the similarity of the two systems. The finding that the bilingual child is able to keep sound systems distinct corresponds to the observations of Engel (1965) and Totten (1960).

In contrast, Oksaar fourd obvious interference and mixing in morphology and syntax. The child attached the endings of one language to stems of the other. He also attached Estonian endings to Swedish verb forms in Estonian sentences. His choice of a particular form seemed to follow a simplicity principle: the more simple the form, the more likely it was to be chosen.

Imedadze (1960, 1967) reported the case of a child whose mother and father spoke to her in Georgian and whose grandmother–nurse spoke to her in Russian. Imedadze felt that the child went through an initial stage of confusion where elements of both languages appeared and—at about 20 months—through a period of differentiation where the elements were separated from each other. There also seemed to be an interaction of corresponding grammatical structures. For example, the genitive and instrumental of both languages emerged at the same time. This Imedadze attributed to the fact that these forms express the same semantic relationships in analogous fashion in the two languages. In contrast, the subject–to–object relation in Georgian was expressed first by analogy with the Russian form, which adds an accusative ending: *Dali unda kabas* (*Dali wants a dress*). Only later did the more complicated Georgian form appear, which demands a dative case ending for the psychological subject and the nominative case for the psychological object: *Dalis unda kaba*.

Occasionally, the same semantic relation may emerge at different times in the languages of a single bilingual child. Such a case was reported by Mikěs (1967; Mikěs & Vlahovīc, 1966) in the study of two Serbo–Croatian–Hungarian bilingual girls. Before the age of 2, these children expressed locative relations in Hungarian but not in Serbo–Croatian. Since the Hungarian language requires only case inflections to express locative relations, and the Serbo–Croatian language requires case inflections and a locative preposition, it seems reasonable to suppose that the difference in complexity of the formal devices needed to express the relationship caused the delay in production.

Volterra and Taeschner (1975) reported that the two children they studied, who acquired Italian and German simultaneously, initially developed a single syntactic system that was applied to the lexicon of both languages. This syntactic system appeared to be different from that of either language. Possibly children initially fashion a unique system; then the system of the language with the more simple syntactic structures becomes dominant; and finally, the two syntactic systems become differentiated.

Itoh and Hatch (in press) studied the language development of a Japanese boy who learned English at the age of 2½. Some structures in the child's first language had already been acquired by this time, although other constructions developed simultaneously. The imbalance led to initial confusion, especially in the sound system.

Of particular interest in this study was the acquisition by the child of formulaic expressions that were acquired wholistically and subsequently broken down. For example, *I wanna* first appeared in such utterances as *I wanna orange juice . . . more* and *I wanna driver*. Later forms such as *I wanna down* and *I wanna cake* appeared. Finally, there were utterances like *I wanna play* and *I wanna open it*. The child appeared to be analyzing such formulaic expressions and working out their appropriate usage. As we shall see in the following chapter, the same process has been noted by other authors studying successive acquisition of a second language.

LANGUAGE ACQUISITION PROCESSES IN BILINGUAL CHILDREN

Table 4.2 summarizes case studies of children who were raised under conditions of bilingual presentation during the first 3 years of life. The studies vary considerably in the topics they deal with and appear to be in several instances contradictory. There are, however, general points of agreement that I will attempt to elucidate by looking at what the studies say about the developmental sequence of acquisition in the bilingual child's two languages, about interference between languages, and about code switching in bilingual children.

Developmental Features

In the discussion of processing models of language acquisition in Chapter 2 I noted that an adequate language acquisition system includes sound system processing, lexical processing, and grammatical processing. Looking at *sound system processing* first, it appears that the bilingual child's development is not very different from that of the monolingual child. The child must recognize and distinguish stress–pitch features of prosodic contours, as well as the quality of stressed vowels, timing and length of stressed syllables, and the location of marked features such as friction and nasal consonants. This requires some kind of analytic ability that permits matching of a particular string in short-term memory with the acoustical features of lexical items as they are stored in long-term memory (Ervin–Tripp, 1970).

TABLE 4.2
Case Studies of Simultaneous Bilingual Acquisition[a]

Author	Languages	Age of child at time of study	Concerns of study
Ronjat (1913)	French–German	First 5 years	Sp S, Sem, Interf
Pavlovitch (1920)	French–Serbian	First 2 years	Sp S, Sem, Ext, Interf
Hoyer & Hoyer (1924)	Russian–German	First year	Bab
Smith (1935)	English–Chinese	Eight children, first 4 years	Sem, Interf
Emrich (1938)	German–Bulgarian	First 3 years	Interf
Leopold (1939, 1947, 1949a, 1949b)	German–English	First 2 years (and from 2 to 12)	Bab, Sp S, Sem, Ext, Sy, Mor, W O, Dvlp Seq, Interf
Burling (1959)	Garo–English	1 year, 4 months, to 2 years, 10 months	Sp S, Sem, Sy, Mor, Interf
Imedadze (1960)	Russian–Georgian	11 months to 3 years	Sem, Ext, Sy, Mor, Dvlp Seq, Interf
Tabouret-Keller (1962)	French–German	1 year, 8 months to 2 years, 11 months	Sem, Interf
Engel (1965)	English–Italian	First 4½ years	Sp S, Sem, Mor, Interf
Murrell (1966)	Swedish–Finnish– English	2 years to 2 years, 8 months	Sp S, Sem, Sy, Mor, W O, Interf
Rūķe-Draviņa (1967)	Swedish–Latvian	Two children, first 6 years	Sp S, Sem, Dvlp Seq, Interf
Mikés (1967)	Hungarian–Serbo- Croatian	Three children, first 4 years	Sy, Mor, Dvlp Seq, Interf
Oksaar (1970)	Swedish–Estonian	2 months to 3 years	Sp S, Sem, Ext, Sy, Mor, Interf
Volterra & Taeschner (1975)	Italian–German	Two children, 1 to 3 years	Sem, Ext, Sy, Mor, Interf
Itoh & Hatch (in press)	Japanese–English	2½ to 3 years, 1 month	Sp S, Sem, Sy, Mor, Interf

[a] Abbreviations: Sp S = Speech Sounds; Bab = Babbling; Sem = Semantics; Ext = Extensions of Word Meanings; Sy = Syntax; Mor = Morphology; W O = Word Order; Dvlp Seq = Developmental Sequences; Interf = Interference Phenomena.

The bilingual child's task is complicated by the fact that two sound systems must be distinguished from each other. A number of observers have noted that there is an initial period of confusion (Leopold, 1947; Rūķe–Draviņa, 1967), especially when the corresponding phonemes in the two languages are differentially difficult to acquire. In such a case, it seems likely that the easier phoneme will be applied in both languages (Murrell, 1966; Rūḵe-Draviṇa, 1965). If the two languages are in balance, the period of confusion is relatively short (Pavlovitch, 1920). In fact, some authors reported no evidence of confusion of sound systems (Engel, 1965; Oksaar, 1970). When one language predominates, however, as with Burling's (1959) son, the sound features of the dominant language may be substituted for those of the subordinate language. Similarly, words that are difficult to pronounce in one language may be systematically avoided (Celce–Murcia, 1975).

Leopold's daughter Hildegard developed by 2 years of age a vowel system consisting of 12 phonemes. She appeared to be experimenting beyond the model provided by English. For example, although English makes no use of the vowel length, Hildegard did: she distinguished [wɔk] *walk* and [wɔ:k] *fork*. Furthermore, she used a number of diphthongs that did not occur in the speech of the adult model: [ɛa], [oi], [oɪ]. She seemed to be using her ability to combine two vowel qualities into a diphthong as a productive process to construct new words with complex vowel nuclei not present in standard English (Moskowitz, 1970). Perhaps such experimentation with sounds from the bilingual repertory is common with bilingual children, but it has rarely been commented upon in the literature.

In the discussion of *semantic processing* in Chapter 2, I noted that one of the tasks involved in semantic development is to attach words to their referents and to abstract concepts. There is a period between the ages of 1 year and 1 month and 2 years and 6 months when overextensions are common (E. Clark, 1973). Detailed studies reveal that overextensions relate to vocabulary growth and rarely last more than 8 months. Only certain words are overextended; others appear to be used in a manner consistent with adult criteria from the moment of their introduction into the child's speech (Leopold, 1949a; Pavlovitch, 1920). When overextensions do occur, their features appear to be derived predominantly from perceptual input—from visual, tactile, and auditory sources (E. Clark, 1973). Both Pavlovitch (1920) and Leopold (1949a) reported that the meaning of overextended terms is narrowed down by the addition of new words that take over subparts of the semantic domain of the overextended word. In Hildegard's speech, for example, *sch* was initially used for all moving objects, but when the words *auto* and *choo–choo* were introduced to her vocabulary, they took over the domain of *sch*. Subsequently *choo–choo* was abandoned (except for *choo–choo train*) when *train, wheelbarrow,* and *airplane* were acquired.

Pavlovitch (1920) provided a number of examples of overextensions in his son's speech. One of the most interesting examples was the word *bébé,* which was initially used to refer to all reflections of the self in mirrors, photos of self and photos in general, pictures, all books with pictures, and books in general. In time, the word was narrowed down and distinguished from other words. This process is schematized in Table 4.3.

TABLE 4.3
The Restructuring of Overextensions[a]

	Word(s)	Semantic domain
Stage I	*bébé*	Reflections of self in mirror; photos of self; all photos; all pictures; books with pictures; all books.
Stage II	*bébé*	Reflections of self in mirror; photos of self; all pictures; books with pictures; all books.
	deda (grandfather)	All photos.
Stage III	*bébé*	Reflections of self in mirror; photos of self; books with pictures; all books.
	deda	All photos.
	káta (karta = card)	All pictures of landscapes, views.
Stage IV	*b´eb´e*	Reflections of self in mirror; photos of self.
	deda	All photos.
	káta	All pictures not of people.
	kigh (book)	All books.
Stage V	*bébé*	Self; small children in pictures.
	deda	Photos.
	káta	Pictures.
	kigh	Books.
	slika (reflection)	Reflections in mirror.
	duda (Douchan, own name)	Photo of self.

[a] Data based on Pavlovitch, 1920 (table from E. Clark, 1973).

Leopold's daughter, Hildegard, used the German word *alle* to mean *all gone* and applied it to persons with this meaning: *Mama alle.* Standard German does not allow this, since *alle* does not have the meaning *all gone* when applied to persons. Leopold thought this construction was due to the influence of the English expression *all gone,* which can be applied to persons and things. Thus some overextensions in a bilingual child's speech may reflect the influence of one language on the other.

It sometimes happens that the bilingual child gives different extensions to words that have a single meaning for an adult. Volterra and Taeschner (1975) found, for example, that the German *da* and the Italian *la (there)* had different meanings for one of their children. *La* was used for things that were not present and not visible; *da* was used for things that were present and visible. They argued that initially all words of the child's speech form a single lexical system; only gradually does the child differentiate the lexical items of the separate languages as these languages are experienced in different linguistic and nonlinguistic contexts.

One problem for the bilingual child is that the meanings of some words have different extensions in the two languages that are being learned. For example, the English word *brush* can be used for a clothes brush, a shoe brush, and a paint brush; but the German word *Bürste* does not extend to paint brush—instead *Pinsel* is used. Similarly the German word *Tuch* (cloth) can be used for handkerchief, towel, and napkin (Leopold, 1948). In such cases the child must learn to utilize a somewhat different set of feature markings for corresponding lexical items in the two languages.

Turning now to *syntactic processing,* we observe once again the importance of word-order regularities (Braine, 1971a; Ervin–Tripp, 1973a). Children probably store features of invariant order and probabilities of order for various semantic relations (Ervin–Tripp, 1973a). In inflected languages there may be morphological realization of semantic relations. As Slobin (1971) noted, linguistic realization of semantic relations can occur at different times within the two languages of a bilingual child, reflecting the perceptual salience of the features needed to mark the relationship in the two languages. Thus Serbo–Croatian–Hungarian bilingual children (Mikeš, 1967; Mikeš & Vlahović, 1966) demonstrated locative relations in Hungarian (where the locative marker is expressed by noun inflection) earlier than in Serbo–Croation (where noun inflection and preposition are needed to express the locative). This seems to reflect a processing strategy according to which word endings are scanned for their linguistic input earlier than prepositions.

Mikeš (1967) pointed out, however, that the order in which various syntactic structures are acquired by bilingual children is the same as for monolingual children. The Serbo–Croatian locative construction is also acquired relatively late by monolingual speakers of that language. Furthermore, the syntactic development in languages of different structural types follows basically the same sequence. Mikeš concluded that bilingual presentation has little effect on syntactic development.

The same conclusion was reached by Imedadze (1960) on the basis of her study of a Russian–Georgian bilingual child. The sequence with which grammatical categories appeared depended on their difficulty—as is true of the monolingual child. Syntactic structures followed the same developmental order in both of the child's languages as they did for monolingual children. If both languages express a semantic relationship similarly, it tends to be acquired simultaneously in both languages; if it is more difficult in one language, it is acquired later in that language—as is true in the development of the monolingual speaker of that language.

One exception to this general rule was reported by Rūķe–Draviņa (1967) who found that her children used the Latvian double negative before the simple negative of Swedish. This was probably because Latvian was acquired earlier, in the home, whereas Swedish was acquired later through contact with playmates. Presumably, the child was exposed to the Latvian construction earlier and hence acquired it before the easier Swedish form.

Morphology usually follows syntax except in some languages that are so structured that morphological and syntactic features must be acquired simultaneously (Burling, 1959). Murrell (1966) found no affix morphemes in his daughter's speech at 2 years and 8 months, and Leopold (1953) also noted that almost no morphological devices indicating declensions and conjugations were acquired by his daughter in the first 2 years. Syntactic relations were made clear by word order, although there were occasional mistakes, especially when a focal word was put first in the sentence (*Meow bites wauwau* at 1 year and 11 months). In the course of time, communication difficulties became a strong source of motivation for Hildegard to learn standard morphological features.

In a study of 3- to 10-year-old, bilingual, Mexican–American children, Carrow (1971) found that there were specific areas where the children studied were, as a group, significantly delayed when compared to a control group of English-speaking children. The comprehension of pronouns, negatives, and some tense markers caused difficulty for children in the bilingual group. Nonetheless, the sequence of development of the various form classes and grammatical structures was the same for both groups and within the Mexican–American group in both English and Spanish. Carrow concluded from this that language development follows systematic growth patterns regardless of language.

Kessler (1971, 1972) also found in her research on 6- to 8-year-old bilingual children who spoke Italian and English that structures shared by both languages were acquired at approximately the same rate and in the same sequence. If the structure is not shared by both languages, it is acquired later—linguistically more simple structural variants being acquired before those that are linguistically more complex. For example, the subject and indirect object relation (e.g., *The boy is handing the book to the mother*) gave the bilingual children very little difficulty in either language, whereas sentences with the prepositions *for* and *to* presented the greatest difficulty in both languages (e.g., *The baby gives the ball for the cat to the dog*). Other constructions such as the object pronoun (*He is giving her the book*) or the possessive adjective (*his ball*) seemed to have been acquired by the children in English but not in Italian. Similarly, the reflexive reciprocal construction (*The girls see themselves*) was not established in English, although it presented no problem in Italian.

Although both the Carrow and Kessler studies compared children at different ages and did not involve the longitudinal study of individual children, their findings are consistent with reports from case studies of bilingual children (e.g., Engel, 1965; Imedadze, 1960; Leopold, 1949a; Mikeš, 1967). The consensus is that language acquisition follows the same basic developmental pattern in the bilingual child as in the monolingual child. In the bilingual child, certain syntactic structures in one language will lag behind those of the other language because they are more complex. The pattern for each language, however, is the same as it is in the monolingual child acquiring that language (although it may be somewhat retarded in some bilingual children).

In short, it seems that the language acquisition process is the same in its basic features and in its developmental sequence for the bilingual child and the monolingual child. The bilingual child has the additional task of distinguishing the two language systems, but there is no evidence that this requires special language processing devices. In fact, the child most likely employs a single set of rules and heuristics with those sounds, lexical items, and formal structures that require differentiation tagged as specific to a particular system. This is a point to which I shall return shortly.

Interference Between Languages

Investigators of childhood bilingualism differ greatly in the amount of interference between languages they report. Both Ronjat (1913) and Pavlovitch (1920) reported that their children showed very few signs of interference and kept both languages separate on all levels. Other investigators, however, found considerable confusion (Burling, 1959; Murrell, 1966; Rūķe–Draviņa, 1967; Tabouret–Keller, 1962).

As we have seen, Rūķe–Draviņa (1965) and Zaręba (1953) both reported substitution of the easier uvular /R/ sound for the more difficult apical /r/. Leopold (1947) also found an early preference for /R/ in his daughter's speech. In addition, all three authors observed a period during which /l/ sounds in the different languages were confused, but all noted that this confusion was of short duration. Leopold (1949a) argued that on close examination those phonetic mistakes that his daughter made could have occurred if his daughter had been exposed to one language only. They were not, he maintained, evidence of interference between languages but could be attributed to processes that operate in the phonological devlopment of monolingual children as well. He pointed out, however, that when the balance between the two languages was shifted in favor of one or the other, his daughter's speech showed signs of interference. The same was true of other bilingual children when one language predominated (Burling, 1959; Zaręba, 1953).

For the most part, children seem to be able readily to acquire and discriminate the sounds they hear in the bilingual environment. Engel (1965) noted that this was the most stable aspect of her son's speech, which otherwise was marked by considerable confusion between English and Italian. She mentioned at one point in her article the case of a French–American family in which children spoke French without an accent to their French mother but French with an American accent to their American father. Apparently such discriminations are readily made by children whose facility in programming the sounds of a language may, as was suggested in Chapter 3, have a physiological basis.

A number of observers have noted a tendency on the part of the bilingual child to mix words from different languages in the same sentence (Burling, 1959; Leopold, 1949a; Rūķe–Draviņa, 1967; Tabouret–Keller, 1962; Totten, 1960). Mixing was especially noticeable in the child observed by Tabouret–Keller, (1962) where 60% of the child's three-word sentences contained words from both languages. In this case the fact that the parents constantly mixed both languages probably played a considerable role in the child's confusion.

Even in cases where this does not happen, however, some mixing occurs. Ronjat (1913) remarked that his son initially tried out words in both languages before settling on the appropriate one. Leopold (1939) found that a small number of bilingual synonyms were used interchangeably in his child's speech. *Hot* and *heiss,* for example, were used synonymously until the 3rd year. Other examples include the words *Schnee* and *snow, ja* and *yes, bitte* and *please, kaputt* and *broke, alle* and *all gone.* In these cases the words were used in both languages concurrently.

In other cases, there seemed to be a struggle going on between two words for predominance. *Nein* and *no* coexisted briefly, but eventually the German word dropped out. *Mehr* was so well established that *more* never appeared in the first 2 years. *Auge* and *eye* appeared at the same time, but only *eye* became active. *Weg* rose ineffectually against *away,* as did *hair* against *Haar. Doggie* entered late as a feeble competitor to the well-established *Wau-wau.* Leopold concluded that such cases indicate that the child is striving to make one unit out of the split presentation. Only when Hildegard became aware that she was being presented two different languages did she begin to use the appropriate word in both languages. Once this realization is achieved, the child may begin simultaneously to learn the words from both languages that refer to objects and abstract concepts (Burling, 1959).

Leopold (1947) also noted that the child may use knowledge of the vocabulary of one language to generate words in the other language. For example, his daughter at 3 years and 6 months did not know the German word for *candle,* so she generated the word *Kandl* with a German *a* sound. Similar examples have been reported by other authors (Engel, 1965; Murrell, 1966; Rūķe–Draviņa, 1967).

Oksaar (1970) observed considerable interference from the predominance of Swedish in the speech of her Swedish–Estonian bilingual child. Swedish morphemes occurred with Estonian endings in the home, where Estonian was spoken; but with playmates the Swedish forms predominated. Engel (1965) also found a great deal of morphological confusion in her son's weaker language, English. Burling (1959) noted morphological and syntactic mixing, although his son seemed aware that he was mixing the two languages. Difficulties with prepositional constructions were noted by Carrow (1971), and Murrell (1966) found no word order regularities in the speech of his English–Swedish-speaking daughter at 2 years and 8 months. Word order and prepositional constructions seem to be the most incorrigible tasks in bilingual language development and may not be entirely mastered in adulthood (Elwert, 1960).

Leopold (1949a) felt that because of the mixture of two languages in his daughter's speech it was impossible to find evidence of syntactic interference. Hildegard's constructions in both languages were so primitive up to the 3rd year and so incomplete that no language differences could be established. It was only when English began to predominate that its influence on German syntactic constructions could be clearly established.

The findings concerning interference seem contradictory until one considers how the two languages were presented to the child. It seems that interference between languages can be held to a minimum if the domains of use are clearly defined and if the two languages are maintained somewhat in balance. This seems to have been true of the children of Ronjat (1913) and Pavlovitch (1920) and initially of Leopold's daughter. These studies suggest that the optimal conditions for reducing interference require that both languages be spoken in the home consistently by different persons. A *caveat emptor* is in order here, however, since in all three cases the children were raised in upper-class or at least upper-middle-class families. No information is available on how this method works in a middle-class or lower-class family environment. Furthermore, Ronjat and Pavlovitch were fairly authoritarian in their upbringing of their children (Tabouret–Keller, 1962), and the rigorous application of the one-person, one-language rule requires considerable discipline on the part of both parents and child.

In looking at other situations of bilingual presentation, one finds that optimal results are rarely achieved. If one language is spoken in the home and the second is acquired through acquaintances and playmates, balance seems to be upset and interference is greater (Murrell, 1966; Oksaar, 1970; Rūķe–Draviņa, 1967; Zarȩba, 1953). Once one language begins to predominate and the other is reduced to subordinate status, interference between languages is clearly in evidence (Burling, 1959; Engel, 1965; Leopold, 1949a). This is not to imply that the child does not achieve bilingual fluency, but the balance is usually tipped in favor of one language or the other.

The greatest amount of interference between languages seems to be produced when adults in the child's environment mix the languages in their own speech (Burling, 1959; Tabouret–Keller, 1962). Another factor contributing to interference is similarity between the two languages (Geissler, 1938; Mikěs, 1967; Rūķe–Draviņa, 1967). However, there has been relatively little systematic research on the effects of various languages on each other's development, and it is not even known if the total amount of interference between two similar languages is less or more than between two dissimilar ones and if the mechanisms of interference differ (Vildomec, 1963). Nor has there been a careful analysis of the errors the bilingual child makes to determine whether the mistakes are indeed the result of interference or whether they reflect developmental errors common in the acquisition data of monolingual children or developmental strategies of various sorts. This type of analysis has been carried out only on children who acquired a second language after the first was established.

Code Switching

I pointed out in Chapter 2 that in addition to their other linguistic tasks, children learn styles, or codes, of talking to different people in different situations. The child, for example, learns to distinguish formal and informal codes, serious, intimate, slang and colloquial codes. One way of viewing the simultaneous acquisition of two languages in children is to regard it as a task not significantly different from that faced by a monolingual child learning to differentiate various linguistic codes.

One argument against this position is that such an interpretation places too great a strain on the child's processing capacities. Yet in some languages, the amount of code switching within the language itself is much greater than what we are accustomed to in European languages. In Javanese, for example, there are a number of different codes among which any Javanese must switch from one situation to another. Many of the most common words vary depending on such variables as the age, sex, kinship, occupation, wealth, education, religion, and family background of the individuals communicating. It is as if a separate language had to be learned for each of these situations (Geertz, 1960).

Furthermore, the frequency of bidialectalism—whereby speakers switch between the standard language and a dialect—in societies throughout the world seems to rule out what Stewart (1971) has dubbed the "single space" theory, according to which an individual has room in the brain for only one language code. The achievement of primitive tribes who master a number of different languages of great complexity (Hill, 1970) would seem to bear eloquent witness to the human's capacity in this respect.

In the development of the child, it seems that initially an effort is made to make a single unit out of the bilingual presentation (Leopold, 1939). Language input remains undifferentiated, and the child does not appear to comprehend that input consists of split presentation. Even when comprehension processing shows that the child can understand the meaning of two words for the same referent or the use of two different forms, children seem to focus on one symbol or form in their spontaneous utterances.

Some evidence that the two languages of bilingual children are initially not encoded separately comes from a study by Swain (1971) of French–Canadian children, aged 2 years and 1 month to 4 years and 10 months, who had been exposed to French and English since birth. Swain argued that separate sets of rules for both codes would be inefficient in terms of memory storage. It is more efficient for the child to employ a common core of rules with those specific to a particular code tagged as such through a process of differentiation. The data indicated that the rules acquired first in the simultaneous acquisition of *yes/no* questions in two languages were those that were common to both languages. Rules that were language-specific or more complex were acquired later.

This seems to be generally true. Imedadze's (1960) finding that the Georgian subject–to–object relation was expressed first by analogy to the Russian in the speech of a bilingual child also suggests that the child initially tries to use a single code for both languages. Other authors also report the initial assimilation syntactically and morphologically of one language to the other (Engel, 1965; Mikěs, 1967; Rūķe–Draviņa, 1967).

At some point the child becomes conscious of speaking two different languages. Ronjat (1913) maintained that his child had this awareness at 1 year and

6 months, and Pavlovitch (1920) also put the date of awareness relatively early, at 2 years. Other authors (Elwert, 1960; Geissler, 1938; Imedadze, 1960; Rūķe–Draviņa, 1967) set the date somewhere in the 3rd or 4th year. Leopold (1949a) saw some signs of awareness on the part of his daughter at 2 years, but it was only at 3 years and 6 months or so that the child had a good feeling for the differences between the two languages.

One reason for the disagreement on this issue is that different authors use different criteria for awareness. Ronjat (1913) thought that the child was conscious of bilingualism when he used synonymous pairs of words from his two languages. Imedadze (1960) argued that this does not necessarily indicate an awareness of bilingualism; the child is simply trying to use the means at her disposal to communicate. For the child, the two words are part of a single linguistic code. Awareness of bilingualism begins when the child starts to use the two languages distinctly to communicate with different people in different languages. It is this practice of "translating" or using rough equivalents in interacting with different people that leads to an awareness of bilingualism, not the use of synonymous word pairs. Imedadze found this stage to begin near the end of the 2nd year in the child she studied and to be complete by 2 years and 4 months, when the child ceased to adopt words from one language to the other but asked for the corresponding word when it was unknown in one of her languages.

Volterra and Taeschner (1975) found that the children they studied passed through three stages. First, they developed a single lexical system with a given meaning expressed in one language or the other, but not in both. The second stage occurred at about 2 years when the child distinguished the two different lexicons, but applied the same syntactic rules to both languages. About ½ year later, in the third stage, the two languages were differentiated both in lexicon and in syntax, and each language was associated with particular persons and situations.

Once the child becomes aware of and differentiates the two linguistic codes, language changing or code switching becomes a normal aspect of behavior with respect to certain known persons or situations. The bilingual child is able to switch codes with remarkable quickness (Gerullis, 1932; Mitchell, 1954) and even, apparently, in his dreams (Braun, 1937; Elwert, 1960). Different codes are associated with different people and age groups (Elwert, 1960; Mitchell, 1954; Oksaar, 1970). Situational specificity was observed by Rūķe–Draviņa (1967), whose children spoke Latvian in the home and Swedish with playmates. When playing in the home, they used Swedish—the language associated with the play situation. Even different locations can be occasions for switching: Meertens (1959) reported that a small Dutch boy spoke Frisian when walking with his parents but switched to Dutch when going into a store and when going by his school and church.

This is not to imply that switching codes is always easy for the child. If parents or other adults try to speak to the child in a language other than the one in which they usually speak, the child is likely to become confused and may not under-stand what is said in spite of knowing the language (Metraux, 1965; Perren, 1972). Once a particular language code becomes temporarily predominant through use, it is difficult to switch back to the other language (Emrich, 1938; Leopold, 1949b). The child may go through a period of silence until some degree of balance is achieved (Engel, 1966; Leopold, 1949b).

There are also cases in which mixing within the same utterance occurs often. For example, Spanish–English bilingual children in the southwestern and west-ern sectors of the United States hear mixed utterances from their parents and others, and mixing occurs in their own speech. Since these children are capable by the age of 3 of distinguishing the two languages and apply different rules to each language (Padilla & Liebman, 1975), it is possible that mixing is for them still another code used for rhetorical purposes. This is a topic I discuss in more detail in the next chapter.

CONCLUSION

In conclusion, a few general comments are in order. As was noted earlier in this chapter, observational studies are fraught with methodological pitfalls. The prin-cipal difficulty is assuring objectivity. How is the investigator (or the reader) to know that all of the data are being gathered, not just the data that fit the inves-tigator's preconceptions as to how things should be? One improvement would be to use more objective methods of assessing the child's linguistic abilities. A large number of techniques are now available for testing young children. These include the Imitation–Comprehension–Production technique (Fraser, Bellugi, & Brown, 1963), Elicited–Imitation (Slobin & Welsh, 1973), Developmental Sentence Scoring (Lee & Canter, 1971), the Bilingual Syntax Measure (Burt, Dulay, & Hernandez, 1975), and the Picture Verification technique (Slobin, 1966b). The use of such methods, in addition to traditional observational information, would greatly improve our knowledge of the processes involved in bilingual language acquisition.

Greater objectivity can also be achieved by technical means. For example, simply keeping notes on the child's speech as it occurs is not sufficient for accurate analysis (Oksaar, 1969). A regular procedure should be instigated for taking tape-recorded samples of the child's speech at different times and in different situations. The use of video tape is also a desideratum, as it frequently happens that the meaning of the child's utterance is clear only from context. Video tapes also could provide a great deal of information as to how the child learns the rules for code switching—presently a murky area.

Finally, investigators have to know what they are looking for. In the typical case study, the data are gathered more or less as they fall from the mouth of the child by an investigator who sits down afterwards and tries to put the pieces together. A better way to proceed is to know what one is looking for beforehand. There is still a lot to be learned. For instance:

- What developmental stages do children exposed to two languages go through in acquiring specific syntactic structures such as negative constructions, interrogative constructions, relative clauses, and so on?
- Are these developmental stages always identical with those followed by monolingual speakers?
- How do specific languages interact with each other phonetically, syntactically, and semantically?
- What regularities are to be found in semantic and morphological mixings?
- Do particular language combinations cause more retardation in individual language development than others?
- Is bilingual language acquisition more difficult for some children than for others? Why is this (if true)?
- What factors of language presentation affect bilingual development?
- What processes are involved in children's achieving an awareness that they are exposed to bilingual presentation?
- How are more subtle aspects of language acquisition—such as the acquisition of implied requests and more complicated grammatical constructions—affected by bilingual presentation?
- What can parents do to facilitate the child's learning of two languages?

The field awaits systematic research directed at answering such questions.

5

Successive Acquisition of Two Languages in Childhood

This chapter deals with research on the successive acquisition of two languages in childhood. The distinction between simultaneous and successive language acquisition is, as we have seen, a rather arbitrary one, the cutoff point being 3 years. If the child is introduced to a second language before that age, I consider acquisition of the two languages to be simultaneous; if the second language is introduced after 3 years, acquisition is successive—one language having been relatively well established (though by no means fully established) by that age.

The questions of interest in this chapter are similar to those that concerned us in the previous chapter. What information can be gained from case studies of children acquiring a second language? What are the developmental consequences of acquiring two languages? Does the acquisition of a second language interfere with the acquisition of the first language, or vice versa? How does the child learn to switch codes—to move from one language code to the other?

The literature on the successive acquisition of two languages is reviewed chronologically, beginning with the early case studies. As was mentioned in the previous chapter, the literature on successive acquisition of two languages in childhood includes some recent studies dealing with particular theoretical issues in second-language acquisition. Some of these are case studies, and others are studies with groups of children that employ a combination of case study and experimental techniques.

The discussion in this chapter deals mainly with studies of children who acquire their second language in a natural milieu (i.e., by living in an environment in which they are constantly exposed to the language). I am less concerned here with second-language learning that occurs exclusively in the classroom and not in the natural environment as well. (Second-language learning in the school is treated in the following chapter.) The format for the present chapter is the same as in the previous one: first an overview of the research and then an examination of the language acqusition process when a second language is acquired following a first language.

STUDIES OF SUCCESSIVE LANGUAGE ACQUISITION

The studies are divided into two groups. The first group consists of case studies that deal for the most part with general phenomena of second-language acquisition. Most studies until recent years were of this sort—the description in broad terms of the linguistic development of children acquiring a second language. Rather than focusing on particular issues, parent–observers and linguists considered the whole process of second-language acquisition, describing some aspects in more detail than others, depending on their interests. Recently, there has been more concern with specific topics, especially particular aspects of syntactic development in children acquiring a second language in a natural setting.

Early Studies

The earliest study in the literature is the report of Volz (cited in Stern & Stern, 1907) of his child's acquisition of German as a second language. The child had lived for the first 3 years of his life in Sumatra, during which time he was exposed almost entirely to Malaysian. From 3 years and 1 month, the child heard only German. Volz observed a transition period from 3 years, 1 month, to 3 years, 3 months, when the child used both languages next to each other but did not mix them. If he did not know a particular German word or expression, he reverted to Malaysian but always added *malayu* (*in Malaysian*). After 3 years and 3 months, Malaysian was used less frequently; and by 3 years and 8 months, the language seemed to be entirely forgotten. Nonetheless, Malaysian syntactic structures and word order persisted for some time. The child experienced a period of relative stagnation between 3 years and 6 months and 3 years and 9 months, attributed by his father to discouragement due to being often misunderstood and not understanding others and to frustration at not being able to express himself adequately. During this period he was often silent. At 3 years and 9 months, the boy began to speak more and tried with considerable effort to express his thoughts accurately. By 4 years of age, his ability in the German language began to approximate that of monolingual children his age. Volz made the interesting observation that when his son had completely forgotten all Malaysian, he displayed the sounds and intonations of Malaysian when speaking nonsensical gibberish or when imitating his parents reading. Apparently he had retained the motor patterns associated with the forgotten language.

Kenyeres (1938) observed her 6½-year-old daughter, Eva, acquiring French after the family had moved from Hungary to Geneva. Up to that point in her life the child had spoken only Hungarian and knew no French. She was strongly motivated to master the language so as to be able to communicate and play with other children. Within 10 months she was able, in her mother's judgment, to speak French as well as native children her age. Phonetic development was especially rapid. At first, only major differences (e.g., nasality) were attended to; after that, more subtle ones. By the end of the 3rd month she had mastered the French sound system.

During these first 3 months Eva tended actively to translate French into Hungarian. She analyzed the differences and began to practice with French forms. Initially she seemed to clutch at a known and dominant word in an otherwise incomprehensible sentence and deciphered the sentence by using that word as a focus and translating into Hungarian. Her French constructions were formed by analogy with the Hungarian. She consciously tried to find rules for gender and to determine to what extent French constructions corresponded to those she already knew. By the 6th month she used words for which she did not possess Hungarian equivalents, and French began to fulfill the function of her native language, although Hungarian continued to be used to supply certain forms not yet acquired in French.

Kenyeres concluded that her daughter had acquired her second language in a manner that was different from the way in which she acquired her first language. Her acquisition of the second language was based on what she knew of her first language. She operated by analogy, using her knowledge of the first language to derive the rules of the second. She consciously rehearsed, especially when playing alone with her dolls, apparently deliberately trying to learn words and phrases in her second language as an adult does via the audio-lingual method.

Malmberg (1945) provided an account of the acquisition of Swedish by a 4½-year-old, Finnish-speaking girl. The child tended to give certain Swedish words, especially those with Finnish cognates, the stress they would receive in Finnish. There was considerable difficulty with certain aspects of the Swedish sound system, especially with voiced stops. Nonetheless, it seemed that certain sounds—such as the uvular /R/—were acquired along with or instead of the sounds—such as the apical /r/—of her first language.

Finnish endings were initially applied to Swedish noun stems, and even after the Swedish suffix was learned, the Finnish postpositional continued to be used. Eventually the Finnish postpositional was replaced by a Swedish preposition, which still, however, followed the noun and its suffix. The final step in this process was the correct placement of the Swedish preposition. There were thus four steps in the child's development:

Stage 1: Substitution of Finnish noun stem by Swedish noun stem with Finnish endings.

Stage 2: Swedish noun stem receives Swedish endings but is followed by the Finnish postpositional as before.

Stage 3: The Finnish postpositional is replaced by a Swedish preposition following the noun and its suffix.

Stage 4: The preposition is correctly placed.

Tits (1948) reported on the language development of a 6-year-old Spanish refugee girl who acquired French and Flemish in Belgium. The child, like Kenyeres's daughter, used her first language as a starting point and demonstrated good progress in French. She declared on the 93rd day after her arrival in Belgium that she did not know Spanish anymore (although her foster parents tried to preserve this language and had her subsequently take Spanish in school). At the age of 8 and again at 10 years, she scored 2 years above the mean for her age on tests of French language skills. In general, Tits maintained that her development in her second language progressed through the same stages as one observes in a child acquiring this language as a first language, although at a much quicker pace and with less clear delineation between stages.

Valette (1964) reported on the acquisition of French by an American child whose parents moved to Paris when he was 3 years and 3 months old. The child was in a French kindergarten from 9 to 5 each day where the only language he heard was French; English was maintained in the home. He mastered a number of standard phrases in the first 6 weeks and by 3 months had acquired a few more functional phrases such as *C'est René qu'a fait ça, Comme ça, Ça y est*. During the period from the 3rd to the 6th month, he showed relatively rapid development, and after this period he could make himself understood to other children. If he did not know a particular French word, he would replace it by the English spoken with a French accent. By 9 months he had acquired an authentic French accent. During the period of his most rapid increase in vocabulary, from 8 to 9 months, Valette observed that he would make a number of mistakes that are typical of native French children, such as deducing from *un avion* or *un autre* that the basic form is *le navion* or *le nautre*. Verbs were learned first in the singular of the present tense; plural verb forms were acquired relatively late, as were other tenses. The infinitive was used in the future and in past constructions and in the subjunctive. Valette noted that acquiring the language was not easy for the child even with so much exposure, and after 1 year he was still a year behind his French peers in his command of the language.

Francescato (1969) found that his children, who learned Italian first and then Dutch, required about a year's time to reach the level of their peers in Dutch. In neither his study nor in Valette's were criteria given for language mastery, so comparison is difficult. In contrast to Kenyeres, Francescato did not feel that his children consciously compared the language system of their second language with their first language, but this is possibly because his children learned the second language at a younger age (3 and 4) than Kenyeres's child. He also argued that the young child of 3 or 4 can serve as a translator, not because the child actually translates from one language to another, but because the situation elicits certain verbal responses. If the child is simply given a sentence out of context to translate, he cannot do so.

Recent Research

To this point the studies under review have been concerned with broad questions of language development and use and have rarely given extended and systematic treatment to phonological, semantic, or syntactic issues. The one exception is Malmberg's valuable analysis of the stages of acquisition of the Swedish prepositional construction by a Finnish-speaking child. Most recent studies are like Malmberg's in that they are centrally concerned with specific problems of theoretical interest, especially aspects of syntactic development and the question of interference between first and second languages.

For example, Ravem (1968) studied the development of English syntactic regularities in the speech of his 6½-year-old, Norwegian-speaking son by attempting to steer the conversation in different directions to elicit from the boy different kinds of sentences referring to past, present, and future events. In addition, he gave his son a translation test at regular intervals involving 50 negative and 50 interrogative sentences that require an auxiliary in adult speech. The test consisted of a request in Norwegian to *Go and ask Mother if . . .* or *Tell Ranny that . . .* , with the indirect sentence containing the auxiliary verb. Comparison of this method with the child's spontaneous utterances showed it to be an accurate index of the child's syntactic development.

Ravem was principally interested in the acquisition of the modal *do* in his son's speech. He found that *do* was learned in a manner that followed the usual developmental sequence for English-speaking, monolingual children. That is, the modal was initially omitted in negative sentences, and the negative was marked by a negator between the subject and the predicate: *I not like that.* The modal was also dropped in *yes–no* questions, although here the Norwegian inversion pattern was retained: *Like you ice cream?* An English-speaking, monolingual child uses intonation without inversion at this stage: *You like ice cream?*

Ravem's son, however, did not usually invert the verb in *wh-* questions. On the basis of his formation of *yes–no* questions, where the Norwegian pattern persisted, one would expect *wh-* questions of the form: *What reading you?* or *What doing you now?* Instead, Ravem found constructions in which the child used the pattern of the declarative sentence in *wh-* question sentences, without inversion: *What you reading to-yesterday?* These constructions are similar to those observed in monolingual, English-speaking children. Ravem suggested that in the *yes–no* questions inversion is used as a question signal, but this does not explain why monolingual children do not use inversion in *yes–no* questions, whereas Ravem's son did. As we shall see, there are other possible explanations for this apparently anomalous finding.

Finally, Ravem's study contained information on the development of *do* as a tense marker. There appeared to be four stages:

Stage 1. *Do* occurs in the context of isolated verbs, probably as a lexical variant of *not: I don't know, I don't talking to you.*

Stage 2. *Do* occurs in the context of and as a variant of you: *What d'you like?*

Stage 3. *Do* emerges as a tense carrier: *What you did in Rothbury? What d'you do to-yesterday?*

Stage 4. *Do* emerges as a separate element with a present and past form. *Did* is used in sentences requiring the past tense, and *do* is almost invariably followed by the infinitive form of the main verb.

In a study using similar procedures, Ravem (1974) examined the development of *wh-* questions in the speech of his son and of his daughter, aged 3 years and 9 months. In general, the mistakes they made reflected English rather than Norwegian developmental features. For instance, the children failed to invert the auxiliary verb and the subject (*What she is doing?*), a mistake similar to that found by Brown (1968) in English-speaking children. They made this mistake although they already had learned the Norwegian rule that requires the subject–verb inversion. Similarly, *why* questions developed late, as they do in monolingual children, even though Ravem's children understood the notion of causality in their first language.

Ravem argued that, taking into account the age and maturity of the children and the fact that they already knew one language, his findings suggested that the similarities in first- and second-language development are more striking than the differences. The children seemed to pass through essentially the same stages that first-language learners pass through. There were occasional exceptions to the rule—instances in which Norwegian forms appeared to influence the English ones—but these were rare.

Hernandez (cited by Ervin–Tripp, 1970) analyzed the language development of a Chicano child of 3 learning English. He found that the influence of the new sound system was initially pre-eminent, suggesting that acquisition of the sound system is especially important for a child of this age learning a second language. Hernandez reported that a number of the Spanish-speaking children he observed attempted to speak English by using English phonological features with Spanish lexicon and grammar.

In a study of the acquisition of Spanish by seven English-speaking children from 4 to 6½ years of age, Dato (1970) reported that the children failed to invert the subject and verb in questions, although word–for–word translation from English to Spanish would lead to inversion. This finding is similar to that of Ravem (1974), suggesting once again that the developmental pattern in second-language learning follows the same sequence as is observed in monolingual speakers of the target language.

In general, Dato found evidence that second-language syntactic development was characterized by a learning sequence in which "base structures" are acquired first and then "transformed structures," a sequence typical of first-language acquisition as well. Although his transformational analysis has been criticized (Dulay & Burt, 1972), his data suggest that second-language acquisition, like first-language acquisition, is characterized by a general trend of increasing complexity.

Dato (1971) extended his transformational analysis in a subsequent study concerned with the auxiliary verb. Again the evidence indicated that even in older children, simple forms are learned before more complex ones. The children in his study learned the imperative and copula first, closely followed by the present indicative. More complex forms developed later. The sequence in which the children learned person-number, tense, and other elements of the auxiliary was the same, although the children differed in age at the time of their introduction to Spanish.

Politzer and Ramirez (1973) conducted a study of Chicano children from 5 to 9 years of age, based on speech samples collected by having the children describe a silent movie they had watched. Their answers were recorded on tape, and deviations from standard English were counted and categorized. The results were interpreted as indicating that Spanish influence was the major cause of error as shown by such mistakes as nominalization by use of the infinitive rather than the gerund (*instead of kill birds*), uncertainty in the use of subject pronouns (omission of the pronoun in sentences such as [*He*] *pinch the man,* [*I*] *liked him, then* [*he*] *flew away*), the use of redundant pronouns (*The bird he save him, The man he came*), and confusion of word order (object–subject–verb constructions). Nonetheless, Politzer and Ramirez admitted that error classification of this sort is problematic. When the child says *He not catch the bird,* this appears to resemble the Spanish construction but may in fact represent a phase in the development of the negative construction that occurs in the monolingual, English-speaking child's language development as well. Whether a particular error can be attributed to the influence of the second language involves the difficult judgmental task of separating those errors that are found in the speech of monolingual speakers from those that are the result of interference between languages.

In a further discussion of this topic Politzer (1974) noted that there is ample evidence that many of the mistakes made by second-language learners are similar or identical to the mistakes made by children in the process of first-language acquisition. He also thought that there was some evidence that complex structures that are difficult in first-language acquisition tend to be difficult in second-language acquisition, so that they are acquired after more simple constructions in both cases. Nevertheless, he argued that the similarity between first- and second-language acquisition should not be taken for granted. His analysis of the Politzer and Ramirez data suggested that the developmental course in second-language acquisition differs from that observed in monolingual children. For the time being we shall defer judgment; a more detailed discussion of this topic follows in the next section. There are, however, other studies that bear on this issue.

Milon (1974) compared the developmental substages of negation in a 7-year-old Japanese boy's acquisition of English with those developmental stages observed by Klima and Bellugi (1966) in the acquisition of negation by monolingual, English-speaking children. As we saw in Chapter 2, Klima and Bellugi documented three stages in the development of negation. In the first stage, the negative appears outside the sentence nucleus (*Not cold, Not me*). In the second stage, the negative appears between the noun phrase and the verb phrase (*He no bite you, I can't catch you*). In the third stage, the adult pattern appears (*You don't want some supper, I not hurt him*).

Through video-tape recordings of 20-minute weekly sessions over a 7-month period, Milon gathered 244 negative utterances. Table 5.1 gives examples of the child's use of negative constructions. Of the child's first 47 negative utterances, 37 fit into Stage I, there were 9 *I don't know* constructions, and 1 anomaly. The *I don't know* construction probably was a phrase borrowed in its entirety. The anomalous sentence was *I don't have a watch,* which occurred once, probably an exact repetition of a sentence heard from other children. Of the next 143 negative utterances, 90 fit into Stage 1 and 48 into Stage 2. There were five anomalous sentences, all of which were negative tag questions (a category not included in Klima and Bellugi's analysis). The final 131 negative utterances fit into all three stages with the majority still described by Stage 1 rules, but with Stage 3 rules emerging (9%).

Milon concluded that the child progressed through the same developmental stages in the same sequence as the children studied by Klima and Bellugi. This is not a priori predictable, since the negative in Japanese is formed by attaching a morpheme to the right of the verb stem. Thus one would expect utterances such as *I give not . . . ,* where the negative structure follows the verb. Instead the child appeared to be replicating the developmental sequence (at least the first two

TABLE 5.1
The Use of Negatives at Three Stages of
Development in a Bilingual Child's Speech[a]

Stage 1	Stage 2	Stage 3
No	I don't know what kind	I never saw yours
Not ocean	I no look	I never do
No more	He can not	I not saw
	Don't look Michael	You no go win
		You never cut yet

[a] From Milon, 1974.

TABLE 5.2
Examples of English to French Translations[a]

Stimulus	5-year-old child 9 months in Geneva	7-year-old child 9 months in Geneva
I see her.	Moi je vois elle.	Je elle vois.
She sees them.	Elle regarde eux.	Elle les voit.[b]
Why does she eat them?	Pourquoi il mange ça?	Pourquoi elle les mange?[c]
He gave her the carrots.	Il a donné les carottes.	Il a donné à elle les carottes.[c]
Who is she waiting for?	Qui elle attend pour?	Elle attend pour qui?
She's waiting for them.	Il attend pour eux.	Elle les attend.[b]
What pushed the door?	Quoi il poussait la porte?	Qu'est-ce qui a poussé la porte?[b]
What fell down?	Quoi il a tombé?	Qu'est-ce qui a tombé?
Why is he pushing her?	Pourquoi il pousse elle?	Pourquoi il elle pousse?
Where is the dog going?	Où le chien il va?	Où va le chien?[b]
Where is he going?	Où lui il va?	Où ils 'en va.[c]

[a] From Ervin–Tripp (1974).
[b] Correct.
[c] Colloquial, possible in native speaker's usage.

stages) observed in monolingual, English-speaking children and not transferring the Japanese structure onto the English.

Ervin–Tripp (1974) was also impressed by the similarities between first- and second-language acquisition in the group of children she studied. Her sample was drawn from English-speaking children between the ages of 4 and 9 living in Geneva. She found evidence that the children, like children acquiring a first language, remember best the items they can interpret. Like Valette's (1964) child, they were capable very early of learning whole phrases because they knew their meaning.

Word order was related to meaning fairly early. The basic subject–verb–object strategy was used in interpreting sentences, even anomalous passive constructions (where the first noun was animate and the second inanimate and a common object of the verb). Although older children correctly interpreted English equivalents, they reverted to the subject–verb–object strategy and misunderstood the French passive. Similarly, indirect objects were often taken to be direct objects if English word order was followed—even though French marks indirect objects with a preposition. This again points to the predominance of the subject–verb–object strategy. In addition, other evidence, such as overgeneralization of lexical forms and the preference for simple sentence production heuristics, seemed to indicate that the process of second-language acquisition was similar to first-language learning.

Table 5.2 gives examples of English to French translations that occurred in the speech of the children in Ervin–Tripp's sample. As she pointed out, at first glance the children seem to be translating word–for–word. Yet this strategy of mapping the French onto the English word order and syntax was actually used in only a few sentences. The basic strategies seemed to be as follows:

- In declarative sentences, use subject–verb–object order. Very few children, for example, had acquired the separate rule for pronominal objects.
- In questions, give the question word then the nuclear word order, either subject–verb–object or subject–verb–locative. Although word–for–word translation would lead to inversion in these sentences, this rarely occurred.
- In a residual number of cases young children used word–for–word translation strategy.

In short, it seems that children either have to relearn the heuristics they use in their first language when acquiring a second, or lose subrules governing indirect object, passives, and word order in questions when acquiring a second language. In either event their performance is similar to that of children learning the target language as their first language.

Cancino, Rosansky, and Schumann (1974, 1975) found some evidence, however, that suggests that different processes are involved in at least some aspects of second-language acquisition. They studied the speech of six Spanish-speaking persons: two children age 5, two adolescents ages 11 and 13, and two adult subjects. All were visited approximately twice monthly for an hour over a 10-month period. The data were based upon speech utterances, elicited imitations or negations of model utterances, and preplanned sociolinguistic interaction at parties, restaurants, museums, sport events, and the like. For none of the individuals did inverted *yes/no* questions precede inverted *wh-* questions, as is typical in the development of native, English-speaking children. Nor did the stages of acquisition of the negative correspond to those observed by Klima and Bellugi (1966) for native speakers.

In discussing the acquisition of negative constructions, Wode (1976) pointed out that utterances that reflect the child's first language may intrude in the developmental sequence. His data were based on the speech of his four German-speaking children acquiring English naturalistically. Constructions such as *I'm steal not the base, Marylin like no sleepy* appear to reflect German word order and are not found in the speech of native, English-speaking children. Wode argued that children acquiring a second language may take what superficially looks like a step backward in their development, reverting to their first language, but that such ''detours'' are the result of the application of acquisition principles that may or may not be the same as those governing first-language acquisition.

In a study of five Spanish-speaking children ages 5 to 7, who were acquiring English as a second language, Lily Wong Fillmore (1976) found considerable variation in the language acquisition of each child. Within 3 months the English of one of the children—as measured by well-formed and varied sentences—had developed beyond the point it would for two other children at the end of a full year of naturalistic exposure. By the end of a year, the child who progressed most rapidly could speak English nearly as well as monolingual children, whereas the other two children would need an additional year of exposure to reach this level of proficiency. These individual differences were seen to be related to cognitive and social factors.

Each of the five children studied by Fillmore was paired with an English-speaking friend so as to make possible observation of the social processes involved in learning to communicate in a second language. Fillmore maintained that the child's principal task in acquiring a second language is to establish social relations with children who speak that language. To do so, the child employs special social (S) and cognitive (C) strategies:

S-I: Join a group and act as if you understand what is going on, even if you don't.

C-I: Assume that what people are saying is directly relevant to the situation at hand or to what they or you are experiencing. Metastrategy: Guess!

The use of these strategies gets the child into a position where acquiring the language is possible. It enables the child to use situational cues to interpret and make sense out of what is being said by native speakers.

The next set of strategies relates to speech production:

S-II: Give the impression—with a few well-chosen words—that you can speak the language.

C-IIa: Give the impression you understand, and start talking.

Children apply these strategies by using formulaic expressions—that is, expressions that are acquired and used as unanalyzed wholes. This enables the child to use the language before knowing anything of its structure. Examples are: *Lookit, Wait a minute, Whose turn is it?* Such formulaic speech, Fillmore argued, is central to the learning of language. Once a repertory of such expressions exists, the child uses the next cognitive strategy:

C-IIb: Look for recurring parts in the formulas you know.

This is the beginning of syntactic development. The child discovers that constituents of formulaic expressions are interchangeable—*I wanna play wi' dese, I don't wanna do dese.* By determining the parts of formulas that can be varied, the child frees constituents to become units in productive constructions. Once the constituents have been freed from the original construction, the child has an abstract structure consisting of a pattern or rule by which the construction of novel utterances becomes possible. Fillmore gave the example of the formulaic expression *How do you do dese?* which became *How do you do dese flower pot?* or *How do you do dese little tortillas?* Eventually *How do you make the flower?* appeared, and then *How do cut it? How do make it?* Finally, *how* is freed: *How you make it?* and *How will take off paste?* Thus *how* is progressively analyzed until only the question word remains. Similar examples were found to be extremely common in the children's speech.

The next set of strategies leads to fluency in the language:

S-III: Count on your friends for help.
C-IIIa: Make the most of what you've got.
C-IIIb: Work on the big things first; save the details for later.

The children learned to use their limited repertory in a wide variety of situations. The important thing was to communicate, even if details of the utterances were incorrect. The native-speaking children cooperated by simplifying their speech, by including the nonnative speakers in their play, and by directing their speech at objects and activities at hand. Furthermore, they believed that their friends would learn the language, encouraged them, and made an effort to figure out what they were trying to say.

Nonetheless, as we noted, the children acquiring English did so at very different rates. Fillmore maintained that one of the most critical ways they differed was in having the social skills necessary to make use of the social strategies mentioned above. The child who progressed most rapidly, Nora, sought out English-speaking children to a much greater extent than was true of the others; she preferred role-playing games to other play activities, and she was highly concerned with peer relationships. In addition, Nora was completely uninhibited in speaking English, which was not true of some of the other children.

Fillmore's research makes a point often missed in case studies. In focusing on a single child, the researcher looses sight of sources of variation. By comparing the progress of several children, Fillmore demonstrated that social factors make a large difference in language acquisition. The child who is outgoing and possesses social confidence has a much greater opportunity to discover structural possibilities in the target language.

Fillmore's observation that children acquiring a second language use formulaic expressions corroborates the observation of some earlier investigators (e.g., Kenyeres, 1938; Valette, 1964) and the findings of Hakuta (1974b, 1975), who studied a 5-year-old Japanese girl acquiring English as a second language. He found that the girl, Uguisu, operated within a simple learning system involving "prefabricated patterns." The child progressed from utterances such as *I don't know where is the money* to *I don't know where is it* to *I don't know where is the woods is* to *I don't know where the bathroom is*. Hakuta thought that the child tries to maintain both internal consistency within the structures already possessed and external consistency, matching structures with those heard in the input from native speakers.

Hakuta (1974a) also studied the development of grammatical morphemes in Uguisu's speech. Samples of spontaneous speech were recorded for about 2 hours biweekly over a 60-week period. Order of acquisition of the morphemes was determined by taking the ratio of actual realizations to potential occurrences in obligatory contexts. The order of acquisition did not invariably parallel that of children acquiring English as a first language. A subsequent analysis of the data (Hakuta, 1976) revealed only a weak correlation (.20) with the data on morpheme accuracy obtained in cross-sectional research (Bailey, Madden, & Krashen, 1974; Dulay & Burt, 1974a). Hakuta (1976) also cited other research with Japanese children that failed to show a stable order of acquisition of grammatical morphemes across children learning English.

Kessler and Idar (1977) also studied the acquisition of grammatical morphemes longitudinally. They gathered English speech samples from a 4-year-old Vietnamese girl during a 9-week period when the girl lived with an American family. The use of four verb phrase morphemes in obligatory contexts revealed an acquisition ordering that was identical to that found by Brown (1973a) for children learning English as a first language: progressive -ing, present irregular, copula, auxiliary. Kessler and Idar pointed out that these similarities do not reflect language similarities. Contrastive analysis of Vietnamese and English predicts a different ordering for the two languages. They concluded that their findings support the hypothesis that second-language acquisition follows the developmental path of first-language acquisition of English.

Table 5.3 recapitulates the case-study literature dealing with the successive acquisition of a second language in childhood. Because they are not strictly case studies but deal with larger samples, the studies of Politzer and Ramirez (1973) and Ervin–Tripp (1974) are not included in the table. There are also a number of unpublished studies that have not been included here (see Hatch, 1977).

LANGUAGE ACQUISITION PROCESSES WHEN A SECOND LANGUAGE IS ACQUIRED SUBSEQUENT TO A FIRST LANGUAGE

In Chapter 3 I discussed the literature dealing with the acquisition of second languages in childhood and adulthood. I argued there that the evidence does not support the assertion that children and adults acquire or learn second languages in essentially different ways. The child and the adult approach a second language in a manner consistent with their cognitive development, but the same processes seem to be involved in both cases. Cook's (1973) research suggests that adults learning a second language pass through essentially the same stages as a child does acquiring that language as a first language. Can the same be said of children acquiring a second language?

Developmental Features

Before discussing syntactic development, a few comments are in order about phonological and semantic development in the second-language acquisition of children. In the previous chapter we saw that *sound-system processing* in chil-

TABLE 5.3
Case Studies of Successive Bilingual Acquisition

Author	Languages	Age of child at time of study	Concerns of study[a]
Volz (Stern & Stern, 1907)	Malaysian–German	3 years, studied for a year	Sp S, Interf
Kenyeres (1938)	Hungarian–French	6 years, 10 months, to 7 years, 8 months	Sp S, Sem, Sy Dvlp Seq, Interf
Malmberg (1945)	Swedish–Finnish	4½ years	Sp S, Sy, Mor, W O, Dvlp Seq, Interf
Tits (1948)	Spanish–French	6 years	Sp S, Interf
Valette (1964)	English–French	3 years, 3 months, for a year	Sp S, Sem, Sy, Mor, Dvlp Seq, Interf
Francescato (1969)	Italian–Dutch	Two children, from 4th year	Interf
Ravem (1968)	Norwegian–English	6 years, 6 months, for 3 months	Sy, Mor, W O, Dvlp Seq, Interf
Ravem (1974)	Norwegian–English	3 years and 9 months for 10 months	Sy, Mor, W O, Dvlp Seq, Interf
Hernandez (Ervin-Tripp, 1970)	Spanish–English	3 years	Sp S
Dato (1970, 1971)	English–Spanish	Son from 4 years, 1 month, for 9 months and 6 other children between 5½ and 6½	Sy, Mor, W O, Dvlp Seq, Interf
Milon (1974)	Japanese–English	7 years for 7 months	Sy, Mor, W O, Dvlp Seq, Interf
Cancino et al. (1974, 1975)	Spanish–English	Two children, two adolescents, two adults for 10 months	Sy, Mor, W O, Dvlp Seq, Interf
Hakuta (1974a, b, 1975)	Japanese–English	5 years for 1 year	Sy, Mor, W O, Dvlp Seq, Interf
Wode (1976)	German–English	Four children	Sy, Mor, W O, Dvlp Seq, Interf
Fillmore (1976)	Spanish–English	Five children, ages 5 to 7 for 1 year	Sy, Mor, W O, Devlp Seq
Kessler & Idar (1977)	Vietnamese–English	4 years for 1 year	Sy, Mor, W O, Dvlp Seq

[a] Abbreviations: Sp S = Speech Sounds; Sem = Semantics; Sy = Syntax; Mor = Morphology; W O = Word Order; Dvlp Seq = Developmental Sequence; Interf = Interference Phenomena.

dren exposed simultaneously to two languages is probably no different than it is when the child is exposed to a single language. The child most likely initially treats the input as part of a single system and only later distinguishes the two sound systems from each other. The amount of confusion between sound systems seems to depend on the way in which the two languages are presented to the child: if they are kept sharply differentiated with respect to persons and situations, interference will be reduced. Similarly, if the two languages are maintained in balance, interference is reduced.

What of successive acquisition of a second language? Unfortunately the data are skimpy. There is some evidence suggesting that the strategy employed in processing the sounds of a second language is similar to that used in processing the sounds of the first language. Children tend to acquire the more simple sounds of a second language earlier than those that are more complex (Hernandez in Ervin–Tripp, 1970; Malmberg, 1945). The problem with this sort of evidence, however, is that it tends to be circular: sounds used later are defined as more difficult to acquire than those used earlier. What is needed is careful documentation of the sequence in which children acquiring given languages acquire the sound systems of those languages as a basis of comparison for examining the developmental sequence followed by children acquiring these languages as second languages.

Wode (1976) found that German-speaking children acquiring English used their knowledge of German phonology to acquire certain English sounds, substituting German phonemes for English phonemes. But this was not the case for all sounds. Some were acquired in a manner that could not be related to first-language phonological capacity. Instead, such sounds as the English /r/ followed the same developmental sequence as is observed in native, English-speaking children.

Ervin–Tripp (1974), upon observing that young children playfully pronounced English words with a French accent, devised a test to determine what phonological principles were involved in this skill. She gave children of different ages stimuli in English, such as *knife, ride, winter, birthday,* and asked them to pronounce these words as if they were French. Even children with limited amounts of exposure to French seemed to have developed certain phonological rules. Younger children tended to reduce all words to a single syllable and to delete most final consonants. The uvular /R/ replaced the apical /r/, and nasal segments were converted to nasalized vowels. In contrast, older children tended to use more complex rules, including more complete /R/ replacement, a shift of stress to second syllables, vowel changes to the French vowel values, and correct nasalization.

These differences are not surprising in view of the fact that the older children have already discovered some basic principles of phonology. If they have learned to read a syllabic written language, they have acquired a fairly abstract knowledge of oral language phonology. Indeed, the greatest differences seemed to occur between children who could read and those who could not read.

Information about *semantic processing* is also relatively meager. Few researchers have concerned themselves with this topic. We know little, for example, about the occurrence of overextensions in the second languages of children—whether they occur and whether they resemble those that are found in first-language acquisition. A common finding is that the first words that children learn when placed in a milieu in which they must acquire a new language relate to greetings and to terms dealing with interactions. These utterances are usually learned as a whole without any syntactic differentiation. Words relating to the self also seem to be learned early (Table 5.4).

Ervin–Tripp (1974) pointed out that the second-language learner, like the child acquiring a first language, tends to learn best items that have meaning. Recurrence in meaningful situations provides the basic categorization device for building a lexicon. The child tends initially to prefer one form for one meaning and rejects two forms for what appears to be an identical meaning on the basis of the

TABLE 5.4
Spontaneous Speech Samples of Two English-Speaking Children[a]

Weeks in French-speaking environment	Speech sample	
	6.7-year-old child	
6	moi sanglier	(me boar) [claiming animal from comic book]
	au-revoir	(goodbye)
	je-ne-comprends	(I don't understand)
	à moi, lait, moi	(mine, milk, me) [gesturing he wants milk]
	allez-y	(hurry up, get going)
8	Nicolas dit non	(Nicolas says no)
	Nicolas dit pourquoi	(Nicolas says why)
	pousse-moi	(push me)
	ça Nicolas vélo	(that Nicolas bike)
	ferme la porte	(close the door)
	toi nez rouge	(you nose red)
	5-year-old child	
8	regarde	(look)
9	regarde, escargots	(look, snails) [for dinner]
	moi bébé	(me baby) [in play]
	moi poupée	(me doll)
	moi princesse	(me princess)
11	regarde, Anna	(look at Anna)
	le crayon bleu, c'est là-bas	(the blue pencil, it's over there)
16	pas moi, toi, moi là	(not me, you, me there) [directing play locations]
	ça moi, ça Alexandre	(that me, that Alexander) [possessions]
	moi, c'est grand	(me, it's big) [mine's big]
	ça va, ça va pas, Eric?	(that's okay, that's not okay, Eric?)
	pas lait là, pas lait, milk	(not milk there)

[a] From Ervin–Tripp, 1974.

referential situation. Children acquiring French in Ervin–Tripp's sample regularly treated *le* (the masculine article) and *la* (the feminine article) as synonymous, because they appeared to have identical meanings. One child reported that he had learned a new word, *Assieds-toi* (*sit down*), pronounced as though it were a single word. The next day he reported that this was a mistake and that the word was *Asseyez-vous*, again pronounced as though it were a single word.

Ervin–Tripp noted that older children have the advantage of possessing more efficient memory heuristics and greater knowledge than younger children. The older children learn word combinations faster than younger children and can map new vocabulary into storage more efficiently. The older child has a more developed semantic system in the first language and so merely needs to discover new symbolic representations. Because of these differences, Ervin–Tripp argued that the major changes that occur between learners of a second language at various ages tend to relate to semantics.

Most research concerned with developmental sequences in second-language acquisition has been directed at *syntactic processing*. There seems to be good evidence that many of the same strategies are employed in second-language acquisition as are used in first-language acquisition. For example, word-order regularities are of initial importance in both first- and second-language acquisition. In both cases children appear to work from simpler to more complex structures, to use meaning as a clue for interpreting syntactic features, to relate word order to meaning, and to prefer simpler word orders to more complex order strategies such as verb–subject inversions (Ervin–Tripp, 1974).

The research of Ravem (1974) on questions and Milon (1974) on negative constructions lends support to the hypothesis that second-language development in children progresses through stages similar to first-language development in monolingual speakers of the target language. The apparently conflicting evidence from Ravem's (1968) study can be interpreted in processing terms that are consistent with the general trend of research findings. That the Norwegian inversion pattern was retained in interrogative sentences but not in negative sentences may be attributed to a strategy, particularly important in *yes–no* questions, of inverting the subject of interrogatives so as to indicate meaning from the start (*Like you ice cream?*). This inversion may be relatively strong at 6 in the Norwegian-speaking child. However, in *wh-* questions, the tendency to invert is not so strongly established, and so the pattern observed in English-speaking children is found. In the negative, location is less important for meaning, and since a separate rule is used for modals and nonmodalized verbs in Norwegian, the English construction is simpler and more likely to be adopted (Ervin–Tripp, 1970).

As we have seen, Politzer (1974) expressed scepticism about the similarity between developmental sequences in first- and second-language acquisition. Although an initial analysis of the Politzer and Ramirez (1973) data showed a developmental trend that suggested a great similarity between first- and second-language acquisition processes, Politzer found that when the data were reanalyzed controlling for length of uttterance and correct utterance, the bilingual children did not show the same developmental pattern as monolingual children.

The difficulty with Politzer's analysis is that the controls he employs are far too rigid. Their application does not so much yield different developmental sequences in bilingual and monolingual children as eliminate developmental sequences entirely. Controlling for length and correctness of utterance wipes out the developmental patterns usually found in the speech of monolingual children. No coherent pattern was found in either group. It is not surprising, then, that this analysis produced inconclusive results.

If we look at the earlier studies of successive language acquisition, we again find support for the hypothesis that first- and second-language learning involve similar processes. Stern and Stern (1907) reported that Volz's son at 3 years and 6 months built the past participle of German verbs in the same manner that the Sterns' son had at 2 years and 4 months (*ge* + infinitive). Furthermore, like young, German-speaking, monolingual children generally (Roeper, 1973), Volz noted that his son adopted the simplification strategy of using the infinitive as the verb in early sentences. Tits (1948) felt that the girl she observed passed through the same stages of development as a monolingual child although at a faster pace. Kenyeres (1938) also observed that her daughter processed sentences like a child acquiring a first language—by seizing on known and dominant words and using these words as clues for meaning.

Kenyeres maintained, nonetheless, that her daughter's development did not simply recapitulate early first-language development; nor did the child learn language as an adult would. Instead, she worked at the level of a child of her age, and her sentences were of the type spoken by children her age. This, however, does not contradict the hypothesis that first- and second-language acquisition involve similar processes. It is certainly the case that second-language acquisition makes use of the cognitive abilities of the child, but this is also the case for first-language acquisition (Ervin–Tripp, 1974). But this does not mean that intrinsically different processes are involved in first- and second-language acquisition.

This distinction is important. Politzer (1974) was doubtless correct in pointing out that the tendency to view second-language acquisition as similar to first-language acquisition depends on the conceptual perspective one adopts toward language acquisition generally. From a cognitive perspective, the experiences are obviously different. There is no evidence that the sequence of cognitive operations to which first-language acquisition is tied is repeated in second-language acquisition. The child, in acquiring a second language, does not have to build up knowledge of the world and of language from scratch. On the other hand, if one views language acquisition in terms of the processes involved and in terms of the strategies used in acquiring language, the similarities between first- and second-language acquisition become more pronounced. In process terms, language acquisition in both cases seems to involve the same operations, although the older child (and the adult) proceeds at a much more rapid rate of development.

Aside from the studies already mentioned, Ervin–Tripp's (1974) data support the contention that the process of second-language acquisition is developmentally like first-language acquisition. As we have seen, she found that children of various ages prefer a simple subject–verb–object strategy for all constructions, although they had already learned the appropriate constructions for passives and questions in their first language. Even when a preposition appeared after the verb, children often ignored the preposition and interpreted the noun following the verb as the object.

Ervin–Tripp (1974) made the interesting observation that two American children, who were in the process of losing English after living 9 months with their Swiss mother and grandparents, had regressed in their English to simpler sentence production heuristics with corresponding syntax degeneration and morphology loss. It is possible that a similar regression to earlier first-language stages occurs in second-language acquisition. That is, the child uses the language skills acquired in the first language when confronted with a second language but at a very primitive and rudimentary level (regression hypothesis). An alternate hypothesis is that the child recapitulates the learning process of a native speaker of the second language (recapitulation hypothesis). Although many studies provide no evidence for deciding between the two hypotheses, the studies of Ravem (1968, 1974) and Milon (1974) favor the recapitulation hypothesis in that developmental sequences characteristic of the second language, rather than those of the child's first language, were observed.

It should be noted, however, that the findings of Cancino, Rosansky, and Schumann (1974, 1975) and Hakuta (1975) indicated that there is individual variation in the way in which learners acquire structures of the second language. These authors did not find the kind of sequences reported by Ravem and Milon for negative and wh- questions, and it may be that Wode (1976) is correct in suggesting that children occasionally use first-language structures to solve the riddle of second-language structures. Reliance on first-language structures may be greater, the more intractable the structural problem.

Additional support for the notion that second-language learners go through (recapitulate) the stages observed in monolingual learners of the target language comes from a number of cross-sectional studies. Natalicio and Natalicio (1971) studied the acquisition of English plurals by native, Spanish-speaking children in grades 1, 2, 3, and 10. Their sample included a control group of native, English-speaking children, and both groups were tested by a procedure similar to that used by Berko (1958) to study children's knowledge of morphological rules (discussed in Chapter 2). Both Spanish-speaking and English-speaking groups acquired the /-s/ and /-z/ plural allomorphs before the /-iz/, though the mean proportion of overall correct responses was lower for the Spanish-speaking group. These findings indicate that Spanish first-language structures are not transferred to the English second language, since transfer from Spanish to English would predict that /-s/ be acquired first with /-z/ and /-iz/ acquired simultaneously (because Spanish plurals are all voiceless and voicing is the new feature English requires).

In a study of the acquisition of Welsh by 21 English-speaking children, Price (1968) found that the Welsh noun phrase constructions produced by the children reflected Welsh rather than English word order. The data were gathered by a classroom observer who took written notes on the children's utterances at various times during the day. Children followed Welsh word order in adjective-noun phrase constructions (*blodyn cock* for *flower red, cyw bach melyn* for *chick little yellow*) and in possessive-noun phrase constructions (*esgidiau Dadi* for *shoes Daddy* and *cadair y babi* for *chair the baby*). This indicates that the children did not follow their first-language word order, but it is not clear whether the developmental sequence the children followed was similar to that followed by monolingual Welsh children since the study did not deal directly with this issue.

Finally, there is a series of important studies conducted by Dulay and Burt (1973, 1974a, 1974c) directly concerned with the question of the developmental sequences followed by 5- to 8-year-old children acquiring a second language (English). They began with Roger Brown's (1973a) finding that there is a common—"invariant"—sequence of acquisition for at least 14 "functors." Functors are little function words in English that have a minor role in conveying sentence meaning—noun and verb inflections, articles, auxiliaries, copulas, and prepositions such as *in* and *on,* etc. Dulay and Burt asked whether children who acquire English as a second language acquire these functors in the same sequence and whether this sequence is the same as that found in children who acquire English as a first language.

Dulay and Burt (1973) used an instrument called the Bilingual Syntax Measure (Burt, Dulay, & Hernandez, 1975) to elicit speech samples from 151 Spanish-speaking children living in California, Tijuana, Mexico, and New York City. Even though the three groups differed in amount and type of exposure to English, they showed roughly the same patterns in their use of the functors in obligatory contexts. The degree of acquisition was somewhat different for the three groups, reflecting differential exposure. Table 5.5 shows the order of acquisition of the functors for the three experimental groups and for native, English-speaking children. Note that the order of acquisition for the three, second-language groups was clearly different from that of the first-language group.

Dulay and Burt attributed this discrepancy between first- and second-language acquisition to the different cognitive abilities of children at different stages of their development. Since older children are more sophisticated than younger children with respect to cognitive and conceptual development, their pattern is different. Nonetheless, there does seem to be a common sequence according to which children acquiring a second language acquire certain structures.

In a subsequent study, Dulay and Burt (1974c) compared Chinese- and Spanish-speaking children's acquisition of 11 English functors to determine

TABLE 5.5
Order of Acquisition of Functors in
First- and Second-Language Learners[a]

Functor	Native English-speaker	California sample	Mexican (Tijuana) sample	Puerto Rican (New York) sample
Present progressive (-ing)	1[b]	2	2	2
Plural (-s)	2	1	1	1
Irregular past (ate, took)	3	7	7	5
Possessive (noun phrases)	4	8	5	7
Article (a, the)	5	5	8	3
Third person singular indicative (-s)	6	3	6	8
Contractible copula (be + adjective or noun phrase)	7	6	4	6
Contractible auxiliary (be + verb + -ing)	8	4	3	4

[a] Table based on Dulay and Burt, 1973.

[b] The first column is the rank order of acquisition for these particular functors in Brown's (1973a) original list of 14 functors.

whether the order of acquisition of functors was the same across children with different language backgrounds. Examination of small corpora of speech from 60 Spanish-speaking children in Long Island and 55 Chinese-speaking children in New York City's Chinatown revealed that the sequence of acquisition of the 11 functors studied was virtually the same for both groups. Rank order correlations using various scoring procedures were remarkably high (averaging .94). Thus, although the grammar of the functors differs greatly in Chinese and Spanish, they were acquired in the same sequence in the second language. Dulay and Burt concluded that their research provided a strong indication that universal cognitive mechanisms are the basis for the child's organization of the target language and that the second-language system, rather than the child's first language, guides the acquisition process.

In the third study in this series, Dulay and Burt (1974a) discussed the nature of the universal cognitive mechanisms they thought guide second-language acquisition in children. Rather than examining developmental data in terms of linguistic complexity, they argued that analysis should focus on critical characteristics or features of syntactic structures that distinguish groups of structures in an acquisition hierarchy from one another. For example, one characteristic common to a group of structures may be that their acquisition involves a strategy of looking for exceptions to syntactic rules, which would mean that this aggregate would tend to be acquired relatively late. Another aggregate of structures might be characterized by some feature expressing a semantic relation. The learner probably uses the strategy of looking for semantic relations relatively early, and so this aggregate would be acquired earlier.

The main thrust of Dulay and Burt's argument is that it is not enough to consider simply the complexity of syntactic structures in linguistic description. Analysis in terms of complexity ignores the possibility that the child, in acquiring a language, organizes linguistic data in accord with certain cognitive strategies. Though their analysis was tentative, Dulay and Burt hoped that analysis in terms of distinctive features of aggregates of structures would provide clues about the actual strategies learners use in acquiring second languages. These strategies may be universal, but not enough is known about acquisition hierarchies in second languages other than English to postulate specific universal language-learning strategies in children.

Nonetheless, we are left with the inconsistency between the findings of Dulay and Burt and those of other investigators discussed in this chapter. Whereas the majority of studies indicate that the child acquiring a second language passes through the same stages of development as the monolingual child acquiring the target language as a first language, Dulay and Burt found that the acquisition sequence is different for first- and second-language learners. The order in which English functors were acquired by children with different first languages correlated relatively weakly with that found in English, monolingual children (the average correlation for different scoring methods was .41). There are several possible reasons for the discrepancy between these findings and those of other investigators:

- Dulay and Burt lumped together children with different amounts of exposure to the second language and measured acquisition sequence by examining the degree to which the functors were correctly supplied in speech samples. Their study was not a longitudinal study, as were most of the studies discussed earlier. They did not, strictly speaking, measure *acquisition sequence* but rather *accuracy of use,* since they measured the percent of times a subject correctly supplied a morpheme in an obligatory context. Longitudinal studies of individual children yield more direct information about the developmental sequence in the acquisition of functors and are more directly comparable to Brown's (1973a) original (longitudinal) data.
- It may be that acquisition of functors, as Dulay and Burt suggested, is especially reflective of cognitive abilities. That is, children acquiring the English functors as grammatical features of a second language bring different and more sophisticated cognitive abilities to this task than do children who acquire the functors as part of their first language (at an earlier age). In contrast, other grammatical structures, such as negative constructions and questions, may not reflect differential cognitive ability to the same extent.

Nonetheless, the morpheme research does suggest that second-language learners do not use their first language as a basis for approaching the target language. There seem to be common strategies that children second-language learners use regardless of their first language. This appears to be true of adults as well. Research with adults (Bailey, Madden, & Krashen, 1974; Fathman, 1975;

Krashen, Sferlazza, Feldman, & Fathman, 1976; Larsen–Freeman, 1976a) indi-cates that despite differences in amount of instruction, exposure to English, and first language, there is a high degree of agreement as to the relative difficulty of the set of grammatical morphemes studied. Moreover, the relative degree of difficulty for the various morphemes found in adult second-language learners corresponded closely to the relative difficulty observed in children second-language learners for the same morphemes. This strongly suggests that children and adults learning English process the language in similar ways.

There is recent evidence that suggests that the principal determinant of accu-racy order of the morphemes in second-language learners is the frequency of occurrence of these same morphemes in the input to which learners are exposed. Larsen–Freeman (1976a) showed that accuracy ordering in adult subjects corre-lated highly with the frequency of the morphemes in the speech of English-speaking parents reported by Brown (1973a). In a subsequent study, Larsen–Freeman (1976b) found high correlations between the frequency of the morphemes in the speech of ESL (English as a Second Language) teachers and her own morpheme accuracy data (average correlation .607) and Dulay and Burt's (1974c) data (average correlation .754). This suggests that the frequency of forms in input influences what the second-language learner produces (Wagner–Gough & Hatch, 1975).

Although these studies point to important variables in second-language learn-ing, there are serious methodological difficulties with the morpheme studies (Rosansky, 1976). One difficulty, for example, is that the morphemes may appear both in correct and incorrect contexts, so that a confusion matrix analysis (Hatch, 1977) might be the best way to determine the extent to which individuals use the morphemes appropriately. There is the further problem that grouping data may obscure individual variation in learning strategies and that group curves may in fact not reflect the accuracy ordering of any individual in the group (Rosansky, 1976).

The fact of individual variation does not, of course, mean that there are no universal strategies employed by second-language learners. Fillmore's (1976) research in particular indicated that children acquiring a second language follow essentially the same strategies but with individual variation. The morpheme studies suggest that children and adults follow similar strategies, although more research is needed to determine whether different types of strategies are used in different situations—the classroom, the home and playground, different classroom situations, and so on.

Interference Between Languages

One argument against the hypothesis that first- and second-language acquisition involve similar processes is based on interference in second-language learning. Usually such authors as Haugen (1953, 1956) and Weinreich (1953) are cited as authoritative sources for the validity of the assumption that interference from the first language influences second-language acquisition. As Dulay and Burt (1972) pointed out, however, both Haugen and Weinreich were concerned with the relationship between the languages and dialects of speech communities in contact with each other and not with individual language development.

The existence of interference between languages in the case-study literature is surprisingly scanty. Children acquiring a second language in a social milieu supportive of that language generally show few signs of first-language interference. Once the languages are distinguished, the child appears to keep them apart and does not impose first-language structures on second-language syntax. Huntsberry (1972) concluded on the basis of parental reports that children who showed the greatest amounts of interference from their first language in their second language were children who were either very young or who had little contact with children and adults speaking the second language. Similarly, the children in the study by Politzer and Ramirez (1973) seem not to have spoken English in their own community but learned and used it principally in the school.

The evidence suggests that when the learning conditions are such that the larger social milieu provides a supportive context, interference from first language is minimal in second-language acquisition. When, on the other hand, the second language is not the language of the child's larger social environment, interference tends to result from the imbalance in exposure and use. This seems to be the case when the second language is learned exclusively in the school and would account for the large amounts of interference observed by educators and those testing school children (e.g., Rivers, 1964; Senn, 1932; Stern, 1970; Vey, 1946).

Ervin–Tripp (1974) also thought that interference is maximized when the second language is not the language of the learner's larger social milieu. In such a case, the learning context is aberrant both in function and frequency of structure. That is, the learner in the classroom is exposed to a different language sample than is a learner in the natural milieu, and the language is learned in isolation without being tied to concrete situations. Presumably, situational specificity is an important factor in minimizing interference between languages (as we saw in discussing simultaneous bilingual acquisition).

Ervin–Tripp speculated that the simpler the semantic task, the less the likelihood that the child will have recourse to first-language formations. When children attempt to communicate at a more complex level, they will tend to fall back on first-language structures. This may be one reason why more inteference is apparently found in the classroom setting than is reported in case studies. In the classroom the child may be expected to communicate about fairly complex topics, whereas in the home or on the playground language may be simpler and more repetitive.

There has, however, been relatively little systematic attention given to interference in the case-study literature. Even in studies directly concerned with the topic of interference, it is not easy to classify the mistakes that learners make as due to interference between languages and nothing else. As we noted in Chapter

3, errors can come about for a number of different reasons: they may reflect interference between languages, they may be developmental errors that occur in the speech of monolingual children acquiring the target language, they may be ambiguous errors that cannot be classified as due exclusively either to interference or developmental factors, or they may be unique errors that do not reflect first-language structures or developmental factors. The attempt systematically to classify errors into such categories is called *error analysis*.

Recently, increasing attention is being given to the errors that second-language learners make because of the information errors give about strategies learners employ (Burt & Kiparsky, 1972; Corder, 1967, 1975). Dulay and Burt (1972, 1974b) have concerned themselves specifically with errors children make in acquiring a second language. They cited the evidence from studies of syntactic development (e.g., Milon, 1974; Natalicio & Natalicio, 1971; Ravem, 1968, 1974) as evidence that errors in children's second-language snytax reflect first-language developmental errors. That is, the mistakes that children make in syntactic development are similar to those made by monolingual children acquiring the target language.

In addition, Dulay and Burt (1972) analyzed data from Spanish-speaking children who were learning English as a second language in terms of the categories mentioned above. Table 5.6 gives some examples of the types of errors found in their data. The critical errors are those classified as interference errors, because such errors supposedly reflect the influence of Spanish constructions on English. These errors, Dulay and Burt argued, could just as well reflect overgeneralizations, which though not found in the speech of monolingual children acquiring the target language, *do* correspond to strategies used by children acquiring the target language as a first language. That is, although errors such as *Now she's putting hers clothes on* are not found in the speech of monolingual children, such errors may be instances of overgeneralizing the possessive /-s/ from English. In contrast, overgeneralizations that reflect Spanish influence, such as *bigs houses* and *talls boys,* are not found in the data.

In short, Dulay and Burt argued that the interference errors do not provide unequivocal evidence that first-language structures interfere with second-language learning. Even sentences such as *I know to do all that* and *I finish to watch TV when it's four o'clock* may reflect overgeneralization from English verb-complement constructions (if *want* is substituted for *know* and *finish,* the result is a common construction in English). What the second-language learner appears to be doing is using a strategy similar to that used by monolingual children—namely, syntactic generalization.

In a subsequent study, Dulay and Burt (1974b) summarized and added to the evidence that there are common strategies used in second-language acquisition by children with various language backgrounds. In this research, error analysis of English speech samples of Spanish-, Chinese-, Japanese-, and Norwegian-speaking children acquiring English as a second language indicated that the types of mistakes made by the children were strikingly similar. Dulay and Burt argued

TABLE 5.6
Errors Found in the Speech of Spanish-Speaking Children
Learning English as a Second Language[a]

Type of error	Construction	Example
Interference	Possessive pronoun + noun agreement: not allowed in English, obligatory in Spanish.	Now she's putting hers clothes on.
	Omission of obligatory *how* in English; obligatory in Spanish.	I know to do all that.
	Use of infinitive for gerund: not allowed in English, obligatory in Spanish.	I finish *to watch* TV when it's four o'clock.
Developmental	Irregular plural treated as regular form.	He took her teeth*s* off.
	Two verbal words tensed; only one required.	I didn't wear*ed* any hat.
	Accusative pronoun with nominative.	*Me* need crayons now.
	Do–subject agreement missing.	Where does the spider*s* go?
	Object pronoun missing.	My mother can fix.
Ambiguous	Wrong *no* placement; *no*–*not* distinction; *do* missing.	It *no* cause too much trouble.
Unique	Use of noun for possessive pronoun.	*She* name is Maria.
	Overuse of *do*.	We *do* got no more book.
	-ing with modal.	Now we will talk*ing* about.

[a] From Dulay & Burt, 1972.

that the similarity of errors, as well as the specific error types, reflect what they referred to as "creative construction"—a process whereby children gradually reconstruct rules for the speech they hear, guided by strategies that derive from certain innate mechanisms that cause them to formulate certain types of hypotheses about the language system being acquired, until the mismatch between what they are exposed to and what they produce is resolved. The construction of linguistic rules is said to be creative, because no speaker of the target language models the kind of sentences regularly produced by children who are still acquiring the language.

The result of this "creative construction" process is a developing language often referred to as *interlanguage* (Richards, 1972; Selinker, 1972). By interlanguage is meant a separate linguistic system that results from the learner's attempted production of the target language norm. Selinker (1972) argued that interlanguage (in adults) resulted from five central processes involved in second-language learning:

- Language transfer: some items, rules, and subsystems of the interlanguage may result from transfer from the first language.
- Transfer of training: some elements of the interlanguage may result from specific features of the training process used to teach the second language.

- Strategies of second-language learning: some elements of the interlanguage may result from a specific approach to the material to be learned.
- Strategies of second-language communication: some elements of the interlanguage may result from specific ways people learn to communicate with native speakers of the target language.
- Overgeneralization of the target language linguistic material: some elements of the interlanguage may be the product of overgeneralization of the rules and semantic features of the target language.

In each case, the process brings about "fossilization," in that linguistic items, rules, and subsystems in the interlanguage are retained, no matter what the age of the learner or the amount of instruction and explanation received. Selinker maintained that such fossilization results especially from language transfer (French speakers who retain the uvular /R/ in their English interlanguage, English speakers who use English word order in German subordinate clauses, etc.), but fossilization also results from the other processes. For example, strategies of communication may dictate to some individuals that they stop learning the language once they have learned enough to communicate.

Most adults, Selinker argued, never master a second language to the point where they are indistinguishable from native speakers of that language. Children, on the other hand, seem to be capable of going beyond interlanguage and achieving mastery in a second language, especially if the two languages are acquired simultaneously or if the child has environmental support for successive acquisition through family and peers. However, if the child's second-language acquisition is nonsimultaneous and if it occurs in the absence of peers who speak the second language, interlanguage is likely to result (Selinker, Swain, & Dumas, 1975). This is consistent with the previous comments about interference being maximized when the second language is not a part of the learner's larger social milieu and is also supported by research that suggests that fossilized, non-developmental errors are found in the speech of school children who learn a language in the absence of native-speaking peers (Naiman, 1974).

In a study of the interlanguage of 7-year-old children learning French in a classroom where French was the medium of instruction and where all students were native English-speakers, Selinker, Swain, and Dumas (1975) found evidence for three types of errors: those due to language transfer, those due to overgeneralization, and those due to simplification (Table 5.7). They viewed these errors as the result of particular cognitive strategies employed by the children to develop their interlanguage. The children had no trouble communicating with each other in this interlanguage, but the presence of language transfer errors in particular leads one to suspect that they would have difficulty communicating with French children who had no knowledge of English. Indeed, as Selinker and his associates pointed out, isolation from native speakers has often led historically to pidginization. Schumann (1974) has also discussed the persistence of pidginization in a second-language learner's speech, viewing it as the result of social and psychological factors.

TABLE 5.7
Errors Found in the Speech of English-Speaking Children
Learning French as a Second Language[a]

Type of error	Construction	Example
Language transfer	English transitive meaning given French intransitive verb.	Elle *marche* les chats. (She's walking the cats.)
	Lexical confusion.	*Des temps* (sometimes)
	Substitution of *être* for *avoir*.	Il *est* trois ans. (He's three years old.)
	English word order.	Je aller le *français* camp. (I'm gonna go to a French camp.)
	Use of English tense agreement for French construction.	*Avant* je *vais* . . . (Before I go . . .)
	Improper pronoun placement.	Le chien *a mangé les.* (The dog ate them.)
Overgeneralization	Overgeneralization of French adjective placement rule to situation where adjective should precede noun.	Une *maison nouvelle* (A new house)
	Past-tense form modeled on most common conjunction.	Il a *couré.* (He ran.)
	Use of subject form where object form is required.	Je lis des histoires *à il* en français. (I read stories to him in French.)
Simplification	Use of one form (infinitive) for all tenses.	Le fille *mettre* du confiture sur le pain. (The girl puts some jam on the bread.)
	Avoidance of French postposition of adjective.	Un *jour qui chaud.* (A hot day.)

[a] From Selinker, Swain, and Dumas, 1975.

　　To summarize, interference between languages resulting from language transfer is probably greatest in those situations where languages are learned in a classroom setting and where there is no daily contact with native speakers. When one is dealing with children who acquire a second language in a natural milieu where they have daily contact with native speakers, evidence for language transfer is more difficult to come by. But this does not mean that transfer errors do not occur. They probably occur in all second-language acquisition situations. The important issue is to determine when and to what extent they occur in different situations (Wode, 1976). Like overgeneralizations and simplifications, transfer errors reflect general strategies used by second-language learners. Precisely what the nature of these strategies is and whether they relate to innate mechanisms, as Dulay and Burt suggested, are unresolved issues at the present time.

Most likely the strategies that second-language learners employ reflect general cognitive abilities and linguistic information processing systems. In fact, as we noted in Chapter 3, errors that appear to result from language transfer can be viewed as reflecting the cognitive strategy of utilizing one's first language as a source of information to crack the code of the second language. From this perspective, interference is not transfer in the learning theory sense, but the result of a particular cognitive strategy.

This discussion ends on the same note as the previous discussion of developmental sequences in first- and second-language learning: it would seem to be more fruitful from a practical and theoretical point of view to direct research attention at the strategies that individuals use in acquiring a second language rather than to argue over the presence or absence of interference from the learner's first language. To do this, more detailed information is needed about the types of errors second-language learners make and about the extent to which these errors reflect the learning situation and the structural similarity between languages. As Dulay and Burt (1974c) noted, the strategies that underlie second-language acquisition should be sufficiently abstract and comprehensive so as to account for learning processes based on different types of language input and based even on types of exposure other than natural speech. This means going beyond ad hoc strategies that apply to specific aspects of specific languages, to the formulation of general cognitive strategies that apply to all languages. Needless to say, we are a long way from possessing the information we need to undertake such an enterprise.

Code Switching

Both Weinreich (1953) and Haugen (1953) noted that bilingual individuals occasionally make use of a separate code that includes interference structures for the sake of enriching their language and for affective purposes. This phenomenon has been found to be especially common in the speech of Mexican–Americans (Gumperz, 1970; Gumperz & Hernández–Chavez, 1972; Lance, 1969) and has been cited as an instance of interference between languages (Mackey, 1965). There is evidence, however, that bilinguals can eliminate such structures from their speech when talking to a monolingual individual (Weinreich, 1953), so that a distinction is necessary between *mixing* and *switching* codes. Some bilinguals mix codes for rhetorical purposes when communicating with members of their own bilingual community, but they are perfectly capable of switching codes without interference structures when dealing with members of a monolingual community.

In their analysis of the mixing phenomenon in Mexican–American speakers, Gumperz and Hernández–Chavez (1972) showed how the choice of speech forms is highly meaningful and serves definite communication needs. Speakers build on the coexistence of alternate forms in their language repertory to create meanings that may be highly idiosyncratic and understood only by members of the same bilingual speech community. For instance, the speaker may insert Spanish words into English sentences as identity markers:

Speaker A: Well, I'm glad that I met you. Okay?
Speaker B: Andale, pues (okay, swell), and do come again, mmm?

The use of Spanish expressions in this context was apparently intended to convey a sense of ethnic similarity. The speakers had been strangers and had met for the first time. By injecting Spanish in the farewell, Speaker B conveyed that since they shared the same ethnic identity, they should get to know each other better.

Another example of this use of mixing codes is the following exchange (Gumperz & Hernández–Chavez, 1972):

Speaker A: . . . I mean do some of the other people in the neighborhood have kids?
Speaker B: They don't associate with no children. . . .There's no children in the neighborhood. Well . . . si hay criatures (There are no children, yes) [p. 96].

Here the use of Spanish serves to single out Mexican children from others, and the speaker goes on to talk about this Mexican family.

Such mixing of Spanish expressions in the flow of English speech seems to be a normal part of Mexican–Americans' style in English. Speakers use such expressions when speaking to others of the same ethnic background in much the same way that American Jews use certain Yiddish expressions or Italians use certain Italian expressions to mark in-group identity. Often they are used by speakers who no longer have effective control of the first language.

In addition to mixing languages, switching from one language to another is often common in the speech of bilingual individuals. The speaker may switch codes because of the nature of the topic or because a topic is more intimate and personal. Such a practice seems to be fairly common among Mexican–Americans, who are often at a loss to explain why it is that they switch languages at certain points in their speech.

Children who live in a bilingual environment where they are exposed to a good deal of switching and mixing may find it difficult to separate the two codes in formal speech. In fact, interference can be thought of in terms of the inability of the child to discriminate between the two codes, rather than in terms of language transfer. The more the people around the child mix codes, the more difficulty the child will have in differentiating between them. It seems, however, that children also learn to mix languages for stylistic purposes (Lance, 1969).

Children—especially young children—seem initially to prefer a single referent or linguistic form to the two codes required in bilingual speech. Occasionally they confuse codes within a single word or phrase. For instance, the child may identify two morphemes because they have functions they share in common. This phenomenon Haugen (1955) referred to as a "diamorph." In the example of the development of the prepositional construction in the Swedish of a Finnish-speaking child described by Malmberg (1945), there was a systematic progression from the Finnish to the Swedish structure, with Swedish diamorphs gradually replacing their Finnish counterparts until syntactic restructuring was achieved. A similar phenomenon was observed in the development of a Swedish–Estonian, bilingual child (Oksaar, 1970).

Malmberg's analysis is valuable in that he showed the stages through which the child progressed in switching from one code to another. Such process descriptions are rare, however, and little is known about the conditions under which children adopt switching rules. It may be that such rules are situationally controlled (Ervin–Tripp, 1970) but precisely how and to what extent remains to be clarified.

In any event, it seems useful to view the successive acquisition of two languages in the same way as we viewed simultaneous bilingual acquisition—as a process of learning to differentiate two linguistic codes. This task is probably no different in terms of the operations involved than is the task of switching codes within a single language. Such a perspective has the advantage of economy: no new processes need be postulated to account for second-language learning, and a similar development seems to be followed, though at a different rate.

CONCLUSION

Methodologically, the early literature on successive acquisition of two languages suffers from the same drawbacks as does much of the literature on simultaneous bilingual acquisition. Early case studies were mostly descriptive and almost anecdotal accounts of children's second-language acquisition. They dealt unsystematically with a broad range of issues and questions.

The recent literature, however, is characterized by a more systematic concern with specific topics. Ravem's (1968, 1974) examination of interrogative and modal constructions, Milon's (1974) work on negatives, and Dato's (1971) study of verb-phrase constructions are examples of the ways in which recent investigators have tackled limited areas of theoretical interest. The tendency has been to try to go beyond description to explanation. Fillmore's (1976) research is especially important in this regard, since she was able to outline specific strategies that each of the five children in her sample followed.

In addition, there has been a number of studies with larger samples directed at resolving specific questions. Natalicio and Natalicio (1971) conducted a comparative study of the acquisition of English plural forms by native and nonnative speakers; Dulay and Burt (1972, 1973, 1974a, 1974b, 1974c) have carried out a number of studies dealing with the analysis of errors and the developmental sequence of the acquisition of English constructions by non-English-speaking children. Selinker, Swain, and Dumas (1975) examined different types of errors made by second-language learners exposed to the target language exclusively in the classroom.

The result of these systematic research efforts is that we have more answers to questions about second-language acquisition in the case where a second language is acquired after the first language is established than we do in the case where the two languages are acquired simultaneously. Some of the questions left unanswered at the end of the previous chapter can, at least tentatively, be answered with respect to the successive acquisition of two languages. For instance, I asked the question:

- What developmental stages do children exposed to two languages go through in acquiring specific syntactic structures such as negative constructions, interrogative constructions, relative clauses, and so on?

Research on successive acquisition of two languages has been directly concerned with this question. The work of Ravem (1968), Milon (1974), and Dato (1971), as well as the evidence from the studies of Ervin–Tripp (1974) and Natalicio and Natalicio (1971), suggests that the developmental stages are much the same as those that monolingual children go through in acquiring the target language, probably because second-language learners recapitulate this process in acquiring the language.

Although the evidence seems to support the similarity between the developmental stages followed by first- and second-language learners of a given language, there are some findings that are not entirely consistent with this notion (e.g., Cancino, Rosansky, & Schumann, 1974, 1975; Wode, 1976). This brings us to the second question asked at the end of the previous chapter:

- Are these developmental stages always identical with those followed by monolingual children?

Dulay and Burt (1973, 1974a, 1974c) found that children who were speakers of different first languages learned English constructions in the same developmental sequence but that this sequence was different from that reported in studies of monolingual, English-speaking children. This appears to contradict other studies, but we noted that there are several possible reasons for this. The most interesting aspect of this research (and the point where it converges with other research) is that the children studied did not resort to the strategies of their first languages but used common strategies in approaching the second language, regardless of the nature of their first language.

The next three questions dealt with interference phenomena:

- How do specific languages interact with each other phonetically, syntactically, and semantically?
- What regularities are to be found in semantic and morphological mixings?

- Do particular language combinations cause more retardation in individual language development than others?

The evidence from error analysis studies appears to indicate that interference is by no means a main cause of error—except possibly when children learn a language in the school that they do not use outside of the classroom with family and peers. Many errors that appear to be interference errors might be errors brought about by overgeneralizing strategies learned from the second language itself (Dulay & Burt, 1972).

One of the most interesting findings in the error analysis research is that children whose first languages were Spanish, Chinese, Japanese, and Norwegian all made the same types of mistakes when acquiring English as a second language (Dulay & Burt, 1974b). This suggests that interaction between different language combinations is a minor factor in second-language acquisition. Whether this counterintuitive finding will hold up in subsequent research remains to be seen.

This brings us to the next question:

- Is bilingual language acquisition more difficult for some children than for others? Why is this (if true)?

Little is known about personality variables and about motivational factors that affect children learning a second language—obviously a serious lacuna in the research literature. Another aspect of this question relates to the variable of age: is it better to introduce a second language to older or younger children? Is there an age at which children are optimally prepared to learn a second language?

Most authors would probably agree that the optimal time to introduce a child to a second language is at birth. That is, the ideal conditions would be simultaneous acquisition where the two languages are kept distinct by being consistently associated with different persons in the child's environment and where they are subsequently maintained in a somewhat balanced state.

Once a language has been established as the child's first language, research suggests that a later, rather than an earlier, start in the second language is better. Older children seem to experience fewer problems adjusting to a second language than do younger ones (Francescato, 1969; Smith, 1935; Yoshioka, 1929). As we saw in Chapter 3, studies of school children showed that older children performed better in second-language learning than younger children (Bühler, 1972; Ervin–Tripp, 1974; Politzer & Weiss, 1969). Asher and Garcia (1969), however, found young children to be superior in acquiring the sound system of the second language.

It is doubtless premature to set a specific age as optimal for the child to begin to acquire a second language. For one thing, the conditions of learning differ depending on whether the child is to be exposed to a second language in the natural milieu, in school, or in both environments. Perhaps there are different optimal ages for each of these situations. The older child has the advantage of superior cognitive skills, but the younger child may be less inhibited and less afraid to make mistakes. Younger children may do more poorly on tests of phonology, morphology, and syntax; but they may be able to communicate better in the language than children with the same exposure who began to acquire the language later.

As we shall see in the next chapter, a great deal of success has been reported in programs in Canada in which children are introduced to a second language from kindergarten on. In Germany, on the other hand, research aimed at demonstrating the superiority of starting second languages earlier than the traditional fifth grade has been inconclusive. We are obviously still a long way from possessing definitive answers for resolving this issue.

Some other unanswered questions:

- What are the differential effects of simultaneous and successive acquisition of two languages?
- Does successive acquisition lead to more or less interference than simultaneous acquisition?
- What is the developmental sequence of more complex grammatical constructions in a language acquired as a second language? Is this sequence similar to that observed when the language is acquired as a first language?
- Does acquiring a second language after a first language is established interfere with the first language, or does it facilitate further development in the first language?

A lot more research is needed before even first approximations can be given toward answering such questions. More information, however, is available about two other major questions relating to second-language acquisition:

- What methods are most effective for teaching a second language in the school context?
- What are the effects on the individual as a child and as an adult of bilingualism?

The first of these questions is dealt with in the next chapter; the second in Chapter 7.

6

Second-Language Programs in the Elementary School

Up to this point, I have restricted discussion, for the most part, to second-language acquisition in children younger than 6. This chapter deals with second-language education in the elementary school. As we saw earlier in this book, bilingual education exists in most countries of the world and is becoming increasingly common. In many countries, an international language must be learned for educational, cultural, economic, and technical purposes. In other countries, the demands of ethnic minority groups for schools in their own language have received varying degrees of official sanction. In the United States there is a growing recognition that it is desirable for English-speaking children to learn a second language in the elementary school and, at the same time, an increasing acceptance of the legitimacy of demands of minority ethnic groups that their children be allowed to maintain and develop their first language while learning English in the school.

My aim in this chapter is to provide a brief overview of second-language programs of various sorts in the United States and Canada. Discussions of programs for children in other parts of the world can be found in Titone (1972), Dodson, Price, and Williams (1968); Stern (1967, 1969), and Gompf (1971), among others. More extended discussion of developments in the United States and Canada can be found in Andersson (1969), Andersson and Boyer (1970),John and Horner (1971), and Swain (1972). Recent developments are discussed by Condon (1974), Stern (1973), Swain (1974), and Zirkel (1975).

TYPES OF PROGRAMS

In Chapter 1 I distinguished two major sorts of second-language programs in the United States. In the first group are programs for teaching second languages to English-speaking children through a language course. The use of the second language is restricted to that course. In bilingual education programs the second language is used as the language of instruction in other subjects besides the language course. Bilingual education programs exist both for children whose first language is not English and also for children whose first language is English (e.g., total immersion programs).

FLES Programs

FLES (usually pronounced to rhyme with *chess*) is an acronym for foreign languages in the elementary school. The term was first used in the 1950s when the number of such programs in existence in the United States dramatically increased. But, as Donoghue (1968) pointed out, the practice of teaching second languages to school children was not new in this country. Latin and Greek were essential parts of the young child's education in the 17th and 18th centuries. Jefferson was an advocate of instruction in the modern languages, and Benjamin Franklin was of the opinion that it was best to begin with modern languages and then proceed to the ancient ones.

In the 19th century, some public schools began offering German as an elective, especially in areas where there was a large concentration of German immigrants. In Texas and California, Spanish was taught as a subject in many elementary schools. In other areas, Dutch, Italian, and French were taught, but around the turn of the century this practice became increasingly less common. By the time World War I broke out, there was widespread public antagonism against second-language programs, especially against German programs, which at that time were the most numerous. Twenty-three states passed laws hostile to foreign language instruction. A statute of the state of Nebraska banning the teaching of all foreign languages in state schools was debated before the United States Supreme Court, where it was eventually declared unconstitutional.

Public feeling against teaching languages other than English persisted until the 1950s. In 1939 about 2,000 pupils were receiving second-language instruction; by 1960, however, 1,227,000 pupils were enrolled in FLES programs (Andersson, 1969). FLES existed in all states, and government support—through the National Defense Education Act of 1958—provided funds for the training of language instructors. This new enthusiasm for modern languages is usually regarded as a by-product of the Spuknik era, but its roots lie in changes that had occurred in attitudes toward modern languages as a result of World War II (Pillet, 1974). The deployment of armed forces personnel in many countries of the world during and after the war resulted in the need for intensive language programs for the military. These programs were for essentially pragmatic reasons directed at the spoken word. New techniques were developed, and modern linguistic knowledge was applied to the practical problem of language training. In time, interest in modern language instruction spread to the universities and eventually to the public school system.

The most significant development was the spread of the *audio-lingual method* to FLES programs. This method—also referred to as the army method, the aural-oral method, the natural method, or the New Key—involves the following principles (adapted from Donoghue, 1968):

- The four linguistic skills are developed in this order: listening, speaking, reading, and writing.
- The spoken language has primacy; children learn by hearing and imitating a skilled user of the language.
- Words are presented in the meaningful context of everyday situations.
- Reading and writing are secondary skills to be acquired only after the child can comprehend and speak the language.
- Grammar is taught inductively once oral mastery of syntactic structures is acquired and only when grammatical description will help learning.
- Repetitive drill is the best device for teaching language habits.
- Language learning involves the overlearning of basic linguistic patterns.
- Speech is to be maintained at a conversational pace.
- Use of the pupil's native tongue is to be avoided.
- Translation is proscribed until advanced learning levels are reached.
- Culture study is an essential part of language learning.
- Contrastive linguistics is a tool for the teacher.

Eventually, the audio-lingual method became the dominant method of language instruction in FLES programs.

Rationale for FLES programs.   There were a number of reasons advanced for the importance of second-language training in the elementary school. The main argument was that of linguists and psychologists who felt that the sooner the child started to learn a language, the better. Research on language development in the late 1950s and early 1960s had convinced many that the child possessed unique capacities for language learning. This doctrine was promulgated by Chomsky and his followers and was generally accepted by members of the intellectual community. Susanne Langer (1958), for example, wrote of an optimal period for language learning during which the "linguistic intuition" must be developed if it is not to miscarry.

In a discussion during the Modern Language Association meeting in 1956 psychologists were asked the optimal age for beginning language training. Most maintained that language training should begin at birth and, if this was not possible, as soon as children began their formal education (Andersson, 1969). Physiological data were also cited as evidence that the brain loses its plasticity for language as the child grows older.

In addition, there was a growing conviction among educators that language training would help children develop an appreciation for cultures other than their own. In the postwar era, a new international outlook had developed in this country that regarded traditional American isolationism as unacceptable in the contemporary world context. The language barrier seemed to be the main obstacle to international communication. Early acquaintance with other countries and their languages was essential to the education of children (Stern, 1967).

Older methods of somehow sneaking a knowledge of other cultures in through the back door during history or geography classes was no longer sufficient. A truly cultural experience required that the student learn to feel and think as people of other cultures do, and language was an essential ingredient in this process. Learning to use the language correctly in the total cultural context required that the child gain an appreciation for such cultural features as the emotional connotation of words and the subtle rules affecting choice of vocabulary and linguistic structure (e.g., *tu–vous* distinctions).

Parents were anxious to have their children acquire such skills. In fact, pressure from parental groups was one of the main reasons for the proliferation of FLES programs in the 1950s and 1960s (Pillet, 1974). Americans were convinced that they were living in a rapidly shrinking world. Modern technology and communication media would bring the people of the world closer, and America's role was bound to be central to future developments. Parents wanted their children to have language skills that would enable them to be part of this new world.

The new techniques of language training held the promise that children—whose native abilities were thought to be superior to those of adults—could quickly and easily master second languages. Professional educators were convinced that they had at their disposal techniques that would work. The day of the grammar-translation method was gone forever. The audio-lingual approach had worked for the military, and it would work in the schools.

The new approach had the blessing of psychologists of various persuasions (Pillet, 1974). It appealed to the new breed of psycholinguists because it paralleled the natural way in which children learned their first language. Traditional methods did not work with children, because they were required to operate at a level of intellectualism that was above their cognitive ability. FLES students were perfect candidates for the audio-lingual technique, because it allowed them to learn a second language as they had their first—through hearing and speaking the language rather than by translating and learning rules of grammar by rote.

The use of audio-lingual techniques also appealed to traditional behaviorist psychologists. The most doctrinaire advocates of such methods regarded language learning as a process of habit development to be inculcated by varying contingencies of reinforcement. Hullian and Skinnerian philosophies were invoked to justify increasing automatization of language instruction. Even more flexible advocates were fond of speaking of sequential control of the learning process, specification of learning goals, and the effectiveness of immediate reinforcement. No wonder that behaviorist psychologists came to see the audio-lingual method as proof of the saving power of behavioral control.

The wedding of cognitively oriented psycholinguists and behavioristic psychologists produced strange bedfellows. The result was a great deal of theoretical debate, mostly centered around the role of linguistics (usually identified with transformational grammar) in the language learning process. The psycholinguists carried over their enthusiasm for Chomskian linguistics to the applied area; the behaviorists felt that such efforts were a waste of energy (and research funds) that could be more profitably spent on the experimental task of developing efficient audio-lingual techniques. The argument was never resolved, perhaps because both sides had overstated their cases.

Practical problems.   In the early 1960s, enthusiasm for FLES reached its peak. The subsequent loss of momentum has been attributed to a number of factors. In many cases qualified teachers were not available. The recruitment, preparation, and certification of teachers proved to be a more serious problem than was anticipated. Some teachers were certified by reputable universities as being capable to teach a language they could neither understand nor speak. On the local level, teachers who could teach one language were sometimes assigned by school administrators to teach a language they did not know. There seemed to be a widely shared willingness among those responsible for controlling educational policy to accept mediocre standards (Andersson, 1969).

Furthermore there was a great deal of inertia in the academic system. Traditional methods were slowly abandoned; new techniques met with resistance. Teachers did not receive adequate training in those methods they would later be expected to teach. Nor was enough attention given in teacher education to contrastive linguistics and comparative linguistic analysis.

It often happened that FLES programs were launched in local school systems with considerable fanfare but with little attention to preparation and no concern for the program's continuity. Once initial enthusiasm dampened and such programs were shown to be an expensive tax burden for the local community, support weakened. People wanted quality in education but were unwilling to vote for tax increases to achieve it. Many school boards met this problem by organizing FLES as an out-of-school program and asking parents to pay for it (Andersson, 1969). Regular in-school programs were often brought to a halt by coalitions of property owners who regarded FLES as an educational frill.

But there was a more subtle reason why the enthusiasm for FLES programs declined in this country. Too much was expected and too little delivered. Children proved to be much slower in learning languages than psychologists and linguists had predicted. The average FLES student bore no resemblance to Chomsky's immigrant child who learns a second language by osmosis in a few months. No miraculous results were obtained. Children had as much difficulty learning a second language as they had learning other subjects. Here, as elsewhere, knowledge maketh a bloody entrance.

Nor were the predicted results obtained from audio-lingual techniques. The promise of a new generation of bilingual citizens seemed beyond practical realization. The methods were by-and-large successful, but—as Pillet (1974) pointed out—their doctrinaire use complicated education in many settings. The practice of completely avoiding English, for example, limited the possibility of achieving student–teacher rapport, made explanation of the program's goals and purposes difficult, and interfered with the establishment of efficient procedures. Many children succeeded in memorizing a well-drilled corpus of material, but the taboo on translation left them with little understanding of when to say what to whom. Nor were they able to generate new meaningful material in the language. The emphasis on oral methods of learning and communication put visually oriented students at a disadvantage. After a few years of exposure, the average child, who normally associated learning with books and written exercises, tended to belittle the language class as frivolous and not worth serious effort.

There was also little recognition of the child's cognitive development. Basically the same procedures were used for children of various ages. Older children, who were capable of a more abstract, rule-oriented approach to language, were denied the opportunity to employ these cognitive skills. The result was that the child was often frustrated and tried to learn by using cognitive strategies employed for other tasks. If the teacher insisted on orthodox audio-lingual methods, the older child's intellectual potential was usually stifled (Page, 1966).

Finally, there was the problem of the way in which FLES programs were assessed. Many programs were begun without any provision for evaluation (Andersson, 1969). Clearly, the experimental nature of FLES programs made evaluation imperative, but carefully conducted evaluation research takes time and money—two commodities in short supply in most school settings. When there was an evaluation, it was often more concerned with the teacher's adherence to audio-lingual precepts than with the student's reaction to the method (Pillet, 1974). FLES programs, in the early years, were the testing grounds for the audio-lingual method; less concern was given to the critical problem of how children at various stages of development learn a second language.

To itemize problems besetting FLES programs is not to imply that the baby should be thrown out with the bath water. There is a tendency today on the part of educators to move away from a doctrinaire application of the audio-lingual approach to a more flexible and eclectic approach. Furthermore, educators have lowered their sights somewhat and have given up as unrealistic the goal of achieving bilingual command through FLES programs.

Bilingual Education Programs

In Chapter 1 I discussed some of the reasons why bilingual education programs have been developed in this country. As was noted, such programs were a response to the need of thousands of non-English-speaking children who each year entered the school system. They were established primarily as a result of pressure from minority linguistic and sociocultural groups who wanted their children to maintain their first language as a sign of ethnic identity. Furthermore, educators were concerned about the problems that ethnic minority children typically have in the traditional school system. They are disadvantaged from the start and usually achieve below their ability. They tend to drop out of school earlier than their English-speaking counterparts because schooling becomes a failure experience.

The principal reasons for bilingual education programs have been summarized by Gaarder (1969) as follows:

- The child's cognitive development and acquisition of knowledge proceed at a normal rate if the first language is used as a medium of instruction, whereas retardation in school work is almost inevitable if the child's first language is not used for instruction.
- The use of the child's first language by teachers provides a mutually reinforcing bond between the home and the school, especially where a substantial number of non-English speakers exist in the community.
- Rejection of the first language of a large number of children in the schools adversely affects the attitude of those children toward themselves, their parents, and their homes. Such an effect is to be expected, since language is the most important medium for the expression of self.
- Unless bilingual adults have achieved reasonable literacy in their first language, they will not be able to use their unique potential career advantage—bilingualism—for a technical or professional career where language matters.
- Competence in a native language other than English and a cultural heritage conveyed by each are a natural resource that should be conserved.

Types of bilingual education programs.   There have been many attempts throughout the world to develop bilingual education programs for children. Mackey (1970) has provided a typology based on various combinations of language use at home, in school, in the community, and in the nation. For example, within the school, one or two languages may be used for instruction. If two languages are used, they may vary in the domains in which each is used—one may be used for literature and history, the other for science and mathematics. Similarly, one or two languages may be used outside the school in play settings. If two are used outside the school, it may be that there are certain domains for each language—in the schoolyard as opposed to the neighborhood, for instance.

Mackey's typology, though thorough and helpful in specifying the characteristics of bilingual programs, is too detailed for our purposes. A more suitable model is that of Fishman and Lovas (1970), who first pointed out that bilingual education programs must be distinguished from English-as-a-second-language (ESL) programs. In a bilingual program, both languages are used as media of instruction; in ESL programs, there is no attempt to include instruction in the child's first language—all instruction is done in the second language, English.

Fishman and Lovas distinguished four types of bilingual programs. The first of these is the *transitional bilingualism* program, in which the child's first language is used in the early grades to the extent necessary to allow the child to adjust to school and master the subject matter. This use of the first language is merely transitional; however, and once the child's skill in English has developed to the point where it can be used as the medium of instruction, the use of the child's first language is abandoned. There is no attempt in such programs to attain fluency and literacy in both languages. The only reason for using the first language at all is to make the transition to a second language easier.

The second type of bilingual program is *monoliterate bilingualism*. Here the aim is to develop aural–oral skills in both languages but reading and writing skills in the second language only. The child's first language is spoken in the school as a link to the home and neighborhood environment. But no effort is made to develop literacy in the child's first language. This is often the case in bilingual programs for American Indians, where no body of written literature exists; but such programs have also been developed for other language groups.

The third type of bilingual program is *partial bilingualism*. Here fluency and literacy in both languages are aimed at, but literacy in the first language is restricted to certain domains, generally those relating to the ethnic group and its cultural heritage. In such programs it is rare, for example, for the first language to be used in science and mathematics. This seems to be characteristic of programs conducted by American ethnic groups in their own supplementary or parochial schools, but it is also common in programs supported by funding under the Bilingual Education Act.

The final type is the *full bilingual program,* where all skills are developed in both languages and both languages are used as media of instruction for all subjects. This seems to provide optimal conditions for the maintenance and development of the minority language. It also allows the individual to attain competence in all domains in both first and second languages.

In 1974, a Supreme Court decision in the case of *Lau* v. *Nichols* required school districts to provide equal educational opportunities for students from non-English-speaking backgrounds. As a result of this decision, the Office of Civil Rights set forth guidelines for school districts, which included the following definition of a bilingual program:

> Bilingual/Bicultural Program. A program which utilizes the student's native language (e.g., Navaho) and cultural factors in instructing, maintaining, and further developing all necessary skills in the student's native language, while introducing, maintaining, and developing all the necessary skills in the second language and culture (e.g., English). The end result is a student who can function, totally, in both languages and cultures.

This definition would seem to apply only to what Fishman and Lovas called a full bilingual program.

Furthermore, in administering funds for the Bilingual Education Act, the Office of Education is governed by guidelines that specify five purposes for bilingual education programs (cited in Pacheco, 1973):

- To insure that children in such programs become more proficient in the use of two languages and have available curriculum material and teaching techniques that prevent them from being adversely affected in their school learning because of their initial disadvantage in English.
- To integrate the study of history and culture associated with the child's first language.

- To insure that the program prepares, develops, and adapts proper material for teaching and provides equipment necessary for implementing the curriculum.
- To insure the proper training of persons who participate in bilingual education programs.
- To insure the development and effective use of evaluation.

These guidelines are certainly not met by transitional bilingualism programs, where the child's history and culture are usually ignored and where the first language of the child is used only until English can be used. Since there is no attempt to attain proficiency in the child's first language, such programs fail to qualify as bilingual education programs. A more difficult question is whether monoliterate and partial bilingualism programs meet the guidelines. Most likely, those who propose such programs could make the case that they do, but such programs seem to be in opposition to the spirit of the Bilingual Education Act. Aside from the case of the American Indians who have no written language, it seems unconscionable not to give bilingual children literacy skills in both languages. Furthermore, the tendency in some programs to restrict the domains in which the first language is used seems ill advised. Partial programs where the non-English first language is not used in science and mathematics courses imply that these languages have no place in the modern technological world. As Fishman and Lovas pointed out, such limiting implications have been consistently rejected by nationalist protest movements since the mid-19th century.

Some practical issues. Pacheco (1973) listed the following problems facing bilingual education programs:

- Instructional personnel.
- Teacher recruitment and training.
- Curriculum materials.
- Community involvement.
- Evaluation.

In many respects, these are similar to the problems facing those who seek to develop FLES programs, but there are important differences. Above all, bilingual education programs are concerned with a wider range of skills than linguistic skills. The program is intended to affect the pupil's general cognitive and attitudinal development as well as language development.

As is true of FLES programs, a central problem for bilingual education programs is the shortage of suitably trained instructional personnel. The ideal teacher unites two traits that are hard to come by: competence as a teacher and empathy with students and their language and culture. The teacher in a bilingual education program needs a sensitivity for the child's culture that can perhaps be found only in a member of that ethnic group. If sufficient teachers from the ethnic group are not available, programs in cultural sensitivity may help to overcome some of the difficulties teachers from the dominant culture face in teaching ethnic minority children (Ulibarri, 1972).

Teacher training for bilingual education exists in a number of universities and colleges, either in the form of special summer sessions supplemented by in-training programs or as full-year programs. In fact, the increase in the number of such programs raises the possibility that history will repeat itself and that these programs will degenerate into diploma mills (as sometimes happened in the training of FLES teachers). The critical issue is not whether enough teachers receive their certificates but whether they receive the kind of training they need to function effectively in bilingual education programs. This means the establishment of specialized graduate and undergraduate courses in bilingual education and careful screening of candidates.

Until recently there was relatively little curriculum material available for bilingual education programs. This situation has changed in the past few years, and today the teacher has an abundance of material to choose from. The Dissemination Center for Bilingual-Bicultural Education is a national project established to select, reproduce, and distribute project-developed materials according to the needs of bilingual programs throughout the country (Swanson, 1974). There have even been attempts to prepare reading materials in Indian languages (Spolsky, 1973).

In contrast to FLES programs, bilingual education programs require community involvement to be successful. This should ideally begin in the planning stage. Pacheco (1973) felt that from the beginning, there should be open communication with the community through school board meetings, newspaper articles, and feature items on radio and television in both languages. During the implementation stage, parents and community leaders should be encouraged to visit the program. Parents and various community members may also be able to take part in the program, especially by contributing their expertise in areas of folklore and cultural tradition. In some programs, there are paraprofessional home visitors who keep the program and the community in constant touch with each other. Such community involvement does not always make the program easier for school administrators to run, and the successful implementation of this aspect of the program requires tact and sensitivity on the part of all concerned.

There is general agreement that evaluation is a necessary component of any bilingual education program. On the other hand, evaluation requires time, energy, expertise, and money that are not always available. As in FLES programs, the evaluation stage of bilingual education programs is often not given the attention it deserves. This situation has changed, however, because of the Office of Education's policy of requiring an educational audit of all federally funded bilingual programs. Still problematic are the questions of what tests to use to ascertain the level and rate of language development in children and how to measure progress in areas of instruction, staff–community relations, effectiveness of curriculum material, and bicultural attitudes.

Swanson (1974) noted that bilingual education programs are highly charged politically. The Bilingual Education Act itself was the product of politicians responding to the needs of their constituents. The passage of the act was a major breakthrough in public school philosophy. As a result, many state laws had to be changed to allow public instruction in a language other than English. There are, however, large segments of the population—and some educators—who are uncomfortable with this change. In some communities, English-speaking groups resent the programs and point out that no bilingual centers were established for their parents and grandparents, who had to assimilate into the dominant culture (Picchiotti, 1969).

Changing the public's attitudes on this score will probably take some time. As Fishman and Lovas (1970) observed, we are just beginning to realize that the public schools belong to parents, pupils, and communities. It may take a bit longer to accept the fact that pupils, parents, and teachers need not talk to each other in English, even when they are in school, and even when they know and can speak English.

THE QUESTION OF METHOD

The question of the best method for teaching children a second language continues to be debated. As we saw, the audio-lingual method used in FLES programs did not produce the wonders expected. Modification, revision, and experimentation seemed called for. The developments in linguistics in the 1960s appeared to hold great promise for the hard-pressed language teacher. Here again, however, no miracles were forthcoming. The old adage of George Ticknor (1833) seemed to hold true: no one method is suitable for all learners, and the language teacher must adapt her methods to individual needs.

The Role of Linguistics

In the 1960s enthusiasm for modern linguistics, especially for Chomskian transformational grammar, spread to the field of second-language training. Transformational theory seemed especially suited for language learning because it was a generative theory. It described the competence of the speaker and accounted for the fact that a speaker was able to produce and comprehend an infinite number of novel utterances. Such a theory seemed to offer a realistic and creative approach to language learning.

In addition, there seemed to be strong theoretical arguments for the transformational method. Traditional theory relies on the learner's intuition. It provides no account, for example, of how it is that a speaker is able to know that there are two meanings for such sentences as *Visiting relatives can be a nuisance*. Transformational grammar, in contrast, attempts to explain such ambiguous sentences by postulating the notion of deep structure. The ambiguity is due to the presence of two deep structures—one meaning *Relatives who visit can be a nuisance* and the other meaning *It can be a nuisance to visit relatives*. Traditional linguistic analysis based on surface structure alone does not satisfactorily explain such ambiguous sentences and other linguistic phenomena. The superiority of transformational grammar in this regard led many to believe that it would be a powerful means of making language more intelligible and therefore more teachable.

Two advocates of the transformational grammar approach to second-language instruction, Jakobovits (1970) and Lakoff (1969), stressed the superior explanatory power of transformational grammar when compared to traditional theory. Traditional theory, by which Jakobovits and Lakoff mean behaviorist–structuralist theory, leaves unexplained many important facts about English and other languages. Good instruction requires a good theory of language, just as good learning requires an adequate theory of the language acquisition process. Languages are not learned by rote memorization; language learning depends on reason—it is rule-governed, not habit-governed (Lakoff, 1969).

Difficulties arose when it came to spelling out specifically how transformational grammar applied to language learning. How do language learners acquire the rules of the language and how is such learning to be taught? Transformational grammar was theoretically interesting but quite tedious in practice. No one seemed to be able to tell language teachers how they were to utilize transformational grammar in the classroom (Lewis, 1972). In fact, there was some question as to whether, in principle, transformational grammar could be applied to second-language instruction. Chomsky and other linguists continued to insist that linguistics was concerned with the theoretical study of languages, and not with practical application. Lamendella (1969) argued that transformational grammar was irrelevant to second-language teaching; a more promising approach was one based on cognitive psychology.

Furthermore, the task of applying transformational grammar to second-language instruction was hampered by developments in linguistics. One could use the "old" or the "new" Chomsky. The theory was constantly shifting, and new approaches such as generative semantics (Seuren, 1974) provided viable theoretical alternatives to classic transformational grammar. Moreover, the language teacher often found linguistic theory too intuitive and arbitrary; there was no way of proving the theory or its derivations empirically (Hebb, Lambert, & Tucker, 1971).

For many, the best solution seemed to be to incorporate transformational grammar with traditional approaches, to the extent that this was possible. Politzer (1965), for example, advocated the use of transformational drills in second-language learning techniques. He felt that audio-lingual techniques could be developed where a change in surface structure was triggered by a cue such as "passive," "negative," or "relative clause," and so forth. Ney (1974) also argued for a best-of-both-worlds approach: an eclecticism based on elements from both cognitive-transformational and behavioral-structural theories. Robin

Lakoff (1969) recommended the use of pattern practice and drills in teaching some aspects of language.

At the present time, a great deal more needs to be known about how transformational grammar is to be translated into pedagogy and how insights from the theory are to be coupled with more traditional approaches. There is a need for curriculum materials that provide the teacher with concrete examples of natural transformation processes and exercises that stimulate students to take a creative approach to language. If transformational grammar is to be useful to language teachers, it is necessary to go beyond lip service to an undefined "generative" method of teaching language and to find ways of maximizing the student's creative use of language capacities.

It also seems apparent that the differing needs of students have to be taken into account. Young children approach language learning differently than older children. For the young child, the audio-lingual approach is more suitable than the analysis of syntax based on transformational grammar. Yet even young children can profit from a transformational grammar approach if such an approach is understood to mean the utilization of those creative processes that human beings bring to the task of learning a language. The unresolved question is how this ideal is to be realized in practice.

Of course, there is more to linguistics than transformational grammar. Linguistics has provided the second-language teacher with a substantial literature on phonetics and on contrastive analysis of the structure of English and many other languages. Such information is especially helpful for the teacher in identifying problem areas in pronunciation and syntax. Yet as Pillet (1974) pointed out, little attention has been given by linguists to the practical problem of how to differentiate—in the context of the total utterance—word boundaries, stems from endings, and the significance of one ending over another. Nor has there been much work on the linguistic differences between the various codes that the speaker of a language employs—for example, in formal versus informal settings. Some other ways in which linguistics can be helpful to second-language teachers include furnishing more information on how the various phonemes of a language are approximated in the development of native speakers, on the stress and intonation patterns characteristic of different languages, and on what skills are involved in the ability to comprehend speech at various speeds of delivery.

Language-Teaching Strategies

In recent years there has been a great deal of concern in both FLES and bilingual education programs about the suitability of current methods for teaching children second languages. In addition to the debate over the role of transformational grammar in language teaching, there has been a number of proposals and experiments concerned with optimizing teaching methods.

FLES.   As we saw earlier in this chapter, the audio-lingual approach has traditionally dominated in FLES programs. Yet some practical problems led to modification and deviance from strict audio-lingual orthodoxy. For example, the spread of FLES programs to schools where students had poor backgrounds required a more flexible teaching strategy. The program had to be structured to meet the needs of the students; less gifted and less motivated students could not be taught in the same way as their more gifted and more highly motivated counterparts (Pillet, 1974).

Once the break with orthodoxy had been made, it was a simple step to revisionism. Perhaps the most fruitful development has been the emphasis on *individualizing instruction* (Altman & Politzer, 1971). This method is predicated on the belief that it is not only the less gifted student who has special needs but the more gifted as well. The notion that all students learn in the same way is erroneous. More concern must be given to the students' perception of the learning process: their interpretation of goals, their reactions to various incentives, the relevance of the task to their expectations, their self-confidence, and motivation. In addition, individualized instruction implies modifying teaching methods, goals, and the pace of the instruction process of individual needs.

Experience with the audio-lingual method had taught educators that many young children lack the skills to sustain themselves for long periods without adult support and assistance (Hunter, 1971). They learn at different rates and are receptive to different methods. Furthermore, they react differently to the teacher: some children respond to praise, others to embarrassment; some need encouragement, others need to be left alone. Teachers have to know the students well on a personal basis. They can then adjust their goals somewhat more realistically to student needs, interests, and capabilities.

Politzer (1971) has observed that there are three basic ways in which individualized instruction is usually conceptualized:

- Learners may be assigned different goals.
- The same goals may be attained by the use of different approaches, methods, or techniques.
- The same goals may be attained by the use of the same approaches, methods, or techniques, but at different rates.

The first approach—individualizing goals—means that students are allowed to structure their own learning objectives, to decide in advance just what they want to do. How this works with small children is rarely made clear.

The second approach—individualization of method—means that students are to be allowed to select those modalities of learning that are most congruent with their own abilities. Again the question of what this means concretely for teachers in FLES programs is left vague. Indeed, it remains to be demonstrated empirically that individual differences in modes and strategies of learning are significant enough to require widely varied techniques and materials in the acquisition of the same skills (Valdman, 1971).

The third approach—individualizing the pace of learning—seems to be the aspect of individualization that is most likely to be widely adopted. In fact, the audio-lingual approach has always given at least lip service to the principle that learners should proceed at their own speed. Recently this tenet has been given greater emphasis, and many authors regard it as a central doctrine of second-language instruction (Altman, 1971; Gougher, 1973; Hunter, 1971).

There are, however, numerous practical problems with individualizing instruction. How are students to be taught at different speeds in the same classroom? What effect does tracking students into fast, middle, and slow groups have on borderline cases? How is the teacher to grade students who have done varying amounts of work? What can be done to lessen the gap between the better and the poorer students? How are busy teachers to cope with the demands that individualized instruction makes on their time? At present, these and other problems continue to beset attempts at individualization.

Bilingual education programs.   Pacheco (1971) has argued that individualized instruction has special relevance in the education of ethnic minority children. He believes that individualization in bilingual education programs involves the following considerations:

* The objectives of the school program.
* The overall school design and teaching philosophy.
* The content and strategies of instruction required of a curriculum responsive to student needs.
* The kinds of learning that best relate to student needs and reinforce other learning experiences.
* The kinds of bilingual education programs that must be designed to be well integrated into the total curriculum.

On the critical last point Pacheco offered no further guidelines.

Generally speaking, there is less concern with language instruction techniques in bilingual education programs than in FLES programs. Much more attention is given to the development of curriculum materials designed to teach children subject matter areas in their first language and to foster their appreciation of their cultural heritage. The language instruction material available for teaching the child in the first language is usually designed for teaching the non-English language to speakers of English. The methods used in teaching English vary considerably: no concerted attempt has been made to employ audio-lingual techniques or the techniques of individualized instruction.

It is not surprising that attention has centered on the design of materials for subject areas other than language itself. One of the characteristics of bilingual education programs is the commitment to second-language learning through exposure to the second language in the context of normal instruction in subject areas other than language itself. Yet the lack of concern for appropriate pedagogy in the language classroom will only be to the detriment of the program as a whole.

Other developments.   One of the upshots of recent developments in linguistics and psycholinguistics has been the increased interest in the relationship between first- and second-language learning. As we saw earlier, there is a great deal of controversy on this point, some authors arguing that the two involve radically different processes and others that the similarities are more impressive than the differences. The position one takes on this issue obviously has practical bearing on the way one approaches language-acquisition.

In a discussion of this topic, Cook (1969) noted three areas where there are different implications depending on the position one takes with respect to the question of the relationship between first- and second-language learning. If one holds that second-language learning is essentially a different process than first-language acquisition, the *development* of a second language is different than the developmental course of first language. The first language is acquired slowly with many wrong turns and dead ends. Second-language learning need not involve this process. Indeed, traditional teachers, committed to the view that second-language learning is different than first-language acquisition, usually demand that second-language learners speak grammatically from the beginning. An approach that stressed the stimilarities between first-language acquisition and second-language learning would leave room for second-language learners to progress through the developmental stages that characterize first-language acquisition.

The second area of divergence is attitude toward *errors*. Once again the more traditional approach, stressing differences between first-language acquisition and second-language learning, structures the teaching situation in such a way that the possibility of errors is minimized. One of the dogmas of the audio-lingual approach is that the student must not experiment with new combinations and analogies, as the child acquiring a first language does. Instead the pupil must make the correct response in the stimulus situation the teacher has arranged. Mistakes do not represent incremental, but decremental, learning (Rivers, 1964). In contrast, an approach that emphasizes the similarities between first-language acquisition and second-language learning regards errors as an integral part of any language learning process.

A final area of divergence is in attitudes toward the *organization of input*. The traditional approach usually restricts and systematically orders material presented to the learner. Learning involves the repetition and overlearning of carefully chosen amounts of material. The learner is expected to learn sentences in their entirety, without expansion and without giving evidence that underlying grammatical relations have been abstracted. In contrast, an approach stressing the similarities between first-language acquisition and second-language learning is less restrictive in the organization of input and attempts to maximize opportunities for the learner to expand sentences in situationally appropriate ways. Moreover, repetition is de-emphasized in such an approach and more freedom given for the learner to experiment with the language.

In summary, Cook (1969) listed the following criteria for an approach to language instruction based on a recognition of the similarities between first-language acquisition and second-language learning:

- The learner is allowed to progress by forming a set of increasingly complete rules about the second language.
- The learner is encouraged to produce sentences that are ungrammatical in terms of full native competence, so that feedback might be obtained about the adequacy of inductively formulated rules.
- Perception of patterns in emphasized rather than intensity of practice.
- Teaching techniques involve partial repetition of sentences, verbal play, and situationally appropriate expansions of the learner's sentences.

Cook felt that no present approach to language teaching satisfies these criteria.

There have, however, been several experimental studies to determine whether second languages can be learned as first languages are acquired. One example is Asher's work examining the effectiveness of incorporating motorlike techniques into second-language training (Asher, 1965, 1969, 1972; Asher, Kusudo, & de le Torre, 1974). Asher cited the research finding that about 50% of all speech directed at a 12-month-old infant involved commands (Friedlander, Jacobs, Davis, & Wetstone, 1972) and asked whether it is possible for a language to be learned with a format in which the student physically responds to commands. This, after all, seems to be an important feature of much of the child's early language acquisition.

In his research, Asher has been able to demonstrate dramatic increases in lexical learning when adults learn as children, by being taught to recognize words referring to actions as they perform those actions in response to commands. By using pictures, Asher (1972) was able to increase the amount of lexical information present through commands such as *Marie, pick up the picture of the ugly old man and put it next to the picture of the government building.* Because it seems closely analogous to the way they learn their first language, this method seems to have considerable potential as a technique with young children.

A number of other interesting methods have been proposed for teaching second languages derived from observation of first-language acquisition. For example, Gauthier (cited in Tucker & d'Anglejan, 1973) reported success with a method that involves prolonged passive exposure to the second language before any attempt is made to speak the language. This method was also advocated by Carroll (1973), who argued that listening comprehension should be developed before attempts are made to inculcate other language skills. Jakobovits and Gordon (1974) have advocated concentrating on highly specific interactions in the use of language, rather than situationally empty pattern drills. This seems to parallel the way in which children acquire their language by repeatedly hearing and uttering word strings in highly specific contexts. A similar point of view was adopted by Oller (1971), who noted that language is primarily a medium of communication and should therefore be learned in the context of the communicative act.

I shall not attempt to catalogue the numerous methods that have been proposed for teaching second languages. The point is that the field is still in flux, that there is growing recognition of the necessity of taking the student's individual needs and abilities into consideration, and that at least some authors have asked what the consequences would be if second-language learning was approached in a manner analogous to the way in which first languages are acquired.

Exposure to the Second Language

An important question for any second-language program is how much exposure the child is to have to the second language. Is the child to be taught by the intensive method or by a more gradual approach? If the approach is to be intensive, how intensive should it be? There seem to be at least three different answers: total immersion, partial immersion, and mixing.

Total immersion.   The most well-known experiment using the total immersion technique is that of Lambert and Tucker (1972) with a group of English-speaking children in the Montreal suburb of St. Lambert. The program was initiated because of the concern of a group of parents from this area who felt that second-language education should begin in the elementary school but who were disillusioned with the traditional FLES-type program. In 1965 these parents placed their children in an experimental, all-French program. The children were thus automatically thrust into a bilingual environment (termed by Lambert and Tucker, "the home–school language switch"). The program aimed at developing complete bilingual competence in both the home and the school language.

An essential feature of the St. Lambert project was that language instruction was made incidental to educational content. The attempt was made to have the children master the second language in a natural manner in their daily interaction with teachers who were native speakers. Lambert and Tucker argued that previous attempts at bilingual education may have been unsuccessful because excessive emphasis was given to the mastery of the second language, which was taught in a mechanical, routinized manner by non-native speakers, rather than to educational content.

The St. Lambert project involved an extensive, longitudinal study in order to determine how the students progressed as compared with control groups of French and English monolingual children enrolled in standard (monolingual) tracks. Attention was given to the problem of assuring that experimental and control groups were equated in terms of socioeconomic background, general intelligence, and parental interest in academic achievement.

The program began at the kindergarten level. The experimental group had a monolingual, French-speaking teacher who stressed the development of French language skills through story telling, vocabulary build-up, songs, and group projects in the plastic arts. The kindergarten was conducted entirely in French and lasted 2 hours a day. Its primary purpose was to give the children enough knowledge of French to handle the contents of the first grade curriculum.

In the first grade and thereafter the children were exposed to the normal curriculum of the French–Canadian school system of Montreal. All material was in French, designed for children who spoke French as a first language. The program of study at each level focused attention on the development of expected academic skills, with language purposely incidental: French language arts were taught as they would have been taught to a class of French-speaking children. In the second grade, English language arts were introduced, again taught as they were normally to English-speaking children.

Pilot and follow-up experimental groups were tested extensively throughout their elementary school career and compared to the French- and English-speaking control groups. A battery of tests was administered, including word knowledge, word associations, and speaking skills in French and English; sentence and paragraph comprehension in English, arithmetic concepts in French and English, and a phoneme discrimination test. The results of this research are discussed in the following section.

The St. Lambert project has inspired similar total immersion programs in Canada (Barik, Swain, & McTavish, 1974; Cameron, Feider, & Gray, 1974) and in the United States (Cohen, 1974). In the Culver City Spanish immersion project (Cohen, 1974), Anglo children were exposed exclusively to Spanish from kindergarten on with English introduced gradually in the first grade. There was no formal language instruction; essentially the same approach was used here as in the St. Lambert project. The kindergarten class consisted exclusively of monolingual English speakers, and in grade one a few monolingual Spanish speakers were added to the class. There was also a follow-up group as in the St. Lambert project. These experimental groups were matched with comparable control classes of monolingual children and extensively tested in both languages and in mathematical skills.

Partial immersion programs.   An alternative approach to the total immersion formula is partial instruction in the second language. This approach has been used in a number of bilingual education programs in the United States. Typical are the programs of the Coral Way Elementary School in Dade County, Florida, and the Laredo Unified Consolidated Independent School District in Texas (Andersson & Boyer, 1970; Gaarder, 1967). In the Coral Way school, students receive instruction in all subjects in both languages—in the morning from an English-speaking teacher and in the afternoon from a Spanish-speaking teacher. In the Laredo system, students receive all instruction from the same teacher who uses English half of the day and Spanish the other half.

A similar approach is used in St. Thomas, Elgin County, Ontario, where French is the medium of instruction for half of the school day and English for the other half (Barik & Swain, 1974). The children in the Elgin program come from an English-speaking community and have been compared through the early grades of elementary school with a group of monolingual, English-speaking children who received one period of French as a foreign language daily and with a group of children enrolled in a total immersion program.

It should be noted that such partial immersion programs differ from FLES programs in that the attempt is made to teach all school subjects in the child's second language, not merely the second language as such. In this sense the programs involve extensive exposure to the child's second language, though obviously less extensive exposure than is the case in total immersion programs.

Mixing.   By mixing I refer to programs in which children are exposed in the school to bilingual presentation but are given considerable latitude as to which language they will use in a particular context. Such an approach seems to characterize many international schools, situated especially in major European cities, where education is provided in a variety of languages to the offspring of a transient population of soldiers, businessmen, and diplomats, as well as to children from the local community whose parents want them to be exposed to a second language.

An example is the John F. Kennedy School in West Berlin (Mackey, 1972). As we saw in Chapter 1, this school was designed to provide bilingual education to American and German children in the primary school. The school policy is to have 50% German students, 40% American students, and 10% from other groups. The staff is international, though not necessarily bilingual. The German students usually continue in the school until they graduate (grade six), but the American turnover is extremely high, most families remaining in Berlin only 2 years.

Instruction is given in both German and English, but children have a great deal of freedom of choice. They can respond in either language. No effort is made to force them to speak in their second language. In many classes, teachers mix English and German, teaching in German for the first part of the period and in English for the second or alternating sentence-by-sentence between the two languages. The teachers also translate questions from one language into the other. Children switch continually from one language to the other, often attempting to say something in the second language and then falling back into their first language.

A similar procedure was used in the Redwood City program (Cohen, 1975) funded by Title VII funds. In this program there was a two–to–one ratio of Mexican–Americans to Anglos in every class, and great pains were taken to assure that the English-speaking students received instruction in English in all classes except Spanish. Thus a mathematics or social science class would be taught in both Spanish and English, with English predominating. Teachers generally provided sentence–by–sentence or idea–by–idea translation in both languages.

One has the impression that the primary focus in such schools is to foster communication and knowledge of the subject matter rather than language skills. The teacher uses the child's dominant language in order to facilitate communication and to maintain the attention of the class as a whole (or at least that part of the class whose language is being spoken). Mixing is therefore justified on the grounds that without relying on the child's dominant language, school learning would be impeded, because the child may miss out on something if it is presented in a second language.

THE EFFECTIVENESS OF SECOND-LANGUAGE PROGRAMS FOR CHILDREN

This brings us to the question of how effective various approaches to second-language instruction are. Is it better for children to be intensively and exclusively exposed to a second language, or should they be allowed to learn this language in the context of their own first language and at their own speed? How effective are programs of various sorts—FLES programs and different types of bilingual education programs? First, however, I shall discuss briefly the issue of evaluating the effectiveness of second-language programs for children.

Evaluation

Evaluation is obviously an integral part of any educational enterprise. It is necessary to ascertain whether the goals of the program are being realized and to identify factors that are troublesome and that interfere with the attainment of the program's goals. This means that periodic consideration must be made of the way in which instruction is conducted, of the effectiveness of curriculum materials, and of student performance. Usually, the student is tested in each of the following areas:

- General competence in first and second languages.
- Writing, reading, and speaking ability in both languages.
- General mental ability (IQ) and cognitive development.
- Ability in nonlanguage areas, especially mathematics.
- Cultural attitudes.

In addition, in many bilingual education programs the child's self-concept is also tested.

Most educators now believe that there are various skills or domains involved in language learning and that these different domains involve different abilities that may vary within the same individual in different contexts and spheres of activity. For this reason, batteries of tests are given to measure different language skills. Discussion of some instruments available for FLES programs can be found in Valette (1967). Andersson and Boyer (1970) and John and Horner (1971) discussed instruments available for bilingual education programs.

The usual test of general language competence contains a fluency test to measure speed of verbal production, verbal response tests to measure quality of verbal production, and dominance tests to measure which of the child's two languages is dominant. In addition, some investigators have studied language usage as assessed by various storytelling techniques (John & Horner, 1971).

An interesting assessment technique, called developmental sentence scoring, has been devised to measure syntactic development in children's spontaneous speech (Lee & Canter, 1971). The procedure involves scoring each consecutive utterance of the child, assigning one point if the sentence is in conformity with accepted adult usage and, in addition, assigning a score on the basis of whether it contains any of the following categories: indefinite pronouns, personal pronouns, main verbs, secondary verbs, negatives, conjunctions, interrogative reversals, and *wh-* questions. Within each category points are assigned from one to eight on the basis of different grammatical phenomena. For example, *wh-* questions containing *who, what,* or *what* + noun receive two points; *when, how,* or *how* + adjective receive five points; and *what, if, how come,* and *why* questions receive eight points. A similar gradation exists for each of the other categories. Norms for developmental sentence scores are available for English-speaking children based on average scores computed from 50 consecutive tape-recorded utterances. This procedure has been used by Politzer (1974) to study second-language acquisition of Mexican–American children in a bilingual program.

To obtain an index of the language dominance of children in bilingual programs, questionnaires have been developed in the two languages for parents and others in contact with the child. Typical questions relate to the use of the child's two languages in various situations at home and in the community. In addition, some tests have been developed to measure dominance through comparison of children's communicative competence in their two languages. There are now tests of oral proficiency for Spanish–English bilingual children and for Navaho–English children (Swanson, 1974). These tests are for children of particular ages, however; tests for other age groups and other bilingual combinations are not available.

A wide variety of tests exist for measuring such skills as comprehension and reading, writing, and speaking ability in first and second languages. The problem here is one of establishing norms and assuring that the measures are reliable and valid. The last two issues are usually not mentioned in research reports, yet it is obvious that no confidence can be placed in results obtained from unreliable and invalid tests.

A number of authors have pointed out the problems involved in using tests designed for children from the dominant English-speaking culture when assessing general mental ability and conceptual development of ethnic minority children. Ulibarri (1972) argued that such tests reflect previous experience and education not available to minority children who have grown up under conditions of poverty and in a "micro-culturalized" world. As a result, ethnic minority children inevitably do poorly. The same is true of instruments designed to measure specific subject matter skills that have been standarized on middle-class, standard, English-speaking populations when these tests are applied to children whose language and social background is different (Pacheco, 1973).

Andersson and Boyer (1970) have argued that assessment of the impact of bilingual education programs in the affective areas is more important than evaluation of their effect on academic or lingual performance. There are, however, few satisfactory instruments for this purpose, although a number of tests to measure the child's self-concept do exist. Instruments to assess the child's cultural attitudes are in a primitive stage of development, and more work in this area is also necessary.

The ideal of a carefully conducted research design, extending over a number of years with control, pilot, and follow-up groups has rarely been achieved. The St. Lambert project certainly comes closest to this ideal. This project has been the model for research designs employed in a number of studies of programs using total and partial immersion methods both in Canada and in the United States. Unfortunately, less rigorous criteria continue to be the norm for evaluation research in most programs.

Some Research Findings

FLES programs.   Generally speaking, the effects of FLES programs seem to have been disappointing in the light of original, optimistic expectations. As was noted earlier, children did not quickly and easily learn foreign languages as a result of being exposed to them for one period a day. What gains there were were modest.

In an examination of the impact of FLES, Pillet (1968) came to the conclusion that the overall effects of FLES programs have been positive. The presence of second-language instruction in the classroom has come to be widely accepted. There is more attention given to individual differences in language instruction through flexible scheduling, tracking, delayed initiation, and terminal scheduling. Better use is made of instructional media than was true before FLES programs appeared. There is an extensive literature on psychological problems of children learning a second language, on curriculum design, on classroom strategies, and on evaluation methods and research.

On the other hand, the audio-lingual approach turned out not to be the panacea it was predicted to be. Children did not take to learning languages as it was expected they would. Motivation was a serious problem; many children dropped language instruction as soon as they could. Once the fun-and-games atmosphere of the third and fourth grades gave way to increased emphasis on more involved pattern drills, further structure manipulation, reading and writing, children in the higher grades often seemed to resent having to learn a language and lost interest (Page, 1966). In addition, when the children later came to study languages in junior high school, the prior experience of FLES sometimes proved a handicap. Students were slow in coming to grips with "the hard realities of language learning, European style" (Gaskell, 1967; Page, 1966). There seemed to be no transfer from their earlier FLES experience (Oller & Nagato, 1974).

There were, of course, exceptional students who did well under FLES. Frequently, however, even these students were dissatisfied because of the slowness and continual repetition of the audio-lingual method. When they were allowed to do so at the junior high school level, they forged ahead happily on their own (Page, 1966). Perhaps this says something about the lack of attention to individual differences in many early FLES programs.

There are some positive findings in the FLES literature. Vocolo (1967), for example, found that a comparison of the French performance of high school students who had studied French in a FLES program with a group equated in intelligence, amount of instruction received, and grade-point average indicated that the FLES students were significantly superior in comprehension and written and oral skills. Other studies also indicated that positive transfer is possible (Brega & Newell, 1967; Justman & Naas, 1956). On the whole, however, dramatic and unequivocal results were not forthcoming. The upshot has been a renewed call for new methods and new ways of thinking about FLES (Pillet, 1974).

Bilingual education programs.   Cohen (1974) discussed two bilingual education programs with which he was involved—the Redwood City project and the Culver City project. In the *Redwood City project,* there was a two–to–one ratio of Mexican–American to Anglo students in each class. Instructors mixed both languages, providing sentence–by–sentence or idea–by–idea translation. The approach was definitely unsuccessful for the Anglo students, who learned very little Spanish because they knew they could shift into English when they wanted to. Moreover, they were reluctant to speak Spanish in front of the Mexican–American students for fear of being teased. Nor did the approach succeed in improving relations between ethnic groups. The Anglos and Mexican–American students tended to stick together socially and to speak their own languages. When Anglos associated with the Mexican–Americans, they usually spoke to them in English. Thus, in these respects at least, mixing proved to be an ineffectual technique.

On the other hand, the Mexican–American students in the program learned English language skills as well as other Mexican–American students taught exclusively in English, although the students in the mixed program lagged behind in vocabulary. Nor were Spanish language skills or performance in mathematics affected by being in the bilingual program. In fact, use of Spanish and attitudes toward Mexican culture were favorably affected (Cohen, 1975).

In the *Culver City project* the total immersion approach was quite successful. The children knew that Spanish was the language of instruction from the start. When Mexican–American children joined the class in the first grade, they were looked upon as models of Spanish and were socially accepted. It no doubt helped that the Mexican–American children constituted only ¼ of the class, in contrast to being a majority in the Redwood City project. Another factor was probably the fact that the Anglo students had been segregated for a year and taught exclusively in their second language. They were therefore able to acquire a rudimentary knowledge of the language and some confidence in its use.

In the Culver City project it was initially intended that English reading be introduced after a reading base in Spanish had been established. Because of a number of factors, including parental concern, English reading was begun midway through the first grade. This resulted in considerable interference with Spanish reading and speaking, and parents were persuaded to postpone the introduction of English reading until grade two in accord with the St. Lambert model.

Cohen reported that a comparison between the bilingual experimental kindergarten group and a comparable kindergarten group in the adjoining classroom showed that the comparison group scored significantly higher when measured for their readiness to read in English than the experimental group. Since the experimental group had been taught exclusively in Spanish, this result was not surprising. The comparison group was significantly more positive to Anglo cultural items than was the experimental group, but the reverse was true with respect to Mexican cultural items. This contrasts with results in the Redwood City project where experimental Anglo groups rated Mexican cultural items significantly lower than did a Mexican–American group. The lack of a Mexican–American comparison group in the Culver City project makes direct comparison impossible, but the findings were consistent with interaction patterns observed in the two studies.

After the first grade, the children in the experimental group were again tested and compared to a comparison group. The results indicated no differences between the two groups on tests measuring English language development. There was no difference between the immersion group and the comparison group in English reading (though the means for the immersion group were higher); nor was there a significant difference in Spanish reading between the immersion group and a group of Ecuadorian students (although the Ecuadorian children's unfamiliarity with the testing procedures might have artificially lowered their scores). Finally, the immersion and comparison groups did not differ significantly on a test of mathematics (although the immersion children learned this subject in their second language).

Cohen's findings were largely consistent with the results of the classic St. Lambert project. Before turning to this study, however, the superiority of the total immersion approach to the mixing approach should be noted. Cohen found that the mixing method used in the Redwood City project was ineffectual for the Anglo students and only minimally effective for Mexican–American students. A similar conclusion can be drawn from Mackey's (1972) account of the *John F. Kennedy School* in Berlin, although no systematic research was undertaken to assess the impact of the school's program. Teachers in the school felt that bilingual instruction slowed down both learning and teaching. There were discipline problems, and cultural segregation seemed to occur. Many of the American students spoke a type of mixed language—more akin to Pennsylvania Dutch than to German.

These results are not so surprising, since no pressure was put on the students to speak in the second language. Complete freedom was the rule in this regard, and the students followed the natural tendency to speak their own language and to stay with their own cultural group. The teachers even seemed to encourage this development, since they accommodated themselves to the students' wishes by switching to their first language when they had difficulty speaking or understanding the second language.

One can go so far as to raise the question of the morality of such an educational program (Teschner, 1973). The John F. Kennedy School had a budget five times in excess of that of the typical Berlin German school. No positive benefits seemed to derive from the enterprise. Exposure to a second language had little effect, since the child had no need to speak the language. Instead, the practice of providing instructions in two languages slowed down instruction and made it boring for all concerned. There were no observable cultural benefits, and one feels that the school's policy of not testing its students is intended to insure that the obvious ineffectiveness of the program is not empirically demonstrated.

In contrast, the results of the *St. Lambert project* were essentially positive. The children were studied via a battery of tests at regular intervals. In their book, Lambert and Tucker (1972) reported on the first five years of instruction. At the end of grade one, experimental groups (pilot and follow-up) were below English control classes on tests of English word knowledge and reading skill. This was not unexpected, since at this point, the children had been exposed solely to French in the school and had had no instruction in English or in English reading. The experimental groups had no difficulty on tests of English comprehension but had a slower rate of verbal output in reconstructing stories when compared to the comparison groups. Nonetheless, in overall expression, enunciation, rhythm, and intonation the experimental groups did as well as comparison groups.

When compared to French-speaking, control children their own age, the experimental groups were definitely poorer on almost all indices of language skill. They were, however, not significantly lower than controls on tests of French word discrimination, sentence comprehension, and word order. Finally, at the end of grade one, experimental groups did just as well as control classes on arithmetic tests presented in either language. Since experimental children were instructed only in French, this indicates that some transfer occurred from one language to the other.

At the end of grade two, the experimental group had progressed in English language skills (they now had two 35-minute periods of English language arts daily) to the point where they were on a par with control groups. The only exception was a retardation in English spelling, and this was counterbalanced by significantly better English vocabulary development. The ease with which the experimental groups caught up to their monolingual peers was attributed by Lambert and Tucker to transference of basic skills of reading, concept development, and word manipulation through French to English. They suggested that the child processes new information presented in a second language both in this language and in his first language, thereby relating the notions presented in the second language to the conceptual knowledge acquired in the first language during infancy and childhood. The result is that the child has a great deal of latent knowledge, processed through the first language, that can be drawn on when learning and being tested in formal aspects of that language.

By the end of the second grade, continuing progress was made in French. The children in the experimental groups were still behind French control groups, especially in matters of grammar. But progress in pronunciation and in control of the basic sound units of French was noticeable. When experimental children were asked to tell a story in French, they performed as well as French controls on overall expression, enunciation, liaison, rhythm, and intonation. Finally, experimental groups performed better than English control groups in arithmetic tests, a finding that Lambert and Tucker suggested may indicate that they had acquired techniques and ideas more thoroughly because of second-language instruction.

In the third and fourth grades, the experimental children continued to narrow the gap between themselves and French control groups in French language skills. By the end of the fourth grade, the children were rated by a team of linguists as at or above the neutral point in competence for all indices of French language arts. They tended to speak in more simple, though correct, constructions than did French-speaking children their age but understood and read the language without difficulty. Their skills in English and in arithmetic continued to be at the same level or higher than that of controls.

Subsequent developments in the St. Lambert project were discussed by Bruck, Lambert, and Tucker (1974), who reported the results of tests conducted through to grade seven for the pilot group and grade six for the follow-up group. Although the tests differ somewhat from those given previously, the pattern of results is much the same. There was no evidence of poorer English-language or arithmetic skills. The follow-up group did show some signs of difficulty with mathematics at grade five, but no differences were found between this group and the control group at grade six. Experimental groups scored higher than controls on measures of cognitive flexibility. In French language tests experimental groups continued to rank behind French control groups, possibly because of the children's relatively low exposure to the language when compared to the control groups (who heard the language at home and in their communities) and their unfamiliarity with certain structures presented in the task. Nonetheless, it is clear that the experimental children reached a high level of competence in their second language, well beyond that, for example, expected of children in FLES programs.

One particularly impressive aspect of the pattern of results obtained by Lambert, Tucker, and their associates is that essentially the same findings were obtained with two groups exposed to different teachers, different teaching techniques, and even different tests as changes were introduced from year to year. This replicability is a strong witness to the validity of the results. The students enjoyed the program, it involved no extra costs, and it was effective in terms of realizing its goals.

There was, however, one area in which the goals of the program were not realized. Lambert and Tucker reported that during the early years of the program the experimental children showed less hostile attitudes toward French Canadians than did English controls, but there was no further moderation in attitudes in subsequent years. Instead, the experimental groups' attitudes tended increasingly to approximate those of the English control groups. The authors attributed this to the desire for peer group conformity and pointed out, in addition, that at the time of testing (the early 1970s) there was considerable tension between English and French Canadians because of strident demands for French unilingualism, kidnapings, bombing, and other violent acts. In the light of these tensions, the authors were reassured to find that no antipathy for the language of the "other" group had developed and that the students were progressing satisfactorily.

The St. Lambert project has become a model for bilingual programs in Canada, which now has an official bilingual policy. There are total immersion programs in operation throughout the country. Generally, the results are as positive as those obtained in the St. Lambert experiment. One rather large-scale attempt, for example, is the *Ottawa project* (Barik & Swain, 1975), which involves over 1,000 English-speaking children who are exposed exclusively to French in the kindergarten and school. These children have been tested in various cohorts from kindergarten to the second grade.

After a year in kindergarten children in this program were found to have learned more French than children who received 20 to 40 minutes of French daily from kindergarden through grade two. Their numerical and English prereading skills were on a par with those of a comparable group of children in an English kindergarten, and they were at the same level in general mental and cognitive development relative to the English control group.

At the end of the first grade, the same lag was found in English language skills as Lambert and Tucker reported at this stage in the St. Lambert project: compared to English controls the experimental groups were behind in word knowledge, word discrimination, and reading. There was, however, some transfer of reading skills to English even without formal instruction. The experimental groups also compared well with English and French control groups on mathematical knowledge and showed no signs of mental or cognitive retardation when compared to English controls. Although their French did not match that of first-language speakers, it was far superior to that of FLES students.

At the end of grade two, the differences in English language skills between experimental and control groups had disappeared due to the introduction of formal English instructions for the experimental children (as in the St. Lambert project, spelling was an exception). French language skills were not on a par with those of first-language speakers but far superior to those of FLES students. Again the experimental groups were equal to French and English control groups in mathematics and did as well as children in the regular English program on tests of general mental and cognitive development.

The evidence to date, therefore, suggests that total immersion programs are remarkably effective means of bilingual education. The pattern of results obtained in the St. Lambert project and the Ottawa program are amazingly consistent. Children in such total immersion programs show an initial retardation in their first language, but this quickly disappears once formal instruction in that language is begun. In the meantime, the children effectively learn the second language so that their ability in the second language more closely approximates that of native speakers than that of their peers in a FLES program.

How do partial immersion programs compare with total immersion programs? This question was examined by Barik and Swain (1974) in their report on the *Elgin program*. This program, it will be recalled, was a half-day French, half-day English, bilingual program established for first grade, English-speaking children in St. Thomas, Ontario. Barik and Swain's report covered grades one through three with a cohort of initially 27 students (20 in grade two, 21 in grade three). In each of these grades the students had their morning classes in French: mathematics, music, and French language arts. Afternoon classes were in English: English language arts, physical education, and other subjects such as science, social studies, art, and health as these were introduced into the curriculum. Reading and writing were initially taught in English in grade one, with reading in French introduced in grade two. Note that this approach differs from that of the usual total immersion program where reading in the child's first language is introduced only after reading in the second language has been established. In addition, in contrast to the usual practice in total immersion programs, the Elgin program began in the first grade rather than in kindergarten. Finally, whereas the teachers in total immersion programs are typically native speakers of the child's second language, the teachers in the Elgin program were fluently bilingual, native, English speakers.

At the end of the first grade, experimental children were compared against a comparison group of the same intellectual capacity and social background enrolled in a monolingual English school, as well as against children in a total immersion program. They were on a par with their peers in the regular program in cognitive development, English language skills, and arithmetic achievement. In French comprehension, they did as well as kindergarten children in a total immersion program who had had as much exposure to French. When they were compared with first grade children in the total immersion program, they were found to perform substantially lower, a not too surprising finding since the first grade total immersion group had had much more exposure to the language. More perplexing was the finding that the partial immersion group did not perform any better than a grade one FLES class that had had 20 to 40 minutes daily instruction in French. In spite of the fact that the FLES children had less exposure to French, they had about the same scores on French comprehension as the partial immersion group.

At the end of grade two, the students in the partial immersion program continued to perform as well as their peers in a regular, English, monolingual program in arithmetic skills but fell behind them in several aspects of English language skills and reading. They also performed worse in English language skills than students in a total immersion program who were formally introduced to English language only in the second grade and only for an hour a day. In French language skills the partial immersion children scored lower than grade one children in a total immersion program but higher than first- or second-grade children in a FLES program.

By the end of the third grade, the partial immersion group still performed more poorly than their peers in an English monolingual program on English language skills, although they were on a par with them in reading comprehension. In mathematics there were no differences between the groups, although the partial immersion group had been instructed in this subject in French. French comprehension still lagged behind that of total immersion students, but it seemed to be commensurate with the amount of exposure to French that the partial immersion group had received.

Barik and Swain interpreted these findings as indicating that the partial immersion program may cause students initial confusion as they attempt to develop linguistic skills in two languages concurrently. This procedure seems to be somewhat detrimental to the development of first-language skills, although there are indications that this effect is a temporary one. What is surprising is that by the third grade the total immersion procedure seems to achieve the same results with respect to first-language skills as the partial immersion technique, in spite of the fact that the total immersion children had much less exposure to the first language in the classroom. It may be that one important factor is the time at which reading in the second language is introduced. In total immersion programs, reading in the second language begins 1 year prior to reading in the first language. In the Elgin program this pattern was reversed, with reading in the first language introduced a year earlier than reading in the second. Perhaps it is easier to transfer reading skills from French to English than vice versa.

The Canadian research in bilingual education has set a high standard for future studies to emulate. The characteristics of this research have been the careful selection of control groups, the use of test batteries that measure different aspects of linguistic and nonlinguistic development, and the study of follow-up groups and different cohorts of students over an extended period of time. Few studies of bilingual education in the United States have been as well conducted.

Some unanswered questions.   Why is it that the St. Lambert project and other similar total immersion programs in Canada achieved such good results, whereas ethnic minority students in the United States usually fare poorly when they are placed in a school situation where they receive all of their instruction in a second language? As Susan Ervin–Tripp (1970) noted, the overt linguistic circumstances seem to be entirely parallel. In all likelihood, the differences are social and psychological.

In the Canadian environment, English-speaking children have no sense of inferiority in the school. The children in total immersion programs were usually chosen from English, monolingual communities. Their social group was the more prestigious and their language was respected. The children were not expected to compete in the classroom with native speakers of French, and their teachers did not have low expectations for their achievement. The same is true of the Culver City project (Cohen, 1974) in the United States, where the children came from the dominant, English-speaking community. These factors are central to the success of such programs: without changing the community's attitudes, the teachers' attitudes, and the attitudes of the children themselves, such immersion programs cannot be expected to succeed with ethnic minority children.

It should be noted that in total immersion programs for English-speaking children, the children are kept segregated, at least initially, from other children who speak French or Spanish as a first language. The typical situation for minority children in the United States is that the child is in a class with a considerable number of native, English-speaking children whose language proficiency gives them an advantage. The situation is more "submersion" than immersion—submersion reflecting the sink–or–swim nature of the experience for the minority student (Cohen & Swain, 1976). Possibly an immersion program structured along the lines of the Canadian programs, with initial segregation until the children feel comfortable in their second language, would be successful in the United States. If the program were to be based on Canadian programs, the teachers would be bilingual, language arts courses in the child's native language would be introduced very early, and parental support of the program would be a sine qua non for its continuation (Cohen & Swain, 1976).

Nonetheless, it should be noted that English-speaking children in the St. Lambert project, in spite of their great facility in French, remained inferior to native French-speaking children in all aspects of that language. Children whose first language is not English in the United States are usually judged against the standard of native speakers of English (Ramirez, Macauley, Gonzalez, Cox, & Perez, in press). Thus it is not at all clear just what the implications of total immersion programs are for public schooling in the United States.

Lambert and Tucker (1972) pointed out that total immersion was not proposed as a universal solution for all communities or nations. They suggested instead the following guiding principles: in any community where there is a serious, widespread desire or need for bilingual education, priority in early schooling should be given to the language or languages least likely to be developed otherwise. If Language A is the more prestigious, children for whom this is the first language should be exposed to Language B until reading or writing skills are developed and then to Language A. Ethnic minority groups whose first language is Language B have a number of options. They can develop partial immersion programs in kindergarten, with a half day in Language B and a half day in A. They can restrict the language of instruction to Language B until reading and writing skills are established, then introduce instruction via Language A. Another possibility is a completely bilingual program based on two monolingually organized educational structures where the children move back and forth from one language of instruction to another in different classes. The languages are not taught as such; rather they are thought of as vehicles for developing competence in academic subject matters.

There is obviously a need for research to determine whether such suggestions are feasible. Are partial immersion programs as effective with ethnic minority students as they are with students from the dominant culture? Are the problems that arise in partial immersion programs magnified when such programs are used with ethnic minority students? Can programs that switch languages for different subjects be so structured that ethnic minority children do not gain the impression that their language is the language of the "soft" subjects (history, literature), whereas the dominant language is the language of the "hard" subjects (mathematics and science)?

In general, careful longitudinal evaluation research on the model of the St. Lambert project is needed to assess the effectiveness of bilingual and FLES programs of various sorts. There is still a dearth of information about such questions as:

- To what extent do children differ in their aptitude for second-language learning?
- To what extent and for what reasons do children differ in their motivation to learn a second language?
- How do children from the dominant culture develop their attitudes toward the language and culture of ethnic minorities?
- How can positive attitudes toward other languages and cultures be fostered?
- What is the meaning of individualized instruction in the context of bilingual education programs for minority children?
- What effect does the child's participation in a bilingual education program have on attitudes toward continuing instruction in the second language or learning other languages?

In addition, there remain the usual questions concerning teacher selection and training, effectiveness of curriculum materials, methods of instruction, and testing procedures.

A great deal of money is currently being invested throughout the world to teach children second languages. The St. Lambert project and other similar projects have demonstrated that it is possible for children from the dominant culture effectively to learn a second language. They have set a high standard for research that must be met by any method or program claiming to be effective. The question remains whether the premise of the St. Lambert project—that the best way to teach children a second language is to expose them to that language in the context of normal classroom instruction—is transferable to second-language training of ethnic minority children.

Furthermore, there is the question of how the attitudes of the child from the dominant culture can be made more positive toward the minority culture. Even the St. Lambert project—so successful in all other respects—was unsuccessful here. Similarly, too little is known about how positive attitudes toward their own culture and toward the dominant culture can be fostered in ethnic minority children. If success is achieved in second-language training but the child develops negative attitudes toward the other culture, one of the major aims of bilingual education has not been realized.

7
Effects of Bilingualism

We come now to the question of what effect bilingualism has on the individual. This has been a topic of empirical investigation for quite some time, and there are literally hundreds of studies in the literature. Answers are not easily come by—at least not the clear-cut and definitive answers early investigators hoped to find. As we shall see, many factors interact to determine the effects of bilingualism.

One of the most obvious factors is the degree of bilingualism. Some method must be employed to determine whether the bilingual individual's two languages are in balance and, if not, to what extent facility in one language surpasses that of the other language. The complexity of this task becomes apparent when one considers that there are numerous skills involved in language; some decision has to be made about what skills to measure. An individual, for example, may have a passive understanding of a second language that is on a par with the first language but may not be able to speak the second language at all. If a researcher attempts to assess the effect of this individual's bilingualism, some distinction must be made between listening ability and speaking ability. In general, at least four major skills can be distinguished: reading, writing, listening, and speaking. All, some, or only one of these skills may be relevant to the investigator.

Assuming that the researcher decides to measure bilingualism in terms of listening comprehension, there is then the task of deciding which test to use. Many tests employ materials that are presented in a formal and standard style that does not tap the individual's ability to comprehend informal, intimate conversation. Other tests are suitable for age groups different than those the investigator is interested in because they have been standardized on different age groups. Or the tests have been standardized on European, rather than American, populations. The socio-economic status of the researcher's sample might be another factor in determining whether certain tests are appropriate.

Some investigators have come to the conclusion that for their purposes the best way to assess the extent of an individual's bilingualism is to use indirect tests of verbal skills. That is, rather than measuring speech or reading ability by standardized tests, the researcher may use one of a number of less direct procedures. Macnamara (1969) discussed the use of four types of indirect measures:

- Rating scales. This procedure involves the use of a questionnaire on which the individual is asked to rate the extent to which each of the two languages is used in the home environment and the extent to which each language is heard on television, radio, in church, and so forth. Another rating procedure involves self-ratings of skills in reading, writing, listening, and speaking each language. Self-ratings have been shown to be more powerful measures of bilingualism than a language behavior questionnaire.
- Fluency tests. There are a variety of different measures involving speed of responding to verbal stimuli or speed of production that have been used to assess the extent of an individual's bilingualism. These include, for example, word-naming tasks where a subject has to give names to pictures of objects or has to say as many words as possible in one language and then in the other. Another procedure is to measure the speed with which individuals follow simple instructions in both languages. The most valid measure seems to be speed of reading, which correlates well with the major language skills of reading, writing, listening, and speaking.
- Flexibility tests. These tests require subjects to provide meanings or synonyms for individual words in both of their languages. By comparison with norms for monolinguals, one can assess the individual's linguistic flexibility in each language.
- Dominance tests. In these tests the subject is presented with an ambiguous stimulus (which could belong to either language) and is asked to pronounce or interpret it. Examples would be *pipe* for French–English bilinguals or *fast* for German–English bilinguals. Such words are given in a list of words from both languages to prevent the subject from developing a set to answer in one language or the other.

Although there are still problems of validity, Macnamara argued that such measures can be appropriate when for some reason or other more direct tests of language skills cannot or should not be administered.

Many of the studies I discuss in this chapter used the weakest of these indirect measures—ratings of home and neighborhood language use—as the basis for assessing degree of bilingualism. When the researcher has to obtain a measure of the individual's bilingualism prior to the time of the study itself—as is usually the case when an investigator is studying the effect of bilingualism on subsequent academic achievement, for example—the approach is likely to be one of relying on the individual's recollection of family usage. This is probably unavoidable, but it does point up an important weakness of such studies—namely, that the measure of bilingualism is not a very valid one. A more satisfactory approach is to measure degree of bilingualism with more valid procedures initially and then study subjects longitudinally with respect to some dependent variable. But such studies are rare.

In addition to the methodological problem of assessing degree of bilingualism, there is the problem of providing a taxonomy of bilingualism. That is, individuals do not only differ in the *extent* to which they have mastered two languages; they also differ in the *way* in which they have mastered (or not mastered) them. Language learning in the classroom is something very different from language acquisition in the natural milieu. We have seen that the child who simultaneously acquires two languages in a bilingual environment seems to experience little interference and competition between linguistic systems, whereas the child who learns in the classroom often experiences a great deal of interference and competition between languages. If the child learning in the classroom does not have contact with native-speaking peers, the second language may take on the special quality of an interlanguage. It is therefore important to keep these differences in mind when comparing the effects of bilingualism on different aspects of intellectual and linguistic functioning. The effects of bilingualism learned in the classroom may be quite different from the effects of bilingualism acquired in the natural milieu; yet many researchers have ignored these differences, just as they have often ignored differences in subjects due to degree of bilingualism.

Aside from qualitative and quantitative differences in bilingualism, the most important methodological problem in attempting to assess the effects of bilingualism is assuring that bilingual and monolingual groups differ in this respect— i.e., their different linguistic backgrounds—and in nothing else. If the bilinguals are members of an ethnic minority—which often happens to be the case—it is impossible to rule out the operation of economic and social factors. As we shall see, this has been the great stumbling block in research on the effects of bilingualism.

With these cautions in mind, what can be learned from the literature? There are five major areas of research interest: bilingualism and intelligence, bilingualism and language skills, bilingualism and educational attainment, bilingualism and emotional adjustment, and bilingualism and cognitive functioning.

BILINGUALISM AND INTELLIGENCE

If one assumes that linguistic functioning is closely dependent on cognitive functioning (Bever, 1970; Macnamara, 1972; Sinclair–de Zwart, 1973), the question of the effect of bilingualism on intelligence seems anomalous. The more interesting question would seem to be the effect of intelligence on bilingualism. But this question has been largely ignored, whereas the effect of bilingualism on intelligence has been the topic of numerous research projects.

Some authors have been quite convinced that bilingualism has a permanent negative effect on intellectual development. Weisgerber (1935) saw bilingualism as capable of impairing the intelligence of a whole ethnic group and crippling its creative ability for generations. This was a position shared by many German authors at the time, who saw it to be their patriotic duty to find scientific evidence for the negative effects of bilingualism, especially of German-speaking people (Porsché, 1975).

As we have seen, the situation was somewhat the same in America where bilingualism was also negatively valued in the 1920s and 1930s. Here investigators were even more "objective" than their German counterparts, whose "scientific" evidence was usually based on personal intuition. American investigators typically employed pencil–and–paper tests designed to measure differences in intellectual functioning between groups of monolingual and bilingual subjects.

Many such studies showed that bilingualism had a negative effect on intellectual development (e.g., Manuel & Wright, 1929; Mitchell, 1937; Rigg, 1928; Seidl, 1937; Smith, 1939). According to these and other authors, bilingual children often must think in one language and speak in another with the result that they become mentally uncertain and confused. In addition, bilingualism is a mental burden for children causing them to suffer mental fatigue. They are handicapped on intelligence tests, especially those demanding language facility.

These generalizations were arrived at, however, on the basis of studies that lacked appropriate controls. There is no way of knowing whether the obtained results were found because of the children's bilingualism or because the children in the bilingual group were disadvantaged socially and economically relative to the children in the monolingual groups. Such studies allow no conclusions to be drawn about the effects of bilingualism on intelligence. Bilinguals may, in fact, have been intellectually disadvantaged relative to monolingual children; but, if so, this need not have been due to their bilingualism.

In a summary of 32 studies carried out in the United States, Arsenian (1937) noted that 60% of the studies reported evidence that bilingualism is an intellectual handicap; 30% reported that the handicap, if it exists, is a minor one; and 10% found no ill effects of bilingualism on intelligence. Arsenian argued that an adequate study must be more careful methodologically and must consist of larger samples than was typical of past research.

Arsenian's own research involved the correlation of mental ability, age–grade status, and socioeconomic background of 1,152 Italian and 1,196 Jewish, bilingual, American-born children, aged 9 to 14 in New York City. He found no significant impact of bilingualism, as measured by a test of bilingual language skills, and found no difference between "high" and "low" bilingual children with respect to mental development.

It should be pointed out, however, that Arsenian's results, though often cited, have been criticized because of the tests of intelligence he employed (Darcy, 1953). In an effort to avoid contamination from verbal ability in the bilingual's second language, he used nonverbal tests of intelligence—the Pintner Nonlanguage Test and the Spearman Visual Perception Test. The validity of these tests was not established, and the Spearman test was not standarized.

Some of the classic work on the relationship between bilingualism and intelligence has been carried out in Wales with children bilingual in Welsh and English. Like the American research, these studies at first suggested that bilingualism has a negative effect on intelligence, but subsequent investigations challenged this conclusion. This line of research began with D. J. Saer's (1923) study of 1,400 children, age 7 to 14, in five rural and two urban districts of Wales. He found the following mean IQs:

	Urban	Rural
Monolingual	99	96
Bilingual	100	86

The inferiority of the rural children was attributed to the fact that these children learned their second language in the school; whereas most urban children had learned their second language earlier, through contact in play with English-speaking children. Saer felt that the urban child was able to resolve the conflict between the two languages earlier and with less inner turmoil, whereas the rural child had to expend "mental energy" to learn a new language and consequently suffered intellectual retardation in other areas.

Saer also tested bilingual university students and found that those from rural areas were intellectually inferior to monolingual individuals from the same areas, whereas no such differences were observed between monolingual and bilingual students from urban districts. On the basis of these findings, he concluded that the mental confusion due to bilingualism appears to be of a permanent nature, since it persists in students throughout their university careers. Doubt has been thrown on the validity of these findings, however, since a reanalysis of the data showed the difference between rural monolingual and bilingual students to be statistically insignificant (Jones, 1966).

Subsequent research with monolingual and bilingual children in Wales (Barke, 1933; Jones, 1952, 1966), in which both verbal and nonverbal types of intelligence tests were used, has indicated that the inferiority of bilingual children is a function of the type of material used: if nonverbal materials are used, no differences between the two groups are found; if the materials are verbal, the monolingual children usually score higher. Bilingual children tested in their second language are at a definite disadvantage in intelligence tests with a verbal factor because of their inadequate reading ability and because of inability to deal conceptually in the second language with the degree of fluency and accuracy that monolingual children possess. Bilingual children are especially disadvantaged if the test emphasizes speed of responding.

Further research on the rural–urban difference has supported Saer's finding that rural children score lower on intelligence tests than urban children. When the analysis is carried further, however, and children are grouped according to the occupational status of their parents, rural–urban differences disappear (Morrison, 1958). Welsh studies in which socioeconomic class has been controlled reveal no differences between bilingual and monolingual children, whether urban or rural, in nonverbal intelligence.

Research in the United States supports these findings. Reviewing the literature, Darcy (1953, 1963) reported that apparently contradictory results arise largely from methodological differences between the various investigations and from the absence of an agreed definition of bilingualism. Investigators have often failed to separate the bilingual factor from environmental factors by not controlling for socioeconomic class. The general trend in the literature indicates that whereas bilingual children suffer from a language handicap in verbal tests of intelligence, there is no evidence of a similar inferiority relative to monolingual children when bilinguals' performance is measured on nonverbal tests of intelligence. Nor is there evidence that bilingualism negatively affects intelligence in the broader sense of basic, universal, cognitive structures.

Indeed, some research appears to indicate that bilingualism can have a positive effect on intelligence as measured by intelligence tests. Peal and Lambert (1962) compared French–English, bilingual children with French, monolingual children, matched for age, sex, and socioeconomic status. The children, 164 in all, were 10 years of age and were selected from a larger pool on the basis of measures of bilingualism. All children were given an intelligence test with verbal and nonverbal subsections. Bilingual children were found to score significantly higher than monolingual children in nonverbal intelligence and in total intelligence (verbal plus nonverbal IQ).

These findings can be questioned, however, since Peal and Lambert chose their bilingual subjects on the basis of bilingual ability as measured by tests in English and French. Children were chosen for the bilingual groups whose English (the second language) matched their French. It seems likely that only more linguistically gifted and intelligent French–Canadian children are capable of acquiring, by the age of 10, a command of English equal to their command of French (Macnamara, 1966). Thus the method of selection may have led to a sample of children who were more intelligent to begin with than the monolingual comparison group.

This research again underscores the difficulty of comparing groups of monolingual and bilingual individuals. The matched group, single measure design almost invariably leaves open the question of whether the groups differ with respect to bilingualism and nothing else. This design can be illustrated as follows:

Matched Groups + Independent Variables → Dependent Variable
Group X   Monolingual experience   IQ
Group Y   Bilingual experience   IQ

Such a design involves matching Groups X and Y on all relevant factors and taking a single measure of IQ. The methodological difficulties in research of this nature discourage any attempt at generalization.

Another methodological approach to investigating the effect of bilingualism on intelligence is to study the longitudinal effects of bilingualism on IQ. That is, rather than comparing monolingual and bilingual groups of children at one point in time, it is possible to see what effect bilingualism has on a group of children over an extended period of time by measuring IQ repeatedly. This design, which can be called a matched groups, repeated measures design, can be illustrated as follows:

Matched + groups	Matching + variable	Independent variable	Dependent variable
Group X	IQ	Monolingual Experience	IQ
Group Y	IQ	Bilingual Experience	IQ

Here the groups are matched on all relevant variables *and* on IQ, as measured at time A. Subsequent measures of IQ at times B, C, and so forth should indicate whether there is some effect of the bilingual experience on measures of intelligence. This was essentially the procedure employed in the St. Lambert project (Lambert & Tucker, 1972). Yearly retesting of the students in the project with standard measures of intelligence revealed no signs of any intellectual deficit or retardation attributable to the bilingual experience. Nor were there any symptoms of their being handicapped on measures of creative thinking. The findings in other Canadian total and partial immersion programs also reveal no long-term effect on intellectual functioning as a result of the bilingual experience.

BILINGUALISM AND LANGUAGE SKILLS

What effect does bilingualism have on the child's language skills in the two languages? We saw earlier that it appears to be difficult for an individual to maintain two languages in perfect balance. The environment is rarely perfectly bilingual, and usually the individual will need to use one language more than the other in daily life. Does this mean that one language inevitably suffers—that the more English French-speaking children use, for example, the more their French suffers, and vice versa? What evidence is there that bilingualism has a detrimental effect on one or both of the speaker's languages?

In a review of the research on the effect of bilingualism on language development, Jensen (1962) reported that much of the literature asserts that the bilingual child encounters many problems in language development. According to some authors, the child's active and passive vocabulary is smaller because the child must learn two words for each referent. Even the total number of terms is likely to be less than the total number for the monolingual child. The bilingual tends to use fewer different words and develops a confused, mixed vocabulary because of lexical borrowings and the tendency to hyphenate words. Bilingual children use shorter sentences, more incomplete sentences, fewer compound and complex sentences, fewer interrogative and more exclamatory sentences. According to these authors, confused structural patterns, unusual word order, and errors in agreement and dependency characterize the bilingual's speech. Bilingual children make many errors in the use of verb and tense, connectives, prepositions, nouns, pronouns, and articles (especially indefinite articles) that the monolingual child does not make. They misuse idiomatic expressions, err in their choice of synonyms, frequently fail to inflect words, and use the negative incorrectly.

Many of these conclusions are based upon research by Smith (1939) in her study of preschool children of non-American ancestry (mainly Chinese) in Hawaii. One confounding factor that limits the generalizability of this research is that pidgin English was quite common in the Chinese community in Hawaii at that time, and perhaps the main reason why the children performed so poorly is that they used this variant of English as their standard.

Other research, as Jensen noted, points to the conclusion that bilingualism is beneficial for the development of language skills. Some authors argue that bilingualism helps individuals become more sensitive to the nuances of language, aids them in their first language, enables them to manipulate languages more effectively, and helps them learn additional languages more easily. Anastasi and de Jesus (1953) found that a group of bilingual, Puerto Rican, preschool children in New York City actually excelled a comparable group of monolingual children in mean sentence length and in maturity of sentence structure in English. Totten (1960) reported that his observation had led him to believe that vocabulary is increased in the bilingual child. Spoerl (1944) concluded that at the college level, bilingual students had no significant language handicap and even possessed some advantages. Authors of case studies (e.g., Leopold, 1949a; Ronjat, 1913; Rūķe–Draviņa, 1967) usually maintain that the advantages in language development outweigh the disadvantages.

There seems to be some evidence that the linguistic disadvantage of the bilingual child disappears with time. Pintner (1932) felt that the language handicap was greatest in the early grades and diminished afterwards, the rate being determined by the individual's intelligence and the opportunity to interact with others in a community where the second language is used. It may be that the chief cause of the early difficulty for many children—especially children from minority ethnic groups—is not so much bilingualism per se as the fact that they are forced to learn a second language in the school.

The literature varies so greatly in quality that almost all general statements are suspect. The usual procedure has been to seek out two groups of children, one monolingual and the other bilingual, to test them in the language common to both, and to compare results. Again, in terms of research design, no conclusion can be made unless the groups are matched on all factors (except bilingualism) that might conceivably affect learning the language. McCarthy (1946) cited several studies that indicate that there is a relationship between socioeconomic status (as determined by father's occupation) and the child's language development. Yet this variable has rarely been controlled. Other important, and often neglected, variables include the child's school, the teacher's language skills, and the teacher's attitudes toward members of ethnic minorities. Finally, there is the child's own intellectual ability and aptitude in language learning. Very few studies have been conducted in which all of these sources of confounding have been controlled.

Among the better, more carefully controlled studies are Carrow's (1957) research with Spanish–English bilinguals and Macnamara's (1966) study of Irish–English bilinguals. Carrow selected 50 bilingual children from the third grade in three San Antonio, Texas, schools, whom she matched for age (mean age 8½ years), nonverbal IQ, and socio-economic status with 50 monolingual children in the same schools. The bilinguals had heard English and Spanish in the home and had been able to converse in both languages from the age of 3. In our terms, they had acquired the two languages simultaneously. Both groups of children were tested in silent reading, spelling, arithmetic reasoning, hearing, vocabulary, reading accuracy and comprehension, and proficiency in articulation. In addition, a 3-minute sample of each child's speech in retelling a story was recorded and analyzed in terms of length of clause, number of types of grammatical error, and so forth.

Significant differences in favor of the monolingual children were obtained in the tests of oral reading accuracy and comprehension and hearing vocabulary. Otherwise the differences between the two groups were not significant, although the means tended to favor the monolingual group. There was no evidence, however, of a detrimental effect due to bilingualism on such linguistic skills as spelling, total verbal output, clause length, degree of subordination, and complexity of sentence structure. Thus Carrow's study suggested that there were some detrimental effects on language skills due to bilingualism but that a surprising number of linguistic skills were unaffected.

Macnamara (1966) studied children ranging in age from 9 to 15, who came from either English- or Irish-speaking family backgrounds in Ireland. The children, who had been exposed to differing amounts of Irish in their education, were compared on various tests of language and arithmetic skills. There were 1,084 boys and girls in the sample from schools in English-speaking districts where instruction was given in English, in Irish, or in both and from schools in Irish-speaking districts where instruction was given in Irish.

All groups were equated statistically for nonverbal IQ, socioeconomic status, and ratings of teacher's skill as teachers (to control for systematic differences between groups due to quality of teaching). The results indicated that children from Irish-speaking families taught in Irish scored significantly higher in Irish than children from English-speaking families taught in Irish. Comparison with British children on English language skills revealed that all Irish samples performed significantly more poorly. Macnamara concluded from this that native speakers of English in Ireland who have spent a substantial proportion of their school time learning Irish achieve a lower score in both written English and written Irish when compared to their English- or Irish-speaking peers whose education is monolingual.

This effect he attributed to amount of exposure. By the nature of things the bilingual child has less exposure to each language than the monolingual child. For this reason, the bilingual's performance in language skills will tend to be inferior in each language separately. Possibly the difference between Carrow's findings and Macnamara's lies in the fact that Carrow had studied bilinguals who acquired their two languages simultaneously, whereas the children in Macnamara's study generally learned their second language after their first language had been established. This difference in the conditions of acquisition—and most likely exposure—is probably responsible for the fact that Carrow's findings indicated that the effect of bilingualism on language development was less negative than Macnamara's did.

The research discussed in the previous chapter on total immersion programs such as the St. Lambert project (Lambert & Tucker, 1972) suggests that instruction in a child's second language need not necessarily have a detrimental effect on the first language. Nonetheless, the second-language skills of the children in total immersion projects never equalled those of monolingual children of the same age. This again is doubtless due to amount of exposure—French monolingual children having much more exposure to the language than English-speaking children who learn French as a second language. The continued progress of the children in the total immersion project in language skills connected with their second language and the lack of evidence that their first language is detrimentally affected appear to indicate that with time the gap is narrowed and that it is possible eventually to achieve what is functionally a high degree of proficiency in two languages.

BILINGUALISM AND EDUCATIONAL ATTAINMENT

What effect does bilingualism have on the child's educational progress? Is it good for a child to have been exposed to two languages, or does such an experience handicap the child educationally? By this point, it should come as no surprise to find that there is considerable disagreement in the literature, some authors arguing that bilingualism retards educational progress and others arguing that it is beneficial to the child's educational progress.

In Jensen's (1962) review of this literature, a number of studies were cited as evidence that the child's interest and aptitude in language learning are adversely affected by bilingualism. According to authors holding this view, the child may become handicapped in reading and studying in general and in specific subjects such as spelling, history, and geography. Interest, initiative, and responsiveness in class may decline, and the child may develop an inadequate adjustment to school and education, which may result in dropping out of school prematurely. Indeed, bilingual children do tend to drop out of class at a lower level than do monolingual children. The bilingual may therefore be severely handicapped in finding future employment. In some countries, such as Wales, the child may be disadvantaged in taking national school examinations.

On the other hand, Jensen also cited research that indicated that the bilingual is in no way handicapped educationally. In fact, according to these authors, bilingualism is more of an educational advantage than a disadvantage. The bilingual child has a sense of prestige and accomplishment that the monolingual child lacks. Knowledge of an additional language stimulates educational efforts in general. Bilingualism provides children with the ability to maintain contact with their immediate cultural group and yet to go beyond it. Their religious and literary interests can be better nurtured through bilingualism. They have an interest in geography and history that monolingual children lack and are more motivated to learn the subjects. Their bilingualism gives them an advantage for social and professional advancement, particularly in the fields of education, religion, diplomacy, writing, and business. They may become interested in travel and art because of their bilingualism.

Some authors reported that bilingualism had no adverse effect on performance at the college level and, in fact, that far from being handicapped the bilingual is superior academically to monolingual counterparts at the college level. This research is especially suspect, however, since there is considerable evidence that bilingual children drop out of education earlier; and so the college sample of bilinguals is a more selective one than is the college sample of monolingual individuals.

Again we are faced with the problem that almost all studies have lacked adequate controls. It has been frequently pointed out that those educational handicaps that were observed in bilingual children were often due to poor home environment, inadequate financial resources, poor health, and negative attitudes toward education generally, rather than to bilingualism per se. Since bilinguals in many of the early studies came from lower socioeconomic brackets and since there was no control for this factor, these studies are of questionable worth. Even more recent studies often fail to take into account such factors as the child's lack of experiential background, acculturation difficulties, lack of teacher awareness of sociocultural differences, the attitudes of the child, and culture conflict (Ulibarri, 1972).

Among the better controlled studies are those of Carrow (1957), Macnamara (1966), and Kellaghan and Macnamara (1967). Carrow, as we have seen, conducted a carefully controlled comparison of Spanish–English bilingual and English, monolingual children in Texas. One of the tests she administered was the California Achievement Test of Problem Arithmetic. Scores on this test indicated that monolingual children performed significantly better, probably because of their superior command of the language of the test—English.

In Macnamara's (1966) study, Irish children were given a test of mechanical arithmetic and a test of problem arithmetic in English or Irish, depending on which language had been their language of instruction for this subject. The results indicated that bilingualism had no effect on mechanical arithmetic but that English-speaking children taught in Irish scored significantly lower than English-speaking children taught in English on problem arithmetic. Macnamara concluded that the use of Irish in teaching problem arithmetic hinders the progress of English-speaking children.

It should be pointed out, however, that the comparison group in this research was tested in Irish, their second language, rather than with an English version of the test given to the other groups. One suspects that this group would have done better relative to other groups had they also been tested on the English version, because such concepts as buying, selling, dividing, and so on would be more vivid in their first language (Lambert & Tucker, 1972).

Reviewing the literature on the effect of instruction in a child's weaker language, Macnamara (1967c) pointed out that millions of students throughout the world are taught subjects such as mathematics, history, and geography in languages other than their first language. He felt that under these circumstances the bilingual child can experience difficulties in the classroom because of ignorance of certain words, idioms, and syntactic structures. Because of a general unfamiliarity with the language of instruction, the child's problem-solving ability can be adversely affected. Macnamara cited the research of Kellaghan and Macnamara (1967) in which children in a bilingual, Irish–English school solved problems in English (their first language) or Irish. There were eight problems such as:

> If the letters of the word *bad* were removed from the alphabet, what would be the fifth letter of the alphabet.

In addition, there was a set of questions for each problem to determine whether the children understood the components of the problem. Children were found to do more poorly when information was presented in Irish, their weaker language, even when the components of the problem were separately understood.

Kellaghan and Macnamara also presented three arithmetic problems expressed in both Irish and English to two groups of children, all of whom spoke English as their first language. Half of the children had been taught all of their subjects in Irish and the other half in English. All children read the problems aloud three times, and the time for each problem was recorded. For both groups the first reading of the Irish version took significantly longer than the first reading of the English version. Kellaghan and Macnamara suggested that one reason why children perform more poorly in their second language is that they have difficulty processing input in that language (relative to their first language) both at the perceptual and at the syntactic and semantic levels.

In further research on this problem Macnamara (1967c) reported that college students had more difficulty determining the semantic value of French words (their second language) than of English words, even when individual differences in perceptual thresholds for the same words and sentences were controlled. Semantic decoding was found to be a more important factor in problem solving in a second language than was articulation of individual words or the differential use of sequential probabilities between words in the person's two languages. Macnamara suggested that other factors are also important: that bilinguals probably encode ideas and carry out syntactic organization more slowly in their second language.

There is some evidence that suggests that as the bilingual becomes more facile in the second language, the deleterious effect of being instructed in that language disappears. Malherbe's (1946) research with South African children taught arithmetic in their weaker language, English or Afrikaans, indicated that the children quickly recovered from an initial handicap to come even with those children taught in their first language. These children seemed to have had a command of their second language that was superior to that of Macnamara's Irish children (Macnamara, 1967c), and it is likely that the critical variable is command of the second language. As the child's command improves, so will academic performance in subjects taught in that language.

Support for this notion comes from the findings of Lambert and Tucker (1972) that English-speaking children taught French from kindergarten on and immersed in a French school environment did as well as their French-speaking classmates in arithmetic in the early grades, although French was their second language. The same result has been obtained in an immersion project with English-speaking children taught arithmetic in Spanish (Cohen, 1974). Follow-up studies of children in the St. Lambert project have shown that these children do as well as English controls on tests of science and social studies skills, on tests of mathematical and scientific knowledge, and on tests of mathematical skills, including problem-solving ability (Bruck, Lambert, & Tucker, 1974).

Since it seems likely that the children in the total immersion projects have better control of their second language than do bilingual children investigated in other studies, the child's skill in the second language appears to be the critical factor influencing the effect that bilingualism has on educational progress. If the child learns a second language in a favorable, nonthreatening environment, progress in this language will probably be rapid and will not detrimentally affect other aspects of learning. In contrast, Chicano or Puerto Rican children thrust into the American school system and not speaking the more prestigious language may be threatened and inhibited by the experience. In this case, the results may be detrimental to the child's academic development.

BILINGUALISM AND EMOTIONAL ADJUSTMENT

Here again we find the familiar pattern. Some studies indicate that bilingualism has a detrimental effect on emotional adjustment and character formation. It has been argued that bilinguals may be morally depraved because they have not received effective religious instruction in their mother tongue (Gali, cited in Weinreich, 1953) and that bilinguals are "mercenary relativists" who switch principles according to the exigencies of the situation, just as they switch languages (Sander, cited in Weinreich, 1953). Bilingualism is seen to cause tension and emotional lability as well as other psychological disorders (e.g., stuttering).

Other authors argue that the emotional conflicts that the bilingual experiences are not caused by learning two languages but by the hostile attitudes of society. The bilingual may be forced to develop protective devices such as a restrained manner of speaking, inconspicuous behavior, and introversion as a shield against social antagonism. Pintner and Arsenian (1937), however, found no emotional handicap in a group of New York City, Jewish, bilingual children, and Weinreich (1953) cited evidence that tends to disprove the alleged detrimental effects of bilingualism on emotional life.

The most sensible conclusion seems to be that it is not bilingualism that leads to whatever maladjustment might be found but socioeconomic considerations such as being in an inferior social group and having poor teachers and schools. In addition, there are the difficulties that arise from the conflicts of biculturalism— that is, having to adjust to two ways of life, customs, and values.

In this sense, the bilingual's problems of emotional adjustment are very real. The bilingual belongs, yet not fully, to two communities. This produces conflicts of behavior and the stigma of inferiority that may bring out undesirable personality traits (Christophersen, 1973). Anomie often leads to mental tension and stress. But this emotional problem is environmentally determined and does not result from any strain caused by having to cope with two languages.

Indeed, the characterization of the bilingual as a "marginal man," lacking a sense of self- and group-identity, has been criticized as overdrawn (Goldberg, 1941). If bilinguals are members of a community of other bilingual individuals as, for example, most Chicano and Puerto Rican Americans are, it is misleading to think of them as marginal, suffering from the psychological repercussions of anomie. It is their culture that is marginal, which is psychologically a quite different experience. Within that culture the individual can develop a strong sense of identification and personal worth.

This sense of belonging to a subculture within the dominant culture may be a central part of the individual's identity. To lose one's accent is to identify with the dominant society and way of life. Resistance to such a personal submersion within the dominant culture may be quite strong in many cases. A foreign accent is often the badge of an individual's ethnic and cultural identity.

Indeed, it is possible for the bilingual to overcome both individual and group marginality and become an integrated member of both dominant and subgroup cultures. In a famous study of second-generation Italians living in New England, Child (1943) found that there were three reactions to the strain of biculturalism: one group of adolescents studied by Child rebelled against their Italian background and attempted to make themselves as American as possible; a second group rebelled in the opposite direction, rejecting everything American and identifying themselves with their Italian heritage; a third group tried to avoid the conflict by refusing to think of themselves in ethnic terms at all.

Following Child's lead, Aellen and Lambert (1969) studied adolescent boys of bicultural parentage in Canada and found the same basic subgroups and one more: a subgroup of individuals who had achieved membership in both groups and had successfully adjusted to their bicultural identity. When compared with English- and French–speaking controls, the boys showed no signs of personality disturbance, anomie, or feelings of alienation. Their attitudes and values suggested cultural fusion—the boys had managed to identify successfully with both parents and both cultures.

A number of researchers have attempted to determine whether bilingualism leads to a reduction in prejudice toward other ethnic and linguistic groups. The best study of this nature is that of Lambert and Tucker (1972) in the St. Lambert project. As we saw in the previous chapter, the children in this study showed initially more favorable attitudes toward French people than control students, but these differences disappeared by the third grade. This development was attributed to a number of causes: an accumulation of French–English tensions that were particularly acute at that time, a desire on the part of the experimental children to be normal (not overly French), and the special experience the children had with a nonrepresentative group of French–Canadian children following a separate French-medium program in the same school.

In the following year, the attitudes of the children were again tested through a comprehensive, interview-type questionnaire. This time the attitudes of the experimental children were unmistakably more positive toward French-speaking people than were those of English-speaking control children. The experimental children appeared to be much more closely identified with the French people and the French way of life. They seemed to think of themselves as both English– and French–Canadians in outlook (Lambert & Tucker, 1972).

In the sixth grade the attitudes of the experimental groups indicated that they identified fully with their own ethnic group as well as with Canadian and European, French-speaking groups. They were not essentially different in this regard from English–Canadian control children, presumably because these children were in a French-as-a-second-language program that should also have fostered favorable views toward French-speaking people. By contrast, the French–Canadian control children were found to draw sharp contrasts between their own ethnic group and other peoples (Bruck, Lambert, & Tucker, 1974).

This seems to provide some evidence at least that bilingual education leads to a more liberal and enlightened perception of other ethnic groups. But a number of questions are unanswered. If Bruck, Lambert, and Tucker had included an English-speaking control group that had no exposure to the French language, more dramatic differences in attitude might have been obtained. It would also have been interesting to see if the more positive attitudes generalized to other ethnic minority groups as well. As in other areas of research on the effects of bilingualism, the results of research concerning bilingualism and attitudes are suggestive but not definitive.

BILINGUALISM AND COGNITIVE FUNCTIONING

What we have learned about the effects of bilingualism to this point seems rather obvious—even uninteresting. Although research is fraught with methodological pitfalls and very few of the hundreds of studies that have been conducted have been adequately controlled, several statements seem possible:

- Bilingualism seems to have little effect on intelligence, if intelligence is measured by nonverbal tests. If tests are employed that have a large language component, the bilingual child is usually at a disadvantage and does more poorly than monolingual children.
- Bilingual children do more poorly on measures of language skills when compared to monolingual control children, depending on the difference in amount of exposure to the language between bilingual and monolingual children.
- Bilingual children tend to do more poorly than monolingual children in academic subjects where verbal ability is a factor, depending on the bilingual's amount of exposure to and skill in the language.
- The effect of bilingualism on emotional adjustment and attitudes toward other ethnic groups appears to depend on a large number of possibly uncontrollable environmental factors.

It should not be surprising that the bilingual child is at an initial disadvantage in the second language when compared to children for whom that language is the first and only language. The negative effects of bilingualism probably diminish with age so that the "bilingual handicap" disappears after a few years of schooling (Christophersen, 1973). Indeed, under certain circumstances, as in the Canadian immersion studies, there seems to have been no bilingual handicap at all. In less favorable circumstances, bilingual children may need some special help with language in the early grades so that their initial disadvantage in command of the language does not prevent them from developing competence in areas with a large verbal component.

In recent years many investigators have turned away from the traditional questions and have begun to probe more deeply into what effects bilingualism has on the individual's cognitive functioning. Instead of focusing on differences between groups on measures of IQ or school performance where one reaches the obvious conclusion that command of the language is important, these researchers have asked what bilingualism can tell us about the nature of intellectual development. There have been essentially two lines of research: the first is concerned mainly with the correlates of bilingualism and specific aspects of cognitive functioning in the bilingual individual; the second line of research is more concerned with what can be learned about human cognitive processes through the study of the bilingual.

Bilingualism and Cognition

One of the earliest statements about the relationship between bilingualism and cognition was that of Leopold (1949a), who felt that the effect of bilingualism on his daughter's development was essentially positive. The chief gain was that the normal childish habit of clinging to a single wording (e.g., in rhymes, songs, or bedtime stories) seemed to be missing in Hildegard. From a very early age, she would render a story freely in both languages. When memorizing rhymes or songs she would often destroy the rhyme with her own insertions of meaningfully related vocabulary. She readily accepted new names for objects already denoted in one language and asked to be given the name in the second language. Leopold attributed this looseness of the link between the phonetic word and its meaning to the fact that the bilingual child hears the same thing constantly designated in two different phonetic forms, so that form and meaning are not rigidly identified with each other.

Ianco–Worrall (1972) tested Leopold's notion that there is a looseness in the link between phonetic word and meaning in bilingual children by comparing the responses of Afrikaans–English, bilingual children and matched control groups of monolingual, English- and monolingual, Afrikaans-speaking children. In her first experiment, she gave the children a semantic or phonetic preference test, a two-choice test on which similarity between words could be interpreted on the basis of shared meaning or shared acoustic properties. For example, the child was asked, *I have three words: "cap," "can," and "hat." Which is more like "cap"—"can" or "hat"?* A response of *can* was interpreted as indicating a phonetic preference, and the choice of *hat* was seen to indicate a semantic preference.

There were two groups of children in each condition, 4- to 6-year-old children and 7-to-9-year-old children. Bilingual children were tested in both languages. Table 7.1 shows the percent of children in each group whose choices reflected semantic or phonetic preferences. Bilingual children showed a significantly greater tendency to respond on the basis of the semantic properties of the stimuli than did monolingual children. As can be seen from the table, this effect was due mainly to the fact that in the bilingual groups, both younger and older children tended to interpret meanings semantically rather than phonetically, whereas only with older, monolingual children was this the case.

In a second experiment, Ianco–Worrall had children perform three tasks:

- Give explanations for names (*Why is a dog called "dog"?*)
- Tell if names could be interchanged (*Suppose you could make up names for things, could you call a dog "cow" and a cow "dog":*)

TABLE 7.1
Preferences for Semantic and Phonetic Dimensions
Among Monolingual and Bilingual Children[a]

			Choice	
Test and age	Group	Number of subjects	Semantic	Phonetic
English:				
4 to 6 years	Monolingual	12	46%	54%
	Bilingual	13	68%	32%
7 to 9 years	Monolingual	16	60%	40%
	Bilingual	17	67%	33%
Afrikaans:				
4 to 6 years	Monolingual	13	49%	51%
	Bilingual	13	60%	40%
7 to 9 years	Monolingual	17	64%	36%
	Bilingual	17	66%	34%

[a] From Ianco–Worrall (1972).

• Interchange names in play (*Let's play a game. Let us call a dog "cow"*) and answer questions about the properties of the object (*Does this "cow" have horns? Does this "cow" give milk?*)

There were no differences on the first task—both bilingual and monolingual children of different ages gave the same types of explanations for why things have specific names (perceptible attributes, social convention, functional attributes, arbitrary justification, etc.). On the second task, less than 20% of the monolingual children but more than 50% of the bilingual children consistently answered that names of objects could be interchanged. Finally, responses to the last task indicated that older children were more willing to interchange the names of objects in play than were younger children, but there were no significant differences between monolingual and bilingual children on this task.

Ianco–Worrall interpreted her findings as indicating that Leopold's observations were valid. Particularly impressive was the fact that of the 4-to-6-year-old children in her sample, 54% of the bilingual children consistently chose to interpret similarity between words in terms of the semantic rather than the phonetic dimension. Of the monolingual children of the same age, only one English-speaking child and no Afrikaans-speaking children showed the same choice behavior. While bilingual children did not perform better than monolingual children on tasks where names were conceived to be aspects of things, they did perform better when the task required the formulated concept that names are arbitrarily assigned to things.

In a study of the relationship between bilingualism and intellectual functioning, Peal and Lambert (1962) gave a battery of tests to 10-year-old bilingual and monolingual children in middle-class schools in Montreal and found that a factor analysis of 31 variables indicated that the bilingual group possessed a more diversified set of mental traits than the monolingual group. The bilingual children performed significantly better than monolingual children on tests of mental flexibility, concept formation, picture completion, and figure manipulation, among others. All of these tests can be viewed as involving some sort of symbolic reorganization, and Peal and Lambert speculated that since bilingual children have two symbols for every object, they must conceptualize environmental events in terms of their general properties without reliance on linguistic symbols. They are thus more skilled than monolinguals in abstract concepts and relations. A similar argument has been made by other authors as well (Christophersen, 1948; Haugen, 1956; Hoffman, 1934).

A caution should be inserted at this point since, as we mentioned earlier, the method of selection used by Peal and Lambert favors the bilingual group. Bilingual children were selected whose English (their second language) was as good as their French ("balanced" bilinguals). Such 10-year-old children are no doubt linguistically gifted, and this could account for their superior performance on language-related tasks.

In a study of the cognitive flexibility of bilingual children, Landry (1974) found that sixth grade children in a FLES program performed significantly better than monolingual children on a test of divergent thinking ability that measured such aspects of cognitive functioning as fluency, flexibility, and originality. At the fourth grade level, however, there was no significant difference between bilingual and monolingual children. This Landry attributed to the fact that children in the younger group had not yet begun to read and write in their second language and hence were not aware of differences in orthography, grammar, and structure. In a similar study, Balkan (1970) found that bilingual 11- to 17-year-old children demonstrated greater cognitive flexibility than monolingual counterparts in a series of tests with socioeconomic class and intelligence controlled. Feldman and Shen (1971) found that bilingual children in a Head Start program performed better in object constancy tests, naming tasks, and in the use of names in sentences than monolingual children in the same program.

This research suggests that bilingual children have greater cognitive flexibility than do monolingual children. Landry felt that bilingual children have learned to overcome the negative transfer of their first language in learning their second, and this experience makes them less susceptible to negative transfer generally. As a result, bilinguals acquire a "flexibility set," which is beneficial in divergent thinking tasks that require inventiveness and originality. The child has developed an adaptability in learning a second language that can be used profitably in other cognitive tasks.

Experimental children in the St. Lambert project also scored higher than control children on tests of divergent thinking used to measure cognitive flexibility. In the most recent report, however, the differences between groups were not significant (Bruck, Lambert, & Tucker, 1974). The authors were content with the observation that the evidence indicated that no harmful effects to cognitive flexibility could be attributed to participation in the bilingual program.

One of the more interesting findings in the St. Lambert project was that English-speaking children, taught in French, transferred the skills of reading and calculating from French to English without being instructed in these skills in English. In discussing this finding, Lambert and Tucker (1972) made reference to the work of the Russian psychologist, L. S. Vygotsky (1962). Vygotsky distinguished two kinds of knowledge: "spontaneous" knowledge and "scientific" knowledge. Spontaneous knowledge referred to familiar, everyday concepts and scientific knowledge to formal, school-learned concepts. In his research with young school children, Vygotsky asked them to complete sentences following such words as *although* and *because*. Spontaneous concepts were incorporated into familiar, everyday situations in sentences like *The boy fell off his bicycle because . . .* , and scientific concepts were incorporated into sentences such as *Economic planning is possible in the USSR because . . . .* Vygotsky found that the scientific concepts were mastered and understood earlier than the spontaneous ones. That is, 8-year-old children made more mistakes in the testing situation when they had to complete sentences having to do with familiar, everyday situations (*The boy fell off his bicycle because he was taken to the hospital*) than when the sentences dealt with scientific concepts (*If a ball rolls off a table, it will fall downwards because of the force of gravitation*).

Vygotsky argued that children lack awareness of everyday concepts—although they use them correctly outside of the formal testing situation. They cannot yet work with spontaneous concepts in a flexible manner, whereas they are more adaptable in dealing with scientific concepts because a teacher has brought them more into consciousness through explanation, examples, questions, and corrections. Because of this learning experience the child makes more intelligent use of spontaneous concepts: Once a number of scientific concepts are mastered, Vygotsky felt that the awareness accompanying their development spreads to everyday concepts, so that by the age of 10 the child is using both types of concepts intelligently.

This brings us to Lambert and Tucker's findings regarding transfer of learning from one language to another. Vygotsky concluded his discussion by making an analogy with second-language learning, a process—like the learning of scientific concepts—that is conscious and deliberate (assuming that the learning takes place in the classroom setting). The child is drilled and made conscious of rules and how these rules apply to new situations. This awareness, like the awareness of scientific concepts, spreads to the more familiar, everyday language, so that a second language facilitates mastering the higher forms of one's own language. The child learns to see the first language as one particular system among many, to view its phenomena under more general categories; and this leads to awareness in everyday linguistic operations.

This transfer of concepts and linguistic principles appears to be quite similar to the abstract form of learning whereby the child, in mastering reading and computational skills in one language, transfers this knowledge to another language. The awareness of principles of reading and arithmetic that the child gained in one language is available in the second language without any conscious learning having to occur. Lambert and Tucker suggested that further research on the process of reading and calculating in a bilingual's weaker language may throw more light on the independent roles played by language and thought in the child's cognitive development than would be possible with monolingual children learning through a single language.

In conclusion, there seems to be some evidence that bilingualism has a positive effect on cognitive functioning. The bilingual child seems to be more aware of the conventional and arbitrary nature of linguistic symbols than is the monolingual child and may have a consequent advantage in tasks that require abstract reasoning skills. Bilingual children also have been shown to be more flexible in cognitive operations than are monolingual children. Bilinguals have the advantage of a learning experience in which they come to understand that the linguistic rules acquired in the first language are not immutable. If they are made conscious of the rules of the new language and are taught to apply the rules to new situations, they may be more skilled in the advanced forms of their first language.

These statements, however, are by no means the final word. Research on the effects of bilingualism on cognitive functioning has just begun, and the amount of ignorance about the topic is still substantial. The initial bias seems to have been toward positive results favoring bilingualism; but this may stimulate iconoclasts, and negative results may begin to appear in the literature.

Cognition and Bilingualism

I would like to turn now to studies concerned with bilingualism as a cognitive operation. This research is directed at understanding how the bilingual's two language systems interact and how they are usually kept functionally independent in usage. Research has tended to focus on three questions: how is it that the bilingual can switch off one language system while utilizing the other and then, without obvious difficulty, switch on the previously inactivated system and switch off the first system? Second, how are the bilingual's two language systems stored in the brain? Third, how does the bilingual translate meaning from one language system into the other?

Switching. The bilingual is able to know the entire phonological, semantic, and syntactic systems of two languages and to store, retrieve, and process these two systems with relatively little interference from one system on the other. One theory of how this is possible is that the neurological systems underlying the two languages are functionally separate in such a way that when one is "on" the other must be "off" (Penfield & Roberts, 1959). This theory is known as the *single-switch* theory since it postulates that the whole system associated with either language is controlled by a single switching mechanism.

In a test of this theory (Preston & Lambert, 1969) used a bilingiual version of the Stroop Color–Word Test, in which subjects were shown a series of color words printed in a variety of colors, the color of the ink always differing from the color of the word that is the name (e.g., the word *red* colored blue). The subject was told to ignore the word and name the color of the ink. The subjects were French–English bilinguals who were given color names in English and French and were asked to respond in either English or French. The response times were compared with control conditions in which patches of color and noncolor words were used.

The subjects took longer to respond to the color of the ink when color words were used than when noncolor words were used, but there were little differences between the various experimental conditions. This was interpreted as evidence against the single-switch theory, since if the system of one language was off when the subject was responding in the other language, conditions in which the color word was printed in French and the response was given in English should have taken less time than conditions in which the color word was printed in French and the response given in French. That is, the theory predicts that when the color word and response are in different languages, subjects will have no trouble ignoring the color word (since that language system is shut off) and will respond just as quickly as if they were merely naming patches of color. In contrast, when the color word and the response are in the same language, the subject should have more difficulty ignoring the color word (since that system is switched on). Yet no differences were found between conditions.

Macnamara (1967b) proposed a *two-switch* model of bilingual functioning, in which one switch governs the interpretation of the language system to be employed in interpreting speech (input switch) and the other governs the selection of the language system that is to be employed in producing speech (output switch). The input switch is not subject to voluntary control, but the output switch is. Such a model would account for the Preston and Lambert findings, since the requirement to respond in French would mean that the language was meant to be the output system, but not necessarily the input system. The input system would automatically be in the language of the color word stimuli. If one assumes that the semantic values of corresponding French and English color words are equally disruptive of the subject's performance, the results appear to be in keeping with the theory.

Subsequent studies by Macnamara and others have focused on various aspects of the two-switch theory. Macnamara, Krauthammer, and Bolgar (1968) examined the operation of the output switch by having bilingual subjects express a linguistically neutral stimulus—for example, a written numeral—in a linguistic form, first in one language, then in another, and then alternating between languages. Subjects were found to require more time under the alternating conditions where the task requires linguistically mixed outputs.

Kolers (1966b) also found that mixed responding takes longer than responding in a single language. In his experiment, French–English bilinguals were asked to read and spontaneously produce passages in which the two languages were either mixed or in one language only. He found that while the comprehension of the mixed passages was not inferior to that of the monolingual ones, speeds for reading and spontaneous production were significantly slower. In addition, he found a tendency, when coming to the end of a string in one language, to switch toward the pronunciation system of the other language (giving English words a French pronunciation and vice versa). This appears to indicate that the two switches are not entirely independent.

Macnamara and Kushnir (1971) conducted three experiments concerned with the input switch of the two-switch model. In the first experiment, bilingual subjects read continuous passages that were bilingual or monolingual. The bilingual passages took more time to read than the monolingual passages, indicating that switching takes an observable amount of time.

In the second experiment, subjects were presented with individual sentences— some of which were bilingual and some monolingual—and had to signal whether the sentences were true or false. Some bilingual sentences required a single switch (*Horses smoke pomme de terre*), some two switches (*Des chevaux must manger*), and some three switches (*Les oiseaux have deux wings*). Table 7.2 gives the mean response times for sentences for bilingual subjects whose native languages were English or French. The results indicated that the amount of time to process sentences increased with the number of required switches.

In the third experiment, Macnamara and Kushnir had subjects listen to tape recordings of sentences, some of which were bilingual and some monolingual, and signal whether they were true or false. Again sentences that required switching took longer to process than sentences that did not. Furthermore, when the subjects were presented with sentences in a fixed pattern, one monolingual and the next mixed, the amount of time required to process the mixed sentences increased even more when compared to a random sequence in which subjects

TABLE 7.2
Mean Response Times to Verify Sentences[a]

	N	English	French	Number of switches One	Two	Three
Native speaker of English	16	1.86	1.92	2.15	2.30	2.38
Native speaker of French	14	1.91	1.88	2.05	2.23	2.38

[a] From Macnamara and Kushnir, 1971.

could not anticipate whether a sentence would be mixed or not. It seemed that attempting to anticipate a switch in input slowed the subject up. This Macnamara and Kushnir interpreted as evidence that the input switch is automatic and not under voluntary control.

If switching takes time, how is it that a bilingual easily and without pausing switches from one language to another for stylistic reasons? Macnamara (1967b) speculated that bilinguals can do this without difficulty because they can carry out semantic encoding and organization in one language system while more or less mechanically producing in the other language material that has already been encoded.

In support of this hypothesis, Macnamara cited a study in which he had Irish–English, bilingual subjects read two types of lists in three different ways. The lists were either random numbers from 1 to 20 or two sums of money arranged in random order. The subject had to read both lists in English, in Irish, and then switching languages for each item. The language in which the item was to be read was cued by the color in which it was written.

As expected, the mixed lists took longer to read than the lists read in either language separately. There was no difference between number and money lists in the monolingual condition, but numbers took longer to read than the money list in the mixed condition. Macnamara reasoned that in the money lists subjects responded more quickly because they could anticipate the language of the next item while responding more or less mechanically to the item at hand. (Why this could not be done as quickly with numbers was left unclear.) When the subjects were given money lists in which they could not anticipate the language of the next item, the reading time increased sharply.

Macnamara concluded that the results support the hypothesis that in normal discourse bilinguals switch without apparent pause because they anticipate the switch while speaking and thus avoid disrupting the flow of their speech. If the switch cannot be anticipated, speech is disrupted. Apparently the anticipation of a language switch is advantageous, even though speakers do not yet know what they are to say in that language. It seems that the language system can be made ready for a response even before the response has been determined.

Note that in a task involving the input switch, such as the sentence verification task used by Macnamara and Kushnir (1971), attempting to anticipate a switch slowed down performance. In a task involving the output switch, such as reading or sentence production, anticipation of a switch facilitates performance. According to the theory, this is due to the fact that the input switch is not under voluntary control, whereas the output switch is. Attempting to anticipate only interferes with the automatic processing of incoming information, whereas it facilitates the organization of information on the output side.

The fact that switching languages requires time means that switching runs counter to psychological "inertia" and is not a random but a deliberate process in language production (Macnamara & Kushnir, 1971). This supports the contention of Gumperz and Hernández–Chavez (1972) that the code switching of

Mexican–American speakers is a meaningful operation, meant to convey to the listener something over and above what is said. It takes some psychological effort to change codes, and speakers switch because there is something to be communicated by doing so.

Macnamara (1967b) typified the bilingual as similar to a musician who observes the notation for key at the beginning of a piece of music and then forgets about it, though in playing the musician performs the actions appropriate to the key. Similarly, bilinguals manage to forget about the language they are speaking and yet obey the rules of that language. When they are required to switch to their other language, they can readily do so, although constant switching may strain their linguistic ability and disrupt performance. The evidence suggests that bilinguals are able to switch easily from language to language when they can anticipate the language switch.

Storage.   Another area of research interest is bilingualism and memory. Psychologists and psycholinguists have studied bilingual individuals to gain insight into the structure of memory and the organization of psychological processes. In this research bilingual subjects typically learn lists of words in each of their languages separately and then a mixed list containing words from both languages. The question posed is whether recall for mixed lists is poorer than recall for lists containing only items from a single language.

According to Macnamara's two-switch theory one would expect that the mixed lists would be more difficult to recall than the monolingual lists, since the two languages are encoded separately and are presumably stored in separate memories, which are kept in relative isolation from each other. Activation of both of these memories in the mixed-list condition requires switching back and forth between systems and should therefore be a more difficult task than activating a single memory system.

An alternate hypothesis has been proposed by Kolers (1966a), who maintained that bilinguals store information in one memory system only. Items are stored in terms of their semantic features, with some means of "tagging" the items with the proper language at the time of output. Since there is some confusion in the literature as to the appropriate nomenclature for these hypotheses (both hypotheses being called by different authors the "independence" hypothesis), I shall refer to Macnamara's position as the *two-tank* hypothesis, since it proposes that there are separate storage tanks for the bilingual's two languages and to Kolers's hypothesis as the *one-tank* hypothesis.

In support of his hypothesis, Kolers (1966a) reported that subjects required to recall items from mixed- and single-language lists did just as well under all conditions and made amazingly few translation errors. Furthermore, repetition of items in translation was just as helpful for recall as repetition in the same language. Apparently, no extra storage space is required for identifying items as being in one language or the other.

These findings were confirmed by Lambert, Ignatow, and Krauthammer (1968) and Nott and Lambert (1968), who found that single- and mixed-language lists were recalled just as well if the lists consisted of unrelated words. When the items in the list could be categorized, however, recall was significantly poorer for the mixed-language lists (Table 7.3). One explanation offered for these findings was that in learning a category list the subject has to decode each word semantically in order to locate it in its appropriate category. This places an extra burden on memory, so that to remember what language the word is in, the subject may have to store the tag and the meaning. In the case of lists of unrelated words, however, no tagging is necessary for storage—each word being remembered as a discrete unit rather than as a concept plus a language tag. This is supported by evidence that translation errors were significantly fewer for the lists of unrelated words than for the category lists. Apparently the category lists made the subjects more confused about language.

Tulving and Colotla (1970) carried this line of research further with trilingual subjects who were given unilingual, bilingual, and trilingual lists to recall. Although primary (short-term) memory (with seven or fewer intervening items) was the same under all conditions, secondary memory (eight or more intervening items) showed that recall of words in unilingual lists was better than for words in bilingual lists; and recall for words in bilingual lists was better than recall for words in trilingual lists. The findings for primary memory were in line with previous research, which indicated that semantic relationships between words in different languages do not influence performance in primary memory tasks (Kintsch & Kintsch, 1969). The findings for secondary memory, however, appeared to contradict those of previous investigators.

Tulving and Colotla interpreted their results in terms of the differential facility with which words from different types of lists can be retrieved from memory. Rather than attributing the difference between unilingual and multilingual lists to differences in the storage of relevant information, they argued that items in the

TABLE 7.3
Mean Number of Items Recalled for Different
Lists by Bilingual Subjects[a]

Languages	Random lists			Category lists			
	English	French	Mixed	English	French	Concordant[b]	Discordant[c]
English–French	10.83	12.65	10.88	19.17	18.21	18.67	15.50
	English	Russian	Mixed	English	Russian	Concordant[b]	Discordant[c]
English–Russian	12.08	12.50	11.40	20.92	17.75	19.04	15.13

[a] From Lambert, Ignatow, and Krauthammer (1968).
[b] Concordant lists are mixed lists in which the items in a category all appear in the same language.
[c] Discordant lists are mixed lists with half of the items in a category in one language and half in the other.

multilingual lists had a lowered accessibility, because such items were not as readily organized into a higher-order unit of information as were items in the unilingual lists. They did not speculate on the reasons why multilingual items were more difficult to organize into higher-order units, but their explanation is congruent with the findings of Lambert and his associates (1968) and Nott and Lambert (1968) in that these investigators also found that there is greater impairment in bilingual lists where greater degrees of organization are required (i.e., when the lists can be categorized).

Kintsch (1970) felt that the organization of learning material into higher-order units involves semantic cues or imagery and not merely language-specific cues. If the lists consist of unrelated words, subjects can apparently rely on language-specific cues, so that if a word is recalled at all it is recalled in the right language. When a list possesses an obvious semantic structure (as in the category lists of Lambert and his associates), the subject uses semantic cues that, in part at least, do not depend on a specific language and are thus more difficult to keep track of in the mixed-list situation. In a series of experiments, Kintsch demonstrated that the demands of the task can be manipulated so that bilingual subjects will respond on the basis of either language-specific or general semantic cues. When subjects were asked to tell whether the language in which a word was presented was changed or not in a recognition memory task, they relied on language-specific cues. When subjects had to tell whether a word or its translated equivalent had appeared in the list before, they responded on the basis of semantic cues. The data indicated, however, that subjects could not completely disregard one set of cues when responding on the basis of the other; there was considerable overlap, suggesting that language-specific cues intrude when subjects are concentrating on word meaning, and meanings interfere with recognition of language-specific forms.

At this point, it is probably a good idea to recall the two original hypotheses that stimulated this line of research. The one-tank hypothesis assumes that bilinguals have one memory store with words identified in terms of their semantic features and somehow tagged at the output stage with language-specific cues. The two-tank hypothesis assumes that there are two memory stores, one for each language. The research of Lambert and his associates (Lambert, Ignatow, & Krauthammer, 1968; Nott & Lambert, 1968) supports the one-tank hypothesis in that there was no difference between mixed and unmixed lists when they consisted of unrelated items. Only when the items were related and the task therefore imposed additional memory requirements on the subjects (stressing semantic cues, rather than language-specific cues) was there poorer recall of mixed material (presumably because the subject must remember semantic aspects of a given item as well as its language).

In contrast to the one-tank hypothesis, Tulving and Colotla (1970) favored the two-tank hypothesis, which specifies that the two languages of a bilingual represent separate, distinct memory stores. They felt that their data with bilingual and trilingual subjects indicated that free recall of items cannot be organized across languages, but that the organizational processes involve in free recall are restricted to the formation of higher-order retrieval units made up of items in only one or the other language.

Recent research has generally supported the one-tank hypothesis. Studies by Lopez, Hicks, and Young (1974) and Lopez and Young (1974) on retroactive inhibition and familiarization effects indicated that bilinguals stored words in memory in terms of the semantic representation of those words, so that the presentation of a word and its translation activated the same semantic representation in memory. Activation of independent representations by a word and its translation in the second language (the two-tank hypothesis) would not account for the results.

Similarly, research by Saegert and his associates with a negative transfer paradigm (Saegert, Obermeyer, & Kazarian, 1973) and the presentation of overlapping lists of stimulus items (Liepmann & Saegert, 1974) indicated that there was little evidence that bilinguals maintained distinct memories for each language. Instead, the results suggested that subjects process items for recall as semantic entities and, at the same time, process information about the language in which the item is to be produced in output.

In short, the majority of studies indicate that there is a single storage for the semantic representation of words in memory and that the language tag is also stored in some way so that it can be correctly applied in output. When semantic cues are emphasized, as they were in the category lists used by Lambert and his associates and, presumably, in the research of Tulving and Colotla, there is an impairment of recall because of the added burden of additional memory requirements.

Nonetheless, the debate will no doubt continue. Kolers (1968) went so far as to suggest that both theories are true. In his research with word association tasks, the one-tank theory was supported when concrete words were used, and the two-tank theory was supported when abstract and emotional words were used. He drew a much more complicated picture of bilingual memory storage, suggesting that there are two or more levels of bilingualism in a single individual. On the other hand, his data do not necessarily contradict the one-tank hypothesis, if one assumes that the task requirements in experiments with abstract and emotional words were such as to emphasize semantic cues rather than language-specific cues.

Translation.   A final area where there has been considerable research activity into the cognitive processes of bilingual individuals relates to translation. Reviewing research in this area, Macnamara (1967b) noted that translation is switching codes with the added limitation that the message already encoded in one language must be encoded in the second language. The new message must have the same meaning as the old, so that the key to translation is meaning. The translator must somehow match the semantic representation of one language with its equivalent in the other.

Some research with bilingual subjects has indicated that speed of translating and degree of bilingualism are independent. Lambert, Havelka, and Gardner (1959) had bilingual subjects translate lists of French and English words and found that the time taken to translate the lists did not correlate with measures of degree of bilingualism. Macnamara (1967d) also found no relationship between translation ability and degree of bilingualism. In his experiment, translation ability was measured by the extent to which the individual could emit, in a given time span, words in one language followed by their translation in the second language. Degree of bilingualism was measured by experience in the two languages and production ability (emitting distinct words) in either language.

In interpreting these findings, Macnamara (1967b) argued that, although they appear to indicate that speeds of decoding and encoding are independent of relative ability in the two languages, it is more likely that the task demands of constantly switching codes required in such situations have such a disruptive effect on production in either language that they wiped out any differences associated with degree of bilingualism. Obviously, when one tests the limits of ability by taking persons with a fragmentary knowledge of a second language and comparing them to fluent bilinguals, there will be a difference in relative speeds of decoding and encoding.

This is supported by the research of Treisman (1965), who examined the speed with which bilinguals could carry out simultaneous translation from French to English and vice versa by measuring the extent to which the subject lagged behind the incoming message. She found a significant difference as a function of degree of bilingualism, as one would expect in such a translation task. She also found that the task of translation was made more difficult by increasing the information load presented. Passages with high information and low redundancy were much more difficult to translate than passages with less information and more redundancy.

In a study of simultaneous translation, Oléron and Nanpon (1965) found that skilled translators varied considerably in the speed with which they carried out the translation. Delays ranged from 2 to 10 seconds, most likely as a function of the difficulty experienced by the translator in organizing the material to be decoded. The time to translate appears to depend largely on the location of certain key words, especially the verbs, in sentences. Ten seconds seems to be the outside limit to the length of delay because of the restrictions of short-term memory.

Barik (1972) found that skilled translators make use of the speaker's pauses to deliver their translation and hence to reduce the extent to which they must listen and speak simultaneously. He also noted that translators speak more, regardless of the language they are translating into, than the speakers themselves. Generally, skilled translators show the same pattern of relationship among temporal and speech variables as is found in the speaker's utterances, but the translator's speech is less rhythmic. Sins of omission were more common than sins of addition and were related to the speaker's speech rate and the frequency of grammatical pauses in delivery.

Another question about bilingual cognitive functioning is whether bilinguals translate in their head from their weaker to their stronger language. Macnamara (1967c) reported that English-speaking children given problems to solve in Irish were not aware of translating and believed that they had done their thinking in Irish. From the mutterings (in Irish) of some of the children, Macnamara tended to feel that they were telling the truth. Other evidence comes from the findings of Macnamara and Kushnir (1971) in their study of switching within sentences. Examination of the data from that study (Table 7.2) reveals that all sentences involving more than a single language took more time to validate than sentences in the weaker of the subject's languages. If the bilingual usually translates input sentences from the weaker language into the stronger language, performance should be better on sentences in which part of the translation is already done (i.e., on the mixed sentences). Instead, these sentences are apparently harder to comprehend. Since the bilingual subjects in the Macnamara and Kushnir study were fluent in both languages, these findings do not necessarily generalize to all bilingual subjects. It seems probable that translation is more common in the initial stages of language acquisition or when a particular difficulty is encountered.

This discussion should suffice to give the reader a taste for the kinds of research that are being conducted with bilingual subjects to determine the effect their bilingualism has on cognitive processes. This is obviously an area in its infancy, where theoretical formulations are considerably in advance of empirical facts. There is not enough information at present to decide between theories, even regarding apparently simple questions such as how the bilingual's language systems are stored in memory. Such questions, upon examination, turn out to be not so simple after all.

Of all lines of research discussed in this chapter, further exploration into the effects of bilingualism on cognitive processes will probably be the most rewarding from a psychological point of view. It seems fairly likely that further research on the effects of bilingualism on intelligence, linguistic skills, educational attainment, and even emotional adjustment—with all the methodological exertions this type of research requires—will only provide more evidence that the individual's command of the second language is crucial in deciding whether bilingualism will be a positive and beneficial or a negative and detrimental experience.

In contrast, research on the effects of bilingualism on the individual's cognitive processes promises surprises. The exciting work done in the last decade on cognition and language in monolingual individuals has opened the way for researchers interested in bilingualism. The bilingual individual, with a command of two systems of language and the ability to switch back and forth between them with apparent ease, is an ideal subject for investigating how linguistic information is stored in and retrieved from memory and for studying the mechanisms and determinants of code switching. Since storage and retrieval of linguistic information and code switching are operations that occur in monolingual behavior as well, research with bilingual subjects should have repercussions for our understanding of normal linguistic performance.

8
Conclusion

In the beginning of this book I mentioned that there are a number of common misconceptions about second-language acquisition in children that do not stand up under empirical scrutiny. In concluding, I look at some of these unproven assertions by way of summarizing what is not known about childhood bilingualism. Once the limits of knowledge have been delineated, I set down some propositions I feel are warranted on the basis of research on second-language acquisition in childhood.

SOME COMMON MISCONCEPTIONS

There are a number of widely held beliefs about second-language acquisition in children that are unsubstantiated. Of course, there is a sense in which no scientific statement is ever definitively proven. Scientific knowledge consists of an accumulation of probabilistic statements, some more likely to be true than others. To say that a scientific statement is proven is merely to say that the evidence to date leads one to the conclusion that the proposition is likely to be true. The propositions I shall examine here, however, although often accepted as proven, seem as likely to be false as true. I shall restrict the discussion to six such statements.

Proposition 1. The young child acquires a language more quickly and easily than an adult because the child is biologically programmed to acquire languages, whereas the adult is not.

This is the famous critical period hypothesis advanced by Eric Lenneberg (1967) in his monumental work on the biological foundations of language. This hypothesis is accepted dogma in the writings of many authors discussing second-language acquisition (e.g., Andersson, 1969; Fodor, Bever, & Garrett, 1974;

Jakobovits, 1972; Wilkins, 1972). There are two parts to this proposition: first, the statement that children acquire languages more quickly and easily than adults, and second, the statement that the reason for this superiority is biologically based.

Let us consider the second statement first. Advocates of a critical period notion argue that the child's brain possesses a plasticity with respect to language that the adult's brain has lost. Lenneberg proposed that the reason for this cerebral plasticity relates to the fact that the child's brain is not completely lateralized with respect to language function, whereas the adult's brain is. As evidence he cited research with aphasic adults and children that indicated that damage to the right hemisphere causes more language disturbance in children than in adults and studies that show that adults cannot transfer language functions after left hemispherectomies, whereas children can. He argued from this that it is only before puberty that the brain possesses the plasticity necessary to acquire languages effortlessly through mere exposure.

Recent reanalysis of the data on which Lenneberg based his conclusion has shown that it is not puberty that is the cutoff point for lateralization of language function but that lateralization is essentially complete by the age of 4 or 5. Other recent research points to the same conclusion. If this is the case, the critical period has to be revised downward to between the ages of 2 and 4 or 5. This seems to be counter to the views of advocates of the critical period notion and ignores a great deal of evidence that language learning continues during the elementary school years (Palermo & Molfese, 1972).

In addition, the question of the extent to which components of language are functionally and neurologically asymmetrical is a topic of a great deal of contemporary research, some of which suggests that there is more plasticity with respect to language function after childhood than was previously thought to be the case. Research with split-brain patients, for example, suggests that the minor hemisphere can perform certain linguistic tasks. There are also data from normal patients that point to the same conclusion.

Returning to the first part of the proposition, what evidence is there that children acquire languages more quickly and easily than adults? Some authors have pointed out that the child's first-language acquisition is by no means as quick as is commonly supposed: given the amount of exposure the child has to the language, acquisition appears to be relatively slow. Furthermore, other authors who have had close contact with children feel that first- and second-language acquisition is not as easy for the child as theorists would have it. The language acquisition process is by no means automatic for the young child: there are many false starts and often considerable frustration. The myth of easy and rapid language acquisition by children is reminiscent of the myth of the happy childhood.

Experimental research in which children have been compared to adults in second-language learning has consistently demonstrated the inferiority of young children under controlled conditions. Even when the method of teaching appears to favor learning in children, they perform more poorly than adults. The one area where children have been found to perform better than adults is in pronunciation; otherwise there is little evidence from such studies for their vaunted language-learning talents.

Nonetheless, the literature abounds with anecdotal and impressionistic evidence that children learn faster than adults. Even the United States Supreme Court, in one of its decisions, cited the superiority of the child in language learning (Donoghue, 1968). Is this superiority illusory? One difficulty in answering this question is that of applying the same criteria of language proficiency in the two cases. Communicative competence for the child is something quite different than for the adult. The child's constructions are shorter and simpler, and vocabulary is relative small when compared with what is necessary for adults to speak at the same level of competence in a second language as they achieve in their first language. The child does not have to learn as much to acquire communicative competence as the adult.

Furthermore, there are psychological and social factors that favor the child. Children are likely to have fewer inhibitions and to be less embarrassed when they make mistakes than are adults. Children are likely to speak more and receive more feedback. They may be more motivated than are adults: there is probably more incentive in the playground and school to communicate in the second language than there is for the adult on the job or with friends (who may speak the individual's first language anyway). It frequently happens that children are placed in more situations where they are forced to speak the second language than are adults.

In short, even assuming that the same criteria are applied in both cases and that children are found to be superior to adults in acquiring a second language, there is no way of ruling out the possibility that this difference is caused by psychological and social factors, rather than by biological factors. When the same criteria are applied and other factors are controlled in experimental research, children have invariably done poorer than adults in second-language learning tasks. The one exception is pronunciation, and it may be that there is, in this case, a biological critical period. Even here, however, not enough is known about relevant neurological processes.

Proposition 2. The younger the child, the more skilled in acquiring a second language.

This statement is essentially a corollary of the critical period notion. The argument is that the brain becomes less flexible with age and that it is therefore best to begin as early as possible with second-language training to utilize this neurological plasticity. Researchers dealing with this question, however, have generally found that older children do better in acquiring a second language than younger children. When appropriate controls are employed for amount of exposure to the language, older children have been found to be superior in all aspects of language acquisition—with the exception of phonology. Research with school children has generally indicated that the fifth grade child—not children in earlier grades—is at the optimal age to begin second-language instruction.

These findings should not be understood as indicating that early instruction in a second language or exposure to a second language is in some way detrimental to the child. What they demonstrate is simply that younger children do not necessarily have an advantage over older children and, because of their cognitive and experiential limitations vis-à-vis older children, are actually at a disadvantage in learning a language—other things being equal. The apparent superiority of younger children is probably due, once again, to different criteria of communicative competence, different amounts of exposure, and certain social and psychological factors.

In many situations these nonlinguistic factors work to the advantage of the young child. The preschool child, for example, may have more exposure to a second language in play situations than the school child who experiences a second language as one subject among many in the school curriculum. The younger child may be less inhibited, less afraid of making mistakes, and more willing to learn the language than an older counterpart learning in the classroom (Schumann, 1975).

Indeed, a good deal of the case-study literature points to the advantage of beginning second-language training early, if possible in the family environment simultaneous with exposure to the first language. If persons and situations are kept linguistically distinct, the child is likely to acquire both languages with no more difficulty than the monolingual child acquires a single language. Ronjat's (1913) motto of "one person, one language" appears to be the most important rule for successful, second-language training of young children.

The success of young children in acquiring two languages under such conditions need not be attributed to superior language learning skills. Given the same amount and quality of exposure, an older child (or an adult) would presumably do just as well, most likely better. This, of course, is not to denigrate the young child's achievement or to downgrade the advantages of early introduction to a second language. Older children and adults do not have the amount of time at their disposal for learning a second language that the young child does. There is no reason not to utilize this advantage and to begin language instruction early. The practice of total immersion programs of introducing children to a second language in kindergarten through games, songs, rhymes, and so forth, has produced extremely favorable results and is in all likelihood a more pleasant way to acquire a second language for the child than the repetitious drills that often characterize later classroom instruction.

Proposition 3. Second-language acquisition is a qualitatively different process than first-language acquisition.

This statement can also be viewed as a corollary of the critical period notion. If one assumes that the individual is biologically preprogrammed to acquire a language before puberty and subsequently loses this facility, some way must be provided of accounting for the fact that adults can also learn a second language. This is done by assuming that second-language learning involves radically different processes before and after puberty. Before puberty, the individual has available a language acquisition device that is preprogrammed for optimal linguistic coding. After puberty, a less optimal language acquisition device must be utilized, one based on general cognitive coding ability. This appears to be the position held by Chomsky (1968), who has argued that the mind is divided into faculties and that whereas first-language acquisition takes place through the faculty of language learning, which atrophies at a certain age, subsequent language learning must rely on other faculties of the mind such as the logical or the mathematical.

It is difficult to disprove such a statement, because it does not lend itself readily to empirical testing. What evidence there is, however, does not support Chomsky's view. Research in which adults acquiring a second language were compared to children acquiring the same language as a first language has shown that the adults pass through essentially the same developmental stages as children do in acquiring the target language (Cook, 1973) and that children and adults process language in basically the same ways (Palermo & Howe, 1970). There has not been enough research of this nature, but what work has been done does not support the view that second-language learning in adults and first-language acquisition in children are radically different processes.

Studies of children acquiring a second language have yielded abundant evidence that second-language acquisition involves a developmental sequence that recapitulates the sequence characteristic of the second language rather than that of the child's first language (e.g., Dato, 1971; Milon, 1974; Ravem, 1974). That is, Japanese-, Norwegian-, or Spanish-speaking children learning English do not apply the structures of their first language to English but rather progress through a developmental sequence that is similar to that characteristic of children acquiring English as a first language (although the rate of development varies depending on the age of the child).

Particularly impressive in this connection are the findings of Dulay and Burt (1973) that Chinese- and Spanish-speaking children acquired English morphemes (''functors'') in the same sequence, although the order of acquisition differed greatly in the child's own first language. This suggests that the children were not using the strategies of their first language as the basis for approaching their second. It should be pointed out, however, that there is some disagreement about the implications of the morpheme studies. Longitudinal case studies sometimes show the same results as cross-sectional research (Kessler & Idar, 1977) and sometimes yield very different results (Hakuta, 1974a; Rosansky, 1976). Furthermore, as Rosansky (1976) pointed out, the morpheme order obtained by analyzing spontaneous speech does not always correlate with the morpheme order obtained by elicitation techniques such as the Bilingual Syntax Measure. Indeed, the cross-sectional studies measure the *accuracy* with which morphemes are supplied in obligatory contexts at one point in time, whereas the case studies deal with the *acquisition* of the morphemes as measured by their presence in obligatory contexts at different points in time.

Nonetheless, there is no evidence from the morpheme studies for the contention that second-language acquisition is radically different from first-language acquisition because second-language acquisition is filtered through the structures of the first language and hence involves different processes (Haugen, 1970; Stern, 1970). The evidence suggests that first-language structures have a minimal effect on the course of second-language development. The child seems in some way to develop strategies that derive from properties of the second language rather than from the child's own first language.

This suggests that there is a unity of process that characterizes all language acquisition, whether of a first or second language, at all ages. In acquiring a second language, the individual uses the same strategies that are employed in acquiring a first language, although these strategies are now adapted to the second language so that the sequence of development reflects this language more than the first language. Although there are differences in input conditions, in ability to store and retrieve information, in linguistic knowledge, and so forth, the adult, the older, and the younger child seem to process language in the same way so that the developmental sequence they pass through is remarkably similar.

Proposition 4. Interference between first and second languages is an inevitable and ubiquitous part of second-language acquisition.

In a discussion of the differences between first- and second-language acquisition, Prator (1969) mentioned interference between languages as a factor so obviously influencing second-language acquisition as not to require amplification. The case-study literature, however, suggests that under certain conditions interference between languages rarely occurs. Especially in the simultaneous acquisition of two languages, where the input conditions are such as to allow the child to keep the two languages separate, little interference is found. In reviewing his findings concerning his daughter's language development, for example, Leopold (1949a) reported little evidence for interference in phonology, semantics, or syntax.

Research with children who acquire a second language after a first language has been established also indicates that under certain conditions very little interference occurs. When the larger social milieu provides a supportive context in the sense that the child has peers to communicate with in the second language, interference is minimized. When, on the other hand, the second language is not the language of the child's larger social environment, interference between languages increases. This was proposed as a reason why so much interference between languages is found when a second language is learned in the school and the child has little or no contact with peers who speak the language.

The attempt systematically to identify sources of errors in the speech of second-language learners reveals that relatively few of the errors that second-language learners make can be attributed to interference from their first language.

Generally, no more than a third of the errors in a speech corpus can be identified as due to intrusion of first-language structures. In fact, even this estimate appears to be high. The majority of the errors that second-language learners make are the result of generalizing and misapplying the rules of the second language before they are mastered, oversimplifying morphology and syntax in the way that first-language learners oversimplify, and other errors also found in the developmental data for first-language learners of the target language. Some errors are unique in that they do not seem to reflect developmental factors or first-language structures.

One problem in this area is the difficulty of deciding whether a particular mistake is due to developmental features or to intrusions from the first language. When a Spanish-speaking child says *It no cause too much trouble,* does this mistake reflect the influence of Spanish or a developmental stage that native, English-speaking children also pass through? No unequivocal answer seems possible, and such errors are best classified as ambiguous.

Particularly impressive evidence for the predominance of developmental errors in children's speech comes from the study of Dulay and Burt (1974b), in which they found that speech samples of Spanish-, Chinese-, Japanese-, and Norwegian-speaking children learning English as a second language indicated that the types of mistakes made by the children were strikingly similar. If first-language structures were the major source of a second-language learner's errors, one would expect that children with such structurally dissimilar first languages would make very dissimilar mistakes in their English. Apparently, the child is guided more by input than by previous learning experience (Wagner–Gough & Hatch, 1975).

Research indicates that even under conditions where interference between languages should be greatest—in classroom learning where children have no contact with native-speaking peers—the majority of errors cannot be attributed to interference from first-language structures. Thus, even in the most disadvantageous circumstances, there is little support for the claim that interference is the main source of a speaker's mistakes in a second language. More likely, the second-language learner's errors reflect the strategies employed to decipher the new language and to discover its rules.

This does not mean, incidentally, that interference or transfer errors are unimportant in second-language acquisition. There is some evidence that such errors are more frequent early in the process of second-language acquisition and when the particular construction to be mastered proves especially intractable. In such cases, the child second-language learner uses what information is available to solve the linguistic riddle. And since a first language is available, the child will use it.

Proposition 5. There is a single method of second-language instruction that is most effective with all children.

This statement, upon consideration, seems obviously false, yet it is an assumption that underlies a large number of educational movements. The most recent example is the audio-lingual approach to second-language instruction in the elementary school. This approach seemed ideally suited to the child: it allowed children to learn a second language as they acquired their first—through hearing and speaking the language rather than by translation and learning rules of grammar by rote. Furthermore, the audio-lingual method had the enthusiastic blessing of psycholinguists and behavioral scientists of various persuasions.

Unfortunately, it turned out that children did not possess the miraculous language-learning skills that were ascribed to them. Even though they were taught via a method that was thought to exploit their ability to acquire languages naturally, no wonders occurred. There are a number of reasons why the audio-lingual approach did not live up to expectations, but one of the main reasons was that the rigid application of the method failed to take the needs of individual students into account.

Presently, emphasis is on individualizing instruction by focusing on the student's perception of the learning process. At least lip service is given to the notion that the student should be allowed to choose those ways of learning and that pace of learning that are most congruent with individual abilities and motivation. The problem is that it becomes difficult to implement such an approach in practice. The more heterogeneity the teacher encourages, the more difficult the task becomes. The difficulties of individualizing instruction are doubtless a major reason for the popularity of the single-method doctrine.

If any single method has proven effective it is that of total immersion. This approach has been so successful that it has been adopted in schools throughout Canada and, recently, in the United States. From the beginning of their school (or kindergarten) experience the children in these programs are instructed exclusively in the second language. Carefully conducted research has indicated that the experience is primarily a beneficial one and that in a few years time the children have a fluent grasp of their second language without showing any ill effects in their academic progress in other subjects.

Yet the experience of the Canadian children is much like the experience of Puerto Rican and Chicano children in the United States in that these children too are instructed from their first day in school in a second language. Why is it that these Spanish-speaking children often appear to do poorly in school as a result of being instructed in a second language? The answer is that there are a number of important differences. The Canadian children were not in competition with French-speaking peers in the classroom, whereas the Spanish-speaking children are usually placed in classrooms with native, English-speaking children who have an obvious linguistic advantage. Second, the Canadian children were not members of an ethnic minority group, subject to the stereotyping that membership in a minority group often entails. And third, the Canadian children spoke a first language that was the more prestigious language in their society and were learning the less prestigious language as a second language; in contrast, Spanish-speaking children and other minority children in the United States learn the more prestigious language as their second language.

Lambert and Tucker (1972) did not advance the total immersion method as an educational panacea. They proposed that priority in early bilingual schooling should always be given to the language least likely to be developed otherwise. Some partial immersion technique or mixed approach might be the best method for children from ethnic minorities to begin to learn a second language early in their school career. The main concern, however, should be that the children develop their language skills in their first language, prior to extended exposure to a second language.

Proposition 6. The experience of bilingualism negatively (or positively) affects the child's intellectual development, language skills, educational attainment, emotional adjustment, and/or cognitive functioning.

There is a long tradition of research on these topics. For at least 50 years researchers have been arguing about the negative and positive effects of bilingualism. The reason why there are very few definitive findings is that it is difficult to rule out extraneous factors to assure that the obtained effects can be interpreted as the result of bilingualism and nothing else. In much of the early research, socioeconomic factors were uncontrolled, so that generalizations based on this research are invalid.

There seems to be general agreement that bilingualism has no negative consequences for intellectual development as measured by intelligence on nonverbal IQ tests. When IQ tests with a large verbal component are employed, the bilingual child is at a disadvantage when compared to a monolingual counterpart and usually does more poorly. The evidence that bilingual children do better on tests of intelligence is methodologically suspect.

The evidence concerning language skills and educational attainment is generally inconclusive, although there is some well-controlled research that suggests that bilingual children are, initially at least, handicapped in language skills and in school subjects with a large verbal element. This need not inevitably be the case, however, as is shown by longitudinal research with children in total immersion projects in Canada. Instruction from the beginning of school in the child's second language did not affect performance on tests of language skill in the first language relative to monolingual control groups; nor were there detrimental effects on other school subjects such as social studies and arithmetic.

The results obtained in the St. Lambert project are particularly persuasive because this research employed a longitudinal research design in which children were matched with control children on relevant variables at the beginning of the study and were tested repeatedly to determine the effect of their bilingual experience. Such a design is a considerable improvement over the usual "one-shot" approach, in which independent and dependent variables are measured at a single point in time.

The evidence regarding the effect of bilingualism on emotional adjustment is inconclusive, as is research on bilingualism and attitudes toward ethnic groups.

Children in the St. Lambert project appeared to develop more favorable attitudes toward French-speaking people, but only in the later phases of this research. Here, however, the lack of an adequate control group limits one's confidence in the findings.

Also inconclusive was research in the St. Lambert project on the effect of bilingualism on cognitive functioning. There was some indication that bilingual children were more flexible cognitively than their peers, but only in the early grades. Other research on this topic generally supports the advantages of bilingual children. Bilingualism seems to free the child from the tyranny of words and to foster adaptability and inventiveness in problem solving. But this research is in need of replication.

In short, almost no general statements are warranted by research on the effects of bilingualism. It has not been demonstrated that bilingualism has positive or negative consequences for intelligence, linguistic skills, educational attainment, emotional adjustment, or cognitive functioning. In almost every case, the findings of research are either contradicted by other research or can be questioned on methodological grounds. The one statement that is supported by research findings is that command of a second language makes a difference if a child is tested in that language—a not very surprising finding.

SECOND-LANGUAGE ACQUISITION PROCESSES

It is, unfortunately, easier to point to what is not known or proven than to attempt to spell out what can be said about second-language acquisition in children. Nonetheless, there are some general statements that seem warranted in the light of the evidence considered. These relate to the three central issues discussed in examining the literature: the similarity between first- and second-language developmental processes, interference phenomena in second-language acquisition, and the process of code switching.

Proposition 1. First- and second-language acquisition involve essentially the same general (perhaps universal) cognitive strategies.

This statement is an elaboration of the argument above that first- and second-language learning involve the same processes. I maintained there that the evidence to date favors the hypothesis that there is a unity of process that characterizes all language acquisition, whether first- or second-language, and that this unity of process reflects the use of similar strategies of language acquisition.

What is known about these strategies? First of all, they relate to all aspects of language acquisition, not just syntactic development. We saw in Chapter 2 that the child, in acquiring a first language, must distinguish sound units, learn phonological rules, and attach sounds to their referents. Furthermore, the child has to develop a dictionary of meanings and give semantic relations grammatical expression. Unfortunately, not enough is known about the strategies that the child uses to solve phonological and semantic tasks. We have some evidence that children learn the more simple rules of phonology before the more complex, that they give the meaning of individual words a broad extension, only gradually assigning words roughly the same set of semantic features they have for adults. But, in general, the processes of phonological and semantic development remain vague. What we do know about the strategies used in first-language learning relates primarily to syntactic tasks.

We know, for example, that the meanings of words are important, since the syntactic features of sentences such as *John hit the ball* become apparent only after the child understands the meaning of the individual words. Word-order regularities are also an important clue for the child in discovering the rules of syntax. In early sentences the child tends to prefer a subject–verb–object sequence, both as a means of comprehending sentences and in production. There is also evidence that the child generally proceeds from the simple to the more complex in syntactic development, acquiring first forms that are structurally more simple and then advancing to those that are structurally more complex.

Research with children acquiring second languages indicates that the process of second-language acquisition looks much like the process of first-language acquisition. Ervin–Tripp's (1974) research in particular shows that early sentences in a second language are similar in their function, their form, their semantic redundancy, their reliance on short-term memory storage to those of the first language. Simple word-order strategies are preferred, even though the child has learned more complex strategies—e.g., for negative and interrogative constructions—in the first language. Overgeneralization of lexical and of morphological forms occurs in second-language acquisition as in first-language acquisition.

Comparison of children acquiring their first language with adults learning second languages shows that the developmental process, mistakes in imitation and comprehension, strategies for dealing with such irregularities as past-tense inflection, are all similar. When confronted with embedded sentences, adults do not utilize the knowledge of how to deal with these sentences they have from their experience with their first language; instead they approach embedded sentences as the child does and make the same mistakes. The evidence again suggests that there is a similarity of process and strategy.

Research comparing children and adults learning English as a second language indicates that both groups show the same accuracy ordering for key morphemes, regardless of first language. What age differences were found between second-language learners related not to the accuracy ordering but to the level of performance achieved. Thus in all likelihood both groups used the same general language processing strategies.

Again, this research (e.g., Bailey, Madden, & Krashen, 1974; Dulay & Burt, 1973) is by no means conclusive. The similarities in the findings may be due to the elicitation techniques used (Rosansky, 1976). Moreover, there is the problem that although adults and children second-language learners showed similar accuracy ordering, the order was not the same as the developmental order found in children acquiring English as a first language. These differences have been attributed to age factors, the second-language learners being older and more mature cognitively than the first-language learners.

There is no denying that the child and the adult perform at levels appropriate to their ages. There are vast differences between the 3-year-old child and the 30-year-old adult. Adults have superior memory heuristics at their disposal that enable them to retain longer input and discover meaning more easily. They have the lexicon of their first language to fall back on in attempting to decipher the lexicon of the second language. The adult can process information more quickly and has more experiential knowledge than the child.

The fact that adults make use of acquired knowledge, skills, and tactics does not, however, distinguish their learning process from that of the child. Children also use their acquired knowledge and skills. The essential question is whether differences in cognitive abilities and knowledge of the world and language mean that different strategies are being used. And the only way to determine whether there are differences in process is by examination of speech production.

Longitudinal studies of syntactic development generally show the same developmental sequences for first- and second-language acquisition (e.g., Dato, 1971; Milon, 1974; Ravem, 1968, 1974). There is some evidence—especially with respect to the acquisition of negative constructions—that the second-language learner will deviate from the pattern of acquisition observed in first-language acquisition (Cancino, Rosansky, & Schumann, 1974; Hakuta, 1975; Wode, 1976). The child may indeed revert to first-language structures—e.g., early in the acquisition of the second language or when faced with a linguistic riddle that remains insoluble. In doing so, the child is simply using the strategy of employing what is known to solve the problem—just as the child does in acquiring the first language.

This strategy can be thought of as an abstract cognitive operation that transcends the pecularities of specific languages. Such abstract operations characterize first- and second-language acquisition. They tell the learner to pay attention to word order, to use meaning as a clue to syntax, to simplify, to interpret what is unknown in terms of what is known, to generalize rules, and so on. In addition, the second-language learner uses a strategy of employing formulaic expressions in speech, which are subsequently broken down as the linguistic features of the constituents are mastered (Fillmore, 1976).

Recent research on discourse analysis also suggests that second-language learners internalize language rules on the basis of patterns acquired in discourse sets (Wagner–Gough, in press). Evelyn Hatch and her coworkers (Huang & Hatch, in press; Peck, in press; Wagner–Gough, in press) have found that children acquiring a second language imitate sentences of considerable length and complexity and recall these sentences in the appropriate context. The strategy of analyzing the internal structure of prepackaged routines acquired through imitation may be one of the most important techniques employed in second-language acquisition. The first-language learner may very well use a similar strategy, although empirical evidence on this point is lacking.

Hatch (in press) has argued that a second language (like a first language) evolves out of learning how to carry on a conversation. To communicate with others, the child or adult must learn how to identify the topic of a conversation and how to keep the conversation going. Asking for clarification, repetition, imitation, eliciting vocabulary, and guessing are strategies learners use to carry on a conversation. Through such conversational strategies the individual learns to interact with others verbally and, eventually, develops the syntactic structures of the language.

It should be pointed out that the use of general strategies by second-language learners does not rule out the possibility of individual differences in acquisition. Fillmore's (1976) research showed how individual variation occurs among children employing the same cognitive and social strategies. Psychological and social psychological variables certainly enter into the process of language acquisition. Children and adults who possess the requisite cognitive styles and social skills are at an advantage when compared to those who lack these personality traits and skills.

Proposition 2. Errors of various types are best described in strategy terms.

I argued above that interference between languages is not as inevitable or ubiquitous as is generally supposed. Under certain conditions of acquisition, very little interference between languages has been observed. Much of what appears to be interference between languages is actually a result of strategies the learner uses to discover regularities in the target language. In fact, I propose that all errors represent learning strategies.

Some evidence that interference between languages plays a minor role in the second-language acquisition process comes from Dulay and Burt's (1974b) finding that children of various linguistic backgrounds made the same types of errors in acquiring English as a second language. That Spanish-, Chinese-, Japanese-, and Norwegian-speaking children made the same types of mistakes suggests that the children go through a similar process in acquiring English and use similar strategies. It seems reasonable to argue, as Dulay and Burt did, that children attempt to construct rules for the speech they hear, guided by general cognitive strategies that lead them to formulate certain types of hypotheses about the language system being acquired. There is also considerable evidence from the errors made by adult learners of English as a second language that suggests that they make similar mistakes regardless of their first language and that their mistakes are analyzable as incorrect attempts to discover the rules of the English language.

Many of the errors that second-language learners make can be clearly categorized as developmental in character. They occur in the same sequence as errors that first-language learners of the target language make. This is especially true of negative and interrogative constructions and modal and auxiliary verbs, where first- and second-language learners of English generally show the same pattern of mistakes. There is, however, some conflicting evidence concerning negative constructions (Cancino, Rosansky, & Schumann, 1974; Wode, 1976).

Another source of errors is simplification. One finds this strategy used by both first- and second-language learners. Both types of learner will tend to prefer simple to more complex constructions, will drop endings, will use the infinitive or imperative verb form for other conjugations, and so forth. The tendency to simplify, in fact, underlies many of the developmental errors observed in first- and second-language learners.

Other mistakes made by second-language learners are more subtle and more difficult to categorize. It seems quite likely, however, that a good many of the errors that appear to reflect the influence of first-language structures reflect instead a strategy of generalizing on the basis of regularities observed in the target language. An example given by Dulay and Burt (1972) is the sentence *I know to do all that* spoken by a child whose first language was Spanish. Although this sentence appears to show the influence of Spanish, it may in fact be an over-generalization of English verb–complement constructions such as would be the case if *want* were the verb rather than *know*. The child may be overgeneralizing from one English construction to another in an effort to determine the range of application of rules.

In other situations, the child may in fact make errors that show unambiguously the influence of the first language. Such errors, however, can also be interpreted in terms of strategies the learner is using to discover linguistic regularities in the target language. In this case, learners resort to what they know about language as a source of hypotheses for discovering regularities that they do not know. The evidence suggests that this is the strategy of last resort, in that such errors appear to be much less frequent than errors showing the influence of the second language. But in some language learning situations this strategy may be frequently employed, especially when the second language is learned in the classroom and . when the learner has little contact with peers who speak the second language.

One of the reasons for preferring a strategy analysis to an analysis based on interference between languages—aside from the fact that an interference approach leaves the majority of errors unexplained—is that an interference analysis rests on a weak theoretical foundation. It derives from a habit theory of learning: interference occurs because old habits have not been extinguished. According to this theory, new learning (of a second language) is only possible when old habits (the first language) have been extinguished. But people obviously do not forget their first language in mastering a second language.

In addition, an analysis of errors in terms of interference has unfortunate pedagogic implications. The teacher and the student tend to regard errors negatively. They are to be exorcised by all possible means; they contribute nothing to the learning process and only retard the student's progress. In contrast, a strategy analysis views errors as a positive source of information about the way in which learners try to make sense out of the second-language input to which they are exposed. It is not so much the error that matters as the strategy that underlies the error. Once the limitations of a particular strategy can be made clear to the student, a whole complex of errors can be avoided.

Proposition 3. There is a single language system that forms the basis for acquisition, storage, and retrieval of first and second languages.

The evidence from studies of children who acquire two languages simultaneously points to the conclusion that the language acquisition process is the same in each language as it is for the monolingual child. This means that in the bilingual child's language development certain structures in one language will lag behind those of the other language because they are more complex, with the pattern in each language replicating that found in monolingual children.

There is also evidence that the bilingual child does not encode the two languages separately. In the early stages there is syntactic and morphological confusion as a result of the child's attempt to apply a single set of rules to both languages. In time the child learns to keep the separate rules straight. What evidence there is, however, suggests that the child learns the rules of language as a single set with those specific to a particular code tagged as such through a process of differentiation. Similarly, the lexical systems of the two languages do not seem to be stored separately, but rather together, with some means of tagging used to keep them separate.

In fact, I would argue that there is a single language acquisition system that is utilized in first- and second-language acquisition at all ages, that the individual's languages are stored together in one memory "tank," and that there are mechanisms at the retrieval stage for keeping the languages separate in output. This is going somewhat beyond the available evidence, since at the present time little is known about storage and retrieval, especially of syntactic aspects of language.

Nonetheless, the postulation of a single language system seems to be consistent with available evidence. To suggest that there is a separate system for each language contradicts evidence from studies of memory processes in adult bilingual subjects. Nor do the data from studies comparing first- and second-language acquisition in children and second-language learning in adults appear to require the postulation of different language acquisition systems before and after puberty.

In addition, the hypothesis of separate language systems is unparsimonious. It is more economical to regard the bilingual's two languages as separate linguistic codes, analogous to the separate codes of a monolingual speaker. There seems to be no reason to argue that the task of switching languages involves additional processes over and above those used to switch codes in a single language.

In some languages—Javanese is the example frequently given—there are a large number of different language codes associated with such variables as age, sex, kinship relation, occupation, wealth, religion, education, and family background. The complexity of code switching in these various communication situations is enormous, relative to what we are used to in European languages. Anthropologists describing the Javenese system report it to be more complex than is bilingualism for Europeans.

Yet we do not usually postulate separate language systems for the various codes of a single language. The ability of the speaker to move from code to code within a language does not seem to require a multiple language system, one system for each code. Each code is part of a single system with some means available for tagging entries or structures as belonging to one code or another.

It seems consistent to hypothesize that the same is true of bilingualism. The bilingual's language system is a single system with some means of discriminating lexical entries and syntactic forms. Switching codes within this system is not any different from switching codes within a single language. Of course, we do not know very much about the mechanisms involved—either in monolingual or bilingual individuals. It may be, however, that research with bilinguals will throw light on the still mysterious process of code switching in monolingual individuals.

In concluding, I should emphasize that the three propositions I have been discussing are not necessarily true. They are merely proposed as being consistent with most research findings to this point, whereas the propositions discussed earlier appear to run counter to what has been learned through research. It may be that future investigations will show that some or all of the statements I feel are warranted are wrong, whereas those that at present seem unwarranted may turn out to be correct. The study of second-language acquisition in children is an exciting area of research precisely because it does not allow apodictic statements.

References

Aellen, C., & Lambert, W. E. Ethnic identification and personality adjustments of Canadian adolescents of mixed English–French parentage. *Canadian Journal of Behavioral Science,* 1969, **1,** 69–86.

Altman, H. B. Toward a definition of individualized foreign language instruction. *American Foreign Language Teacher,* 1971, **1,** 12–13.

Altman, H. B., & Politzer, R. L. (Eds.). *Individualizing foreign language instruction.* Rowley, Mass.: Newbury House, 1971.

Anastasi, A., & de Jesus, C. Language development and nonverbal IQ of Puerto Rican preschool children in New York City. *Journal of Abnormal and Social Psychology,* 1953, **48,** 357–366.

Andersson, T. *Foreign languages in the elementary school.* Austin: University of Texas Press, 1969.

Andersson, T. Children's learning of a second language: Another view. *Modern Language Journal,* 1973, **57,** 254–259.

Andersson, T., & Boyer, M. *Bilingual schooling in the United States.* Washington, D.C.: U.S. Government Printing Office, 1970.

Anglin, J. M. *The growth of meaning.* Cambridge, Mass.: MIT Press, 1970.

Arsenian, S. *Bilingualism and mental development.* New York: Columbia University Press, 1937.

Asch, S. E., & Nerlove, H. The development of double function terms in children: An exploratory investigation. In B. Kaplan & S. Wagner (Eds.), *Perspectives in psychological theory: Essays in honor of Heinz Werner.* New York: International Universities Press, 1960.

Asher, J. J. The strategy of total physical response: An application to learning Russian. *International Review of Applied Linguistics in Language Teaching,* 1965, **3,** 291–300.

Asher, J. J. The total physical response approach to second language learning. *Modern Language Journal,* 1969, **53,** 3–17.

Asher, J. J. Children's first language as a model for second language learning. *Modern Language Journal,* 1972, **56,** 133–139.

Asher, J. J., & Garcia, R. The optimal age to learn a foreign language. *Modern Language Journal,* 1969, **53,** 334–341.

Asher, J. J., Kusudo, J. A., & de le Torre, R. Learning a second language through commands: The 2nd field test. *Modern Language Journal,* 1974, **58,** 24–32.

Asher, J. J., & Price, B. S. The learning strategy of a total physical response: Some age differences. *Child Development,* 1967, **38,** 1219–1277.

Bailey, N., Madden, C., & Krashen, S. D. Is there a "natural sequence" in adult second language learning? *Language Learning*, 1974, **24**, 235–243.

Balkan, L. *Les effets du bilingualisme français-anglais sur les aptitudes intellectuelles*. Brussels: AIMAV, 1970.

Barik, H. C. Interpreters talk a lot, among other things. *Babel, Revue Internationale de la Traduction*, 1972, **18**, 3–10.

Barik, H. C., & Swain, M. English–French bilingual education in the early grades: The Elgin Study. *The Modern Language Journal*, 1974, **56**, 392–403.

Barik, H. C., & Swain, M. Three-year evaluation of a large scale early grade French immersion program: The Ottawa Study. *Language Learning*, 1975, **25**, 1–30.

Barik, H. C., Swain, M., & McTavish, K. Immersion classes in the English setting: One way for les Anglais to learn French. *Working papers on bilingualism*. Ontario Institute for Studies in Education, 1974. *No. 2*, 38–56.

Barke, E. M. A study of the comparative intelligence of children in certain bilingual and monoglot schools in South Wales. *British Journal of Educational Psychology*, 1933, **3**, 237–250.

Basser, L. W. Hemiplegia of early onset and the faculty of speech with special reference to the effects of hemispherectomy. *Brain*, 1962, **85**, 427–460.

Bates, E. *Language and context*. New York: Academic Press, 1976.

Berko, J. The child's learning of English morphology. *Word*, 1958, **14**, 150–177.

Berlin, C. S., Lowe–Bell, R., Hughes, L., & Berlin, H. Dichotic right ear advantage in males and females—ages 5 to 13. *Journal of the Acoustical Society of America*, 1972, **53**, 368 (Abstract).

Bever, T. G. The cognitive basis for linguistic structures. In J. R. Hayes (Ed.), *Cognition and the development of language*. New York: Wiley, 1970.

Bever, T. G. The nature of cerebral dominance in speech behavior of the child and adult. In R. Huxley & E. Ingram (Eds.), *Language acquisition: Models and methods*. New York: Academic Press, 1971.

Bierwisch, M. Some semantic universals of German adjectives. *Foundations of Language*, 1967, **3**, 1–36.

Bloom, L. *Language development: Form & function on emerging grammars*. Boston: MIT Press, 1970.

Bloom, L. *One word at a time: The use of single word utterances before syntax*. The Hague: Mouton, 1973.

Bloomfield, L. *Language*. London: Allen & Unwin, 1935.

Bowerman, M. *Early syntactic development: A cross-linguistic study with special reference to Finnish*. Cambridge: Cambridge University Press, 1973.

Bradshaw, W. L., & Anderson, H. E. Developmental study of the meaning of adverbial modifiers. *Journal of Educational Psychology*, 1968, **59**, 111–118.

Braine, M. D. S. On two types of models of internalization of grammars, In D. I. Slobin (Ed.), *The ontogenesis of grammar*. New York: Academic Press, 1971. (a)

Braine, M. D. S. The acquisition of language in infant and child. In C. E. Reed (Ed.), *The learning of language*. Englewood Cliffs, N.J.: Prentice–Hall, 1971. (b)

Braine, M. D. S. Length constraints, reduction rules, and holophrastic processes in children's word combinations. *Journal of Verbal Learning and Verbal Behavior*, 1974, **13**, 448–456.

Bransford, J. D., & Franks, J. J. The abstraction of linguistic ideas: A review. *Cognition*, 1972, **1**, 211–249.

Braun, M. Beobachtungen zur Frage der Mehrsprachigkeit, *Göttingische Gelehrte Anzeigen*, 1937, **199**, 115–130.

Brega, E., & Newell, J. M. High school performance of FLES and non-FLES students. *Modern Language Journal*, 1967, **51**, 408–411.

Brown, A. L., & Scott, M. S. Recognition memory for pictures for preschool children. *Journal of Experimental Child Psychology*, 1971, **11**, 401–412.

Brown, R. The development of the *Wh-* questions in child speech. *Journal of Verbal Learning and Verbal Behavior,* 1968, **7,** 279–290.

Brown, R. *A first language: The early stages.* Cambridge, Mass.: Harvard University Press, 1973. (a)

Brown, R. Development of the first language in the human species. *American Psychologist,* 1973, **28,** 97–106 (b)

Brown, R., & Bellugi, U. Three processes in the acquisition of syntax. *Harvard Educational Review,* 1964, **34,** 133–151.

Brown, R., & Fraser, D. The acquisition of syntax. In C. N. Cofer & B. Musgrave (Eds.), *Verbal behavior and learning.* New York: McGraw–Hill, 1963.

Bruck, M., Lambert, W. E., & Tucker, G. R. Bilingual schooling through the elementary grades: The St. Lambert project at grade seven. *Language Learning,* 1974, **24,** 183–204.

Brudhiprabha, P. *Error analysis: A psycholinguistic study of Thai—English compositions.* Unpublished masters thesis, McGill University, 1972.

Bühler, K. *The mental development of the child.* New York: Harcourt, Brace, 1930 (translated from 5th German edition).

Bühler, U. B. *Empirische und lernpsychologische Beiträge zur Wahl des Zeitpunktes für den Fremdsprachenunterrichtsbeginn: Lernpsychologisch interpretierte Leistungsmessungen im Frage Französischunterricht an Primärschulen des Kantons Zürich.* Zürich: Orell Füssli, 1972.

Burke, S. J. Language acquisition, language learning, and language teaching. *International Review of Applied Linguistics in Language Teaching,* 1974, **12,** 53–68.

Burling, R. Language development of a Garo and English speaking child. *Word,* 1959, **15,** 45–68.

Burt, M. K., Dulay, H., & Hernandez, C. E. *Bilingual syntax measure.* New York: Harcourt Brace & Jovanovich, 1975.

Burt, M. K., & Kiparsky, C. *The gooficon: A repair manual for English.* Rowley, Mass.: Newbury House, 1972.

Cambon, J., & Sinclair, E. Relations between syntax and semantics: Are they "easy to see"? *British Journal of Psychology,* 1974, **65,** 133–140.

Cameron, A., Feider, H. H., & Gray, V. *Pilot evaluation of French immersion: Grade I in Fredericton N. B.,* Spring 1974. Interim report, Fredericton, New Brunswick, 1974.

Cancino, H., Rosansky, E. J., & Schumann, J. H. Testing hypothesis about second language acquisition: The copula and the negative in three subjects. *Working Papers in Bilingualism,* 1974, **3,** 80–96.

Cancino, H., Rosansky, E. J., & Schumann, J. H. The acquisition of the English auxiliary by native Spanish speakers. *TESOL Quarterly,* 1975, **9,** 421–430.

Carroll, J. B. Psychological and educational research into 2nd language teaching to young children. In H. H. Stern (Ed.), *Language and the young school child.* London: Oxford University Press, 1969.

Carroll, J. B. Development of native language skills beyond the early years. In C. E. Reed (Ed.), *The learning of language.* Englewood Cliffs, N.J.: Prentice–Hall, 1971.

Carroll, J. B. Some suggestions from a psycholinguist. *TESOL Quarterly,* 1973, **7,** 355–367.

Carrow, E. Comprehension of English and Spanish by preschool Mexican–American children. *Modern Language Journal,* 1971, **55,** 299–307.

Carrow, M. A. (E) Linguistic functioning of bilingual and monolingual children. *Journal of Speech and Hearing Disorders,* 1957, **22,** 371–380.

Casagrande, J. B. Comanche baby language. *International Journal of American Linguistics,* 1948, **14,** 11–14.

Celce–Murcia, M. *Simultaneous acquisition of English and French in a two-year-old child.* Paper presented at TESOL Conference, Los Angeles, 1975.

Child, I. L. *Italian or American? The second generation in conflict.* New Haven: Yale University Press, 1943.

Chomsky, C. *The acquisition of syntax in children from 5 to 10.* Cambridge, Mass.: MIT Press, 1969.

Chomsky, N. *Syntactic structures.* The Hague: Mouton, 1957.

Chomsky, N. Review of B. F. Skinner, *Verbal Behavior. Language,* 1959, **35,** 26–58.

Chomsky, N. Noam Chomsky & Stuart Hampshire discuss the study of language. *The Listener,* 1968, **79,** No. 2044.

Chomsky, N. A., & Halle, M. *The sound pattern of English.* New York: Harper and Row, 1968.

Christian, C. C., & Sharp, J. M. Bilingualism in a pluralistic society. In D. L. Lange & C. J. James (Eds.), *Foreign language education: A reappraisal.* Skokie, Ill.: National Textbook Co., 1972.

Christophersen, P. *Bilingualism.* London: Methuen, 1948.

Christophersen, P. *Second-language learning: Myth and reality.* Baltimore: Penguin, 1973.

Clark, E. V. What's in a word? On the child's acquisition of semantics in his first language. In T. E. Moore (Ed.), *Cognitive development and the acquisition of language.* New York: Academic Press, 1973.

Clark, E. V. Some aspects of the conceptual basis for first language acquisition. In R. L. Schiefel-busch & L. L. Lloyd (Eds.), *Language perspectives: Acquisition, retardation & intervention.* New York: Macmillan, 1974.

Clark, H. H. The primitive nature of children's relational concepts. In J. R. Hayes (Ed.), *Cognition and the development of language.* New York: Wiley, 1970.

Clark, H. H. Space, time, semantic, and the child. In T. E. Moore (Ed.), *Cognitive development and the acquisition of language.* New York: Academic Press, 1973.

Clark, H. H., & Chase, W. G. On the process of comparing sentences against pictures. *Cognitive Psychology,* 1972, **3,** 472–517.

Clark, H. H., & Haviland, S. E. Psychological processes as linguistic explanation. In D. Cohen (Ed.), *Explaining linguistic phenomena.* Washington, D.C.: Hemisphere, 1974.

Cohen, A. D. The Culver City Spanish immersion project: The first two years. *Modern Language Journal,* 1974, **58,** 95–103.

Cohen, A. D. *A sociolinguistic approach to bilingual education.* Rowley, Mass.: Newbury House, 1975.

Cohen, A. D., & Swain, M. Bilingual education: The "immersion" model in the North American context. *TESOL Quarterly,* 1976, **10,** 45–53.

Condon, E. C. Bilingual education. *System,* 1974, **2,** 16–32.

Cook, V. J. The analogy between first- and second-language learning. *International Review of Applied Linguistics in Language Teaching,* 1969, **7,** 207–216.

Cook, V. J. The comparison of language development in native children and foreign adults. *International Review of Applied Linguistics in Language Teaching,* 1973, **11,** 13–29.

Cooper, R. L. What do we learn when we learn a language? *TESOL Quarterly,* 1970, **4,** 312–320.

Corder, S. P. The significance of learners' errors. *International Review of Applied Linguistics in Language Teaching,* 1967, **5,** 161–170.

Corder, S. P. Error analysis, interlanguage, and second language acquisition. *Language Teaching and Linguistics,* 1975, **8,** 201–217.

Cromer, R. F. Children are nice to understand: Surface structure clues for the recovery of a deep structure. *British Journal of Psychology,* 1970, **61,** 397–408.

Cukovský, K. *From two to five.* Berkeley: University of California Press, 1965.

Curran, C. A. Counselling skills adapted to the learning of foreign languages. *Bulletin of the Menninger Clinic,* 1961, **25,** 79–83.

Dale, P. S. *Language development: Structure and function* (2nd ed.). New York: Holt, Rinehart, & Winston, 1976.

d'Anglejan, A., & Tucker, G. R. The acquisition of complex English structures by adult learners. *Language Learning*, 1975, **25**, 281–293.

Darcy, N. T. A review of the literature on the effects of bilingualism upon the measurement of intelligence. *Journal of Genetic Psychology*, 1953, **82**, 21–58.

Darcy, N. T. Bilingualism and the measurement of intelligence: A review of a decade of research. *Journal of Genetic Psychology*, 1963, **103**, 259–282.

Dato, D. P. *American children's acquisition of Spanish syntax in the Madrid environment. Preliminary edition*, U.S. Office of Education. Institute of International Studies. Project No. 3036. Contract No. OEC 2-7-002637, May 1970.

Dato, D. P. The development of the Spanish verb phrase in children's second-language learning. In P. Pimsleur & T. Quinn (Eds.), *The psychology of 2nd language learning*. Cambridge: Cambridge University Press, 1971.

deVilliers, P. A. & deVilliers, J. G. Early judgments of semantic & syntactic acceptability by children. *Journal of Psycholinguistics Research*, 1972, **1**, 299–310.

Diller, K. C. "Compound" & "coordinate" bilingualism: A conceptual artifact. *Word*, 1970, **26**, 254–261.

Dodson, C. S., Price, E., & Williams, I. T. *Toward bilingualism*. Cardiff: University of Wales Press, 1968.

Donaldson, M., & Balfour, G. Less is more: A study of language comprehension in children. *British Journal of Psychology*, 1968, **59**, 461–472.

Donaldson, M., & Wales, R. On the acquisition of relational terms. In J. R. Hayes (Ed.), *Cognition and the development of knowledge*. New York: Wiley, 1970.

Donoghue, M. R. *Foreign languages and the elementary school child*. Dubuque, Iowa: Brown, 1968.

Dulay, H. C., & Burt, M. K. Goofing: An indication of children's second language learning strategies. *Language Learning*, 1972, **22**, 235–252.

Dulay, H. C., & Burt, M. K. Should we teach children syntax? *Language Learning*, 1973, **23**, 245–258.

Dulay, H. C., & Burt, M. K. A new perspective on the creative construction processes in child second language acquisition. *Language Learning*, 1974, **24**, 253–278. (a)

Dulay, H. C., & Burt, M. K. Errors and strategies in child second language acquisition. *TESOL Quarterly*, 1974, **8**, 129–138. (b)

Dulay, H. C., & Burt, M. K. Natural sequence in child second language acquisition. *Language Learning*, 1974, **24**, 37–53. (c)

Echeverría, M. S. On needed research in 2nd language learning in the light of contemporary developments in linguistic theory. *International Review of Applied Linguistics in Language Teaching*, 1974, **12**, 69–77.

Elwert, W. T. *Das zweisprachige Individuum: Ein Selbstzeugnis*. Wiesbaden: Steiner, 1960.

Emrich, L. Beobachtungen über Zweisprachigkeit in ihrem Anfangsstadium. *Deutschtum im Ausland*, 1938, **21**, 419–424.

Engel, W. von R. Del bilinguismo infantile. *Archivio Glottologico Italiano*, 1965, **50**, 175–180.

Engel, W. von R. Linguaggio attivo e linguaggio passivo. *Orientamenti Pedagogici*, 1966, **13**, 893–894.

Ervin-Tripp, S. M. Imitation and structural change in children's language. In E. H. Lenneberg (Ed.), *New directions in the study of language*. Cambridge, Mass.: MIT Press, 1964.

Ervin-Tripp, S. M., & Osgood, C. E. Second language learning and bilingualism. *Journal of Abnormal and Social Psychology*, 1954, **49**, 139–146.

Ervin-Tripp, S.M. Language development. In L. W. Hoffman & M. L. Hoffman (Eds.), *Review of child development research*. New York: Russell Sage Foundation, 1966.

Ervin-Tripp, S. M. An Issei learns English. *Journal of Social Issues*, 1967, **23**, 78–90.

Ervin–Tripp, S. Commentary on a paper by R. M. Jones. In L. G. Kelley (Ed.), *Description and measurement of bilingualism: An international seminar*. Toronto: University of Toronto Press, 1969.

Ervin–Tripp, S. Structure and process in language acquisition. *Monograph Series on Language and Linguistics*, 1970, **23**, 313–344.

Ervin–Tripp, S. Children's sociolinguistic competence and dialect diversity. In I. J. Gordon (Ed.), *Early childhood education*. Chicago: University of Chicago Press, 1972.

Ervin–Tripp, S. Some strategies for the 1st two years. In T. E. Moore (Ed.), *Cognitive development and the acquisition of language*. New York: Academic Press, 1973. (a)

Ervin–Tripp, S. The structure of communicative choice. In S. Ervin–Tripp. *Language acquisition and communicative choice*. Edited by A. S. Dil. Stanford: Stanford University Press, 1973. (b)

Ervin–Tripp, S. Is second language learning like the first? *TESOL Quarterly*, 1974, **8**, 111–127.

Fathman, A. K. *Age, language background, and the order of acquisition of English structures*. Paper presented at annual TESOL conference. Los Angeles, 1975.

Feldman, C., & Shen, M. Some language-related cognitive advantages of bilingual 5-year-olds. *Journal of Genetic Psychology*, 1971, **118**, 235–244.

Ferguson, C. A. Diglossia. *Word*, 1959, **15**, 325–340.

Fillmore, L. W. *The second time around: Cognitive and social strategies in second-language acquisition*. Unpublished Ph.D. dissertation. Stanford University, 1976.

Fischer, J. L. Social influences on the choice of a linguistic variant. *Word*, 1958, **14**, 47–56.

Fishman, S. A. Language maintenance and language shift as fields of inquiry. *Linguistics*, 1964, **9**, 32–70.

Fishman, S. A. *Language loyalty in the United States*. The Hague: Mouton, 1966.

Fishman, S. A. *Sociolinguistics: A brief introduction*. Rowley, Mass.: Newbury House, 1970.

Fishman, S. A., & Lovas, J. Bilingual education in sociological perspective. *TESOL Quarterly*, 1970, **4**, 215–222.

Flavell, H. H. Developmental studies of mediated memory. In H. W. Reese & L. P. Lipsitt (Eds.), *Advances in child development and behavior* (Vol. 5). New York: Academic Press, 1970.

Fodor, J. A., Bever, T. G., & Garrett, M. F. *The psychology of language*. New York: McGraw–Hill, 1974.

Francescato, G. Appunti teorico-pratici sul bilinguismo infantile. *Lingua e Stile*, 1969, **4**, 445–458.

Fraser, C., Bellugi, U., & Brown, R. Control of grammar in imitation comprehension and production. *Journal of Verbal Learning and Verbal Behavior*, 1963, **2**, 121–135.

Friedlander, B. Z., Jacobs, A. C., Davis, B. B., & Wetstone, H. S. Time-sampling analysis of infants' natural language environments in the home. *Child Development*, 1972, **43**, 730–740.

Fromkin, V., Krashen, S., Curtiss, S., Rigler, D., & Rigler, M. The development of language in Genie: A case of language acquisition beyond the critical period. *Brain and Language*, 1974, **1**, 81–107.

Gaarder, A. B. Organization of the bilingual school. *Journal of Social Issues*, 1967, **23**, 110–120.

Gaarder, A. B. Bilingualism. In D. D. Walsh (Ed.), *A handbook for teachers of Spanish and Portuguese*. Lexington, Mass.: Heath, 1969.

Gaer, E. P. Children's understanding and production of sentences. *Journal of Verbal Learning and Verbal Behavior*, 1969, **8**, 289–294.

Garrett, M. F., & Fodor, J. Psychological theories and linguistic constructs. In T. R. Dixon & D. L. Horton (Eds.), *Verbal behavior and general behavior theory*. Englewood Cliffs, N.J.: Prentice–Hall, 1968.

Garrod, S., & Trabasso, T. A dual-memory information processing interpretation of sentence comprehension. *Journal of Verbal Learning and Verbal Behavior*, 1973, **2**, 155–167.

Gaskell, W. G. They dropped the ball on FLES. *Modern Language Journal*, 1967, **51**, 79–81.

Gazzaniga, M. S. *The bisected brain*. New York: Appleton–Century–Crofts, 1970.

Geertz, C. *The religion of Java*. New York: The Free Press, 1960.

Geissler, H. *Zwiesprachigkeit deutscher Kinder im Ausland.* Stuttgart: Kohlhammer, 1938.

George, H. V., *Common errors in language learning.* Rowley, Mass.: Newbury House, 1972.

Gerald, J. A. *The sea dreamer.* Hamden, Conn.: Archon Books, 1967.

Gerullis, G. Muttersprache und Zweisprachigkeit in einem preussisch-litauischen Dorf. *Studi Baltici,* 1932, **2,** 59–67.

Ginsberg, V. S. An experiment in teaching pre-school children a foreign language. Soviet Education Reprints, *Sovetskala Pedagogika,* 1960, **5.**

Gleason, J. B. Code switching in children's language. In T. E. Moore (Ed.), *Cognitive development and the acquisition of language.* New York: Academic Press, 1973.

Goldberg, M. A qualification of the marginal man theory. *American Sociological Review,* 1941, **6,** 52–58.

Gompf, G. *English in der Grundschule.* Weinheim: Beltz, 1971.

Gordon, D., & Lakoff, G. Conversational postulates. *Papers from the 7th Regional Meeting, Chicago Linguistic Society,* 1971.

Gougher, R. L. Individualization of foreign language learning: What is being done? In D. L. Lange (Ed.), *Pluralism in foreign language education.* Skokie, Ill.: National Textbook Co., 1973.

Grégoire, A. *L'apprentissage du language: les deux premières années.* Liège: Bibliothèque de la Faculté de Philosophie et Lettres, 1937.

Grider, R. E., Otomo, A., & Toyota, W. *Comparison between second, third, and fourth grade children in the audio lingual learning of Japanese as a second language.* Research report. Honolulu: University of Hawaii, 1961.

Gumperz, J. J. Types of linguistic communities. *Anthropological Linguistics,* 1962, **4,** 28–40.

Gumperz, J. J. Verbal strategies in multilingual communication. *Monograph Series on Languages and Linguistics,* 1970, **23,** 129–143.

Gumperz, J. J., & Hernández–Chavez, E. Bilingualism, bidialectalism, & classroom interaction. In C. B. Cazden, V. P. John, & D. Hymes (Eds.), *Functions of language in the classroom.* New York: Teachers College Press, 1972.

Hakuta, K. A preliminary report on the development of grammatical morphemes in a Japanese girl learning English as a second language. *Working Papers in Bilingualism,* 1974, **3,** 18–38. (a)

Hakuta, K. Prefabricated patterns and the emergence of structure in second language acquisition. *Language Learning,* 1974, **24,** 287–297. (b)

Hakuta, K. Learning to speak a second language: What exactly does the child learn? In D. P. Dato (Ed.), *Georgetown University Round Table on Languages and Linguistics.* Washington, D.C.: Georgetown University Press, 1975.

Hakuta, K. A case study of a Japanese child learning English as a second language. *Language Learning,* 1976, **26,** 321–351.

Halle, M. Phonology in a generative grammar. *Word,* 1962, **18,** 54–72.

Halliday, M. A. K., McIntosh, A., & Strevens, P. *The linguistic sciences and language teaching.* London: Longman, 1964.

Harshman, R., & Krashen, S. D. An "unbiased" procedure for comparing degree of lateralization of dichotically presented stimuli. *Journal of the Acoustical Society of America,* 1972, **52,** 174 (Abstracts).

Hatch, E. *An historical overview of second language acquisition research.* Paper presented at the Los Angeles Second Language Acquisition Forum, February 1977.

Hatch, E. Discourse analysis and second language acquisition. In E. Hatch (Ed.), *Second language acquisition.* In press.

Haugen, E. *The Norwegian language in America.* Philadelphia: University of Pennsylvania Press, 1953.

Haugen, E. Problems of bilingual description. *General Linguistics,* 1955, **1,** 1–9.

Haugen, E. *Bilingualism in the Americas.* University, Ala.: University of Alabama Press, 1956.

Haugen, E. Linguistics and dialinguistics. *Georgetown Monograph Series on Languages and Linguistics,* 1970, **23,** 1–7.

Hebb, D. O., Lambert, W. E., & Tucker, G. R. Language, thought, and experience. *Modern Language Journal*, 1971, **55**, 212–222.

Hécain, H. Acquired aphasia in children and the ontogenesis of hemispheric functional specialization. *Brain and Language*, 1976, **3**, 114–134.

Hill, J. Foreign accents, language acquisition and cerebral dominance revisited. *Language Learning*, 1970, **20**, 237–248.

Hoffman, M. N. H. *The measurement of bilingual background*. New York: Bureau of Publications, Teachers College, Columbia University, 1934.

Hoyer, A. E., & Hoyer, G. Über die Lallsprache eines Kindes. *Zeitschrift für angewandte Psychologie*, 1924, **24**, 363–384.

Huang, J., & Hatch, E. A Chinese child's acquisition of English. In E. Hatch (Ed.), *Second language acquisition*. In press.

Hunter, M. Individualizing FLES. In H. B. Altman & R. L. Politzer (Eds.), *Individualizing foreign language instruction*. Rowley, Mass.: Newbury House, 1971.

Huntsberry, R. *Second language acquisition in childhood*. Unpublished manuscript. Language Acquisition Laboratory, University of Connecticut, 1972.

Hymes, D. *Language in culture and society*. New York: Harper & Row, 1964.

Ianco–Worrall, A. D. Bilingualism and cognitive development. *Child Development*, 1972, **43**, 1390–1400.

Imedadze, N. V. K psckhologicheskoy prirode rannego dvuyazychiya. *Voprosy psikkologii*, 1960, **6**, 60–69.

Imedadze, N. V. On the psychological nature of child speech formation under conditions of exposure to two languages. *International Journal of Psychology*, 1967, **2**, 129–132.

Ingram, D. Phonological rules in young children. *Journal of Child Language*, 1974, **1**, 49–64.

Itard, J. *The wild boy of Aveyron*. Englewood Cliffs, N.J.: Prentice–Hall, 1962.

Itoh, H., & Hatch, E. Second language acquisition: A case study. In E. Hatch (Ed.), *Second language acquisition*. In press.

Jakobovits, L. A. *Foreign language learning: A psycholinguistic analysis of the issues*. Rowley, Mass.: Newbury House, 1970.

Jakobovits, L. A. The physiology and psychology of second language learning. In E. M. Birkmaier (Ed.), *Foreign language education: An overview*. Skokie, Ill.: National Textbook Co., 1972.

Jakobovits, L. A., & Gordon, B. *The context of foreign language teaching*. Rowley, Mass.: Newbury House, 1974.

Jakobson, R. *Kindersprache, Aphasie und allgemeine Lautgesetze*. Uppsala: Almquist und Wiksell, 1941.

James, C. The exculpation of contrastive linguistics. In G. Nickel (Ed.), *Papers in contrastive linguistics*. London: Cambridge University Press, 1971.

Jensen, J. V. The effects of childhood bilingualism. *Elementary English*, 1962, **39**, 132–143, 358–366.

Jespersen, O. *How to teach a foreign language*. London: Allen & Unwin, 1947.

John, V. P., & Horner, V. M. *Early bilingual education*. New York: Modern Language Association of America, 1971.

Jones, W. R. The language handicaps of Welsh-speaking children. *British Journal of Education*, 1952, **22**, 114–123.

Jones, W. R. *Bilingualism in Welsh education*. Cardiff: University of Wales Press, 1966.

Justman, J., & Naas, M. L. The high school achievement of pupils who were and were not introduced to a foreign language in the elementary school. *Modern Language Journal*, 1956, **40**, 120–123.

Katz, J. J. *The philosophy of language*. New York: Harper, 1966.

Kellaghan, T., & Macnamara, J. Reading in a second language. In M. D. Jenkinson (Ed.), *Reading instruction: An international forum*. Newark, Del.: International Reading Association, 1967.

Kelley, K. L. *Early syntactic acquisition*. P-3719, The Rand Corporation, Santa Monica, California, 1967.

Kenyeres, A. Comment une petite Hongroise de sept ans apprend le français. *Archives de Psychologie*, 1938, **26**, 321–366.

Kessler, C. *The acquisition of syntax in bilingual children*. Washington, D.C.: Georgetown University Press, 1971.

Kessler, C. Syntactic contrasts in child bilingualism. *Language Learning*, 1972, **22**, 221–233.

Kessler, C., & Idar, I. *The acquisition of English syntactic structures by a Vietnamese child*. Paper presented at the Second Language Research Forum, UCLA, February 1977.

King, R. D. *Historical linguistics and generative grammar*. Englewood Cliffs, N.J.: Prentice–Hall, 1969.

Kintsch, W. Recognition memory in bilingual subjects. *Journal of Verbal Learning and Verbal Behavior*. 1970, **9**, 405–409.

Kintsch, W., & Kintsch, E. Interlingual interference and memory processes. *Journal of Verbal Learning and Verbal Behavior*, 1969, **8**, 16–19.

Kirstein, B., & de Vincenz, A. A note on bilingualism and generative grammar. *Praxis des neusprachlichen Unterrichts*, 1974, **12**, 159–161.

Klima, E. S., & Bellugi, U. Syntactic regularities in the speech of children. In J. Lyons & R. J. Wales (Eds.), *Psycholinguistic papers*. Edinburgh: Edinburgh University Press, 1966.

Kobrick, J. W. The compelling case for bilingual education. *Saturday Review*, 1972, **55**, 54–58. No. 18.

Kolers, P. A. Interlingual facilitation of short-term memory. *Journal of Verbal Learning and Verbal Behavior*, 1966, **5**, 314–319. (a)

Kolers, P. A. Reading and talking bilingually. *American Journal of Psychology*, 1966, **79**, 357–376. (b)

Kolers, P. A. Bilingualism and information processing. *Scientific American*, 1968, **218**, 78–87.

Kramer, S. N. *The Sumerians: Their history, culture, and character*. Chicago: University of Chicago Press, 1963.

Krashen, S. D. Lateralization, language learning, and the critical period: Some new evidence. *Language Learning*, 1973, **23**, 63–74.

Krashen, S. D. The development of cerebral dominance and language learning: More new evidence. In D. P. Dato (Ed.), *Georgetown University Round Table on Language and Linguistics*. Washington, D.C.: Georgetown University Press, 1975.

Krashen, S. Formal and informal linguistic environments in language acquisition and language learning. *TESOL Quarterly*, 1976, **10**, 157–168.

Krashen, S. D., Sferlazza, V., Feldman, L., & Fathman, A. K. Adult performance on the SLOPE test: More evidence for a natural sequence in adult language acquisition. *Language Learning*, 1976, **26**, 145–151.

Lado, R. *Language teaching: A scientific approach*. New York: McGraw–Hill, 1964.

Lakoff, R. Transformational grammar and language teaching. *Language Learning*, 1969, **19**, 117–140.

Lambert, W. E. A social psychology of bilingualism. *Journal of Social Issues*, 1967, **23**, 91–109.

Lambert, W. E., Havelka, J., & Gardner, R. C. Linguistic manifestations of bilingualism. *American Journal of Psychology*, 1959, **72**, 77–82.

Lambert, W. E., Ignatow, M., & Krauthammer, M. Bilingual organization in free recall. *Journal of Verbal Learning and Verbal Behavior*, 1968, **7**, 207–214.

Lambert, W. E., & Tucker, G. R. *Bilingual education of children: The St. Lambert experiment*. Rowley, Mass.: Newbury House, 1972.

Lamendella, J. T. On the irrelevance of transformational grammar to second language pedagogy. *Language Learning*, 1969, **4**, 255–270.

Lance, D. *A brief study of Spanish–English bilingualism: Final report*. Research Project Orr–Liberal Arts—15504. College Station, Texas: Texas A. and M., 1969.

Landry, R. G. A comparison of 2nd-language learners and monolinguals on divergent thinking tasks at the elementary school level. *Modern Language Journal*, 1974, **58,** 10–15.

Langer, S. K. *Philosophy in a new key: A study in the symbolism of reason, rite, and art.* New York: The New American Library, 1958.

Larsen–Freeman, D. An explanation for the morpheme acquisition order of second language learners. *Language Learning*, 1976, **26,** 125–134. (a)

Larsen–Freeman, D. ESL teacher speech as input to the ESL learner. *Workpapers in Teaching English as a Second Language*, 1976, **10,** 45–50. (b)

Lee, L. L., & Canter, S. M. Developmental sentence scoring: A clinical procedure for estimating syntactic development in children's spontaneous speech. *Journal of Speech and Hearing Disorders*, 1971, **50,** 315–339.

Lee, W. R. Language, experience, and the language teacher. *English Language Teaching Journal*, 1973, **27,** 234–245.

Lenneberg, E. H. Understanding language without ability to speak: A case report. *Journal of Abnormal and Social Psychology*, 1962, **65,** 419–425.

Lenneberg, E. H. *Biological foundations of language.* New York: Wiley, 1967.

Leopold, W. F. *Speech development of a bilingual child: A linguist's record.* (Vol. 1): *Vocabulary growth in the first two years.* (Vol. 2): *Sound learning in the first two years.* (Vol. 3): *Grammar and general problems in the first two years.* (Vol. 4): *Diary from age two.* Evanston, Ill.: Northwestern University Press, 1939, 1947, 1949a, 1949b.

Leopold, W. F. Semantic learning in infant language. *Word*, 1948, **4,** 173–180.

Leopold, W. F. Patterning in children's language learning. *Language Learning*, 1953, **5,** 1–14.

Lewis, E. G. *Linguistics & second language pedagogy: A theoretical study.* The Hague: Mouton, 1974.

Lewis, K. R. Transformational–generative grammar. A new consideration to teaching foreign languages, *Modern Language Journal*, 1972, **56,** 3–10.

Liepmann, D., & Saegert, J. Language tagging in bilingual free recall. *Journal of Experimental Psychology*, 1974, **103,** 1137–1141.

Limber, J. The genesis of complex sentences. In T. E. Moore (Ed.), *Cognitive development and the acquisition of knowledge.* New York: Academic Press, 1973.

Littlewood, W. T. A comparison of first language acquisition and second language learning. *Praxis des Neusprachlichen Unterrichts*, 1973, **20,** 343–348.

Lopez, M., Hicks, R. E., & Young, R. K. Retroactive inhibition in a bilingual A–B, A–B' paradigm. *Journal of Experimental Psychology*, 1974, **103,** 85–90.

Lopez, M., & Young, R. K. The linguistic interdependence of bilinguals. *Journal of Experimental Psychology*, 1974, **102,** 981–983.

Luria, A. R. *The working brain.* Baltimore, Maryland: Penguin, 1973.

Mackey, W. F. Bilingual interference: Its analysis and measurement. *Journal of Communication*, 1965, **15,** 239–249.

Mackey, W. F. A typology of bilingual education. *Foreign Language Annals*, 1970, **3,** 596–608.

Mackey, W. F. *Bilingual education in a bilingual school: A study of equal language maintenance through free alternation.* Rowley, Mass.: Newbury House, 1972.

Macnamara, J. *Bilingualism and primary education.* Edinburgh: Edinburgh University Press, 1966.

Macnamara, J. Bilingualism in the modern world. *Journal of Social Issues*, 1967, **23,** 1–7. (a)

Macnamara, J. The bilingual's linguistic performance: A psychological overview. *Journal of Social Issues*, 1967, **23,** 58–77. (b)

Macnamara, J. The effect of instructions in a weaker language. *Journal of Social Issues*, 1967, **23,** 121–135. (c)

Macnamara, J. The linguistic independence of bilinguals. *Journal of Verbal Learning and Verbal Behavior*, 1967, **6,** 729–736. (d)

Macnamara, J. How can one measure the extent of a person's bilingual proficiency? In L. G. Kelly (Ed.), *Description and measurement of bilingualism.* Toronto: University of Toronto Press, 1969.

Macnamara, J. Cognitive basis of language learning in infants. *Psychological Review*, 1972, **79**, 1-14.

Macnamara, J. Nurseries, streets, & classrooms. *Modern Language Journal*, 1973, **57**, 250-254.

Macnamara, J., Krauthammer, M., & Bolgar, M. Language switching in bilinguals as a function of stimulus and response uncertainty. *Journal of Experimental Psychology*, 1968, **78**, 208-215.

Macnamara, J., & Kushnir, S. L. Linguistic independence of bilinguals: The input switch. *Journal of Verbal Learning and Verbal Behavior*, 1971, **10**, 480-487.

Malherbe, E. G. *The bilingual school*. London: Longmans, Green, 1946.

Malmberg, B. Drag ur en fy råarig finsk flichas språkliga utvectling. *Nordisk Tidskrift för Vetenskap*, 1945, **21**, 170-181.

Manuel, H. T., & Wright, C. E. The language difficulty of Mexican children. *Journal of Genetic Psychology*, 1929, **36**, 458-466.

Mason, M. K. Learning to speak after six and one-half years. *Journal of Speech Disorders*, 1942, **7**, 295-304.

McCarthy, D. Language development in children. In L. Carmichael (Ed.), *Manual of child psychology*. New York: Wiley, 1946.

McLaughlin, B. *Learning and social behavior*. New York: The Free Press, 1971.

McLaughlin, B. Second-language acquisition in childhood. *Psychological Bulletin*, 1977, 84, 438-459.

McNeill, D. Developmental psycholinguistics. In F. Smith & G. A. Miller (Eds.), *The genesis of language*. Cambridge, Mass.: MIT Press, 1966.

McNeill, D. *The acquisition of language: The study of developmental psycholinguistics*. New York: Harper and Row, 1970.

Meertens, P. J. Sprachforschung im Noordoostpolder der Zuidersee. *Zeitschrift für Mundartforschung*, 1959, **26**, 239-256.

Menn, L. Phonotactic rules in beginning speech. *Lingua*, 1971, **26**, 251-255.

Menyuk, P. *The acquisition and development of language*. Englewood Cliffs, N.J.: Prentice-Hall, 1971.

Metraux, R. W. Study of bilingualism among children of U.S.-French parents. *French Review*, 1965, **38**, 650-665.

Mikès, M. Acquisition des catégoires grammaticales dan le language de l'enfant. *Enfance*, 1967, **20**, 289-298.

Mikès, M., & Vlahović, P. Razvoj gramatickik kategorija u decjem govoru. *Prilozi Proucavanjy jezika*, 1966, II, Novi Sad, Yugoslavia.

Miller, N. E., & Dollard, J. *Social learning and imitation*. New Haven, Conn.: Yale University Press, 1941.

Milon, J. P. The development of negation in English by a second language learner. *TESOL Quarterly*, 1974, **8**, 137-143.

Mitchell, A. J. The effect of bilingualism in the measurement of intelligence. *Elementary School Journal*, 1937, **38**, 29-37.

Mitchell, P. M. Tresprogethed. *Berlingske Tidends Kronik*, 1954, 30/7.

Montessori, M. *Education for a new world*. Adyas, Madras, India: Kalakshetra Publications, 1959.

Morrison, J. R. Bilingualism: Some psychological aspects. *The Advancement of Science*, 1958, **56**, 287-290.

Moscovitch, M. Language and the cerebral hemisphere. Reaction-time studies and their implications for models of cerebral dominance. In P. Pliner, L. Krames, & T. Alloway (Eds.), *Communication and affect: Language and thought*. New York: Academic Press, 1973.

Moscovitch, M. On the representation of language in the right hemisphere of right-handed people. *Brain and Language*, 1976, **3**, 47-71.

Moskowitz, A. I. The two-year-old stage in the acquisition of English phonology. *Language*, 1970, **46**, 426-441.

Mowrer, O. H. *Learning theory and behavior*. New York: Wiley, 1960.

Murrell, M. Language acquisition in a trilingual environment: Notes from a case study. *Studia Linguistica,* 1966, **20,** 9–35.

Naiman, N. The use of elicited imitation in second language acquisition research. *Working Papers in Bilingualism,* 1974, **3,** 1–37.

Natalicio, D. S., & Natalicio, L. F. S. A comparative study of English pluralization by native and non-native speakers. *Child Development,* 1971, **42,** 1302–1306.

Newmark, L., & Reibel, D. Necessity and sufficiency in language learning. *International Review of Applied Linguistics in Language Teaching,* 1968, **6,** 145–161.

Ney, J. W. Contradictions in theoretical approaches to the teaching of foreign languages. *Modern Language Journal,* 1974, **56,** 197–200.

Nott, C. R., & Lambert, W. E. Free recall of bilinguals. *Journal of Verbal Learning and Verbal Behavior,* 1968, **7,** 1065–1071.

O'Donnell, R. C., Griffin, W. J., & Norris, R. C. *Syntax of kindergarten and elementary school children: A transformational analysis.* (Research Report 8.) Champaign, Ill.: National Council of Teachers of English, 1967.

Oksaar, E. Besprechung vom V. Rūǩe–Draviņa *Mehrsprachigkeit im Vorschulalter. Die Sprache,* 1969, **15,** 187–190.

Oksaar, E. Zum Spracherwerb des Kindes in zweisprachiger Umgebung. *Folia Linguistica,* 1970, **4,** 330–358.

Oléron, P., & Nanpan, H. Recherches sur la traduction simultanée. *Journal de Psychologie Normale et Pathologique,* 1965, **1,** 73–94.

Oller, J. W., Jr. Language communication and 2nd language learning. In P. Pimsleur & T. Quinn (Eds.), *The psychology of 2nd language learning.* Cambridge: Cambridge University Press, 1971.

Oller, S. W., Jr., & Nagato, N. The long-term effect of FLES. *The Modern Language Journal,* 1974, **58,** 15–19.

Olson, G. M. Developmental changes in memory and the acquisition of language. In T. E. Moore (Ed.), *Cognitive development and the acquisition of language.* New York: Academic Press, 1973.

Osgood, C. E. Where do the sentences come from? In D. D. Steinberg & L. A. Jacobovits (Eds.), *Semantics: An interdisciplinary reader in philosophy, linguistics, & psychology.* Cambridge: Cambridge University Press, 1971.

Oyama, S. A sensitive period for the acquisition of nonnative phonological system. *Journal of Psycholinguistic Research,* 1976, **5,** 261–284.

Pacheco, M. T. Some implications of individualized instruction for bilingual education, English as a second language, and English as a second dialect. In H. B. Altman & R. L. Politzer (Eds.), *Individualizing foreign language instruction.* Rowley, Mass.: Newbury House, 1971.

Pacheco, M. T. Approaches to bilingualism: Recognition of a multilingual society. In D. L. Lange (Ed.), *Pluralism in foreign language education.* Skokie, Ill.: National Textbook Co., 1973.

Padilla, A. M., & Liebman, E. Language acquisition in the bilingual child. *Bilingual Review,* 1975, **2,** 34–35.

Page, M. M. We dropped FLES. *Modern Language Journal,* 1966, *50,* 139–141.

Palermo, D. S., & Howe, H. E., Jr. An experimental analogy to the learning of past tense inflection rules. *Journal of Verbal Learning and Verbal Behavior.* 1970, **9,** 410–416.

Palermo, D. S., & Molfese, D. L. Language acquisition from age five onwards. *Psychological Bulletin,* 1972, **78,** 409–428.

Palmer, H. E. *The teaching of oral English.* London: Longmans, 1940.

Pavlovitch, M. *Le langage enfantin: Acquisition du serbe et du français par un enfant serbe.* Paris: Champion, 1920.

Peal, E., & Lambert, W. E. The relation of bilingualism to intelligence. *Psychological Monographs,* 1962, **76,** 1–23 (No. 546).

Peck, S. Child–child discourse in second language acquisition. In E. Hatch (Ed.), *Second language acquisition.* In press.

Penfield, W., & Roberts, L. *Speech and brain mechanisms*. Princeton, N.J.: Princeton University Press, 1959.

Perren, G. New languages and young children. *English Language Teaching*, 1972, **26**, 229–238.

Picchiotti, N. *Community involvement in the bilingual center*. Paper presented at TESOL convention, Chicago, 1969.

Pillet, R. A. The impact of FLES: An appraisal. *Modern Language Journal*, 1968, **52**, 486–490.

Pillet, R. A. *Foreign-language study: Perspective and prospect*. Chicago: The University of Chicago Press, 1974.

Pintner, R. The influence of language background on intelligence tests. *Journal of Social Psychology*, 1932, **3**, 235–240.

Pintner, R., & Arsenian, S. The relation of bilingualism to verbal intelligence and school adjustment. *Journal of Educational Research*, 1937, **31**, 255–263.

Politzer, R. L. *Foreign language learning: A linguistic introduction*. Englewood Cliffs, N.J.: Prentice–Hall, 1965.

Politzer, R. L. Toward individualization in foreign language teaching. *Modern Language Journal*, 1971, **55**, 207–212.

Politzer, R. L. Developmental sentence scoring as a method of measuring second language acquisition. *Modern Language Journal*, 1974, **58**, 245–250.

Politzer, R. L., & Ramirez, A. G. An error analysis of the spoken English of Mexican–American pupils in a bilingual school and monolingual school. *Language Learning*, 1973, **23**, 39–61.

Politzer, R. L., & Weiss, L. Developmental aspects of auditory discrimination, echo response, and recall. *Modern Language Journal*, 1969, **53**, 75–85.

Porsché, D. Urteile und Vorurteile über Zweisprachigkeit im Kinderalter. *Linguistik und Didaktik*, 1975, **23**, 179–189.

Prator, C. H. Adding a second language. *TESOL Quarterly*, 1969, **3**, 95–104.

Preston, M. S., & Lambert, W. E. Interlingual interference in a bilingual version of the Stroop color–word task. *Journal of Verbal Learning and Verbal Behavior*, 1969, **8**, 295–301.

Preyer, W. *Die Seele des Kindes: Beobachtungen über die geistige Entwicklung des Menschen in den ersten Lebensjahren*. Leipzig: Schaefer, 1882.

Price, E. Early bilingualism. In C. J. Dodson, E. Price, & L. T. Williams (Eds.), *Toward bilingualism*. Cardiff: University of Wales Press, 1968.

Ramirez, M., Macauley, R. K. S., Gonzalez, A., Cox, B., & Perez, M. *Spanish–English bilingual education in the United States: Current issues, resources and recommended funding priorities for research*. Arlington, Va.: Center for Applied Linguistics, in press.

Ramsey, C. A., & Wright, E. N. Age and second language learning. *Journal of Social Psychology*, 1974, **94**, 115–121.

Ravem, R. Language acquisition in a second language environment. *International Review of Applied Linguistics in Language Teaching*, 1968, **6**, 175–185.

Ravem, R. The development of Wh- questions in 1st and 2nd language learners. In J. C. Richards (Ed.), *Error analysis: Perspectives on second language acquisition*. London: Longmans, 1974.

Richards, J. C. Error analysis and second language strategies. *Language Sciences*, 1971, **17**, 12–22.

Richards, J. C. Social factors, interlanguage, and language learning. *Language Learning*, 1972, **22**, 159–188.

Rigg, M. Some further data on the language handicap. *Journal of Educational Psychology*, 1928, **19**, 252–256.

Rivers, W. *The psychologist and the foreign-language teacher*. Chicago: University of Chicago Press, 1964.

Roberts, J. T. The LAD hypothesis and L2 acquisition: The relevance of the former for the latter. *Audio-Visual Language Journal*, 1973, **11**, 97–112.

Roeper, T. Connecting children's language and linguistic theory. In T. E. Moore (Ed.), *Cognitive development and the acquisition of language*. New York: Academic Press, 1973.

Ronjat, J. *Le développement du langage observé chez un enfant bilingue*. Paris: Champion, 1913.

Rosansky, E. J. Methods and morphemes in second language acquisition research. *Language Learning*, 1976, **26**, 409–425.

Rosch, E. H. On the internal structure of perceptual and semantic categories. In T. E. Moore (Ed.), *Cognitive development and the acquisition of language*. New York: Academic Press, 1973.

Rūḳe-Draviṇa, V. The process of acquisition of apical /r/ and uvular /R/ in the speech of children. *Linguistics*, 1965, **17**, 56–68.

Rūḳe-Draviṇa, V. *Mehrsprachigkeit im Vorschulalter*. Lund: Gleerup, 1967.

Russell, W. R., & Espir, M. L. E. *Traumatic asphasia*. Oxford: Oxford University Press, 1961.

Saegert, J., Obermeyer, J., & Kazarian, S. Organizational factors in free recall of bilingually mixed lists. *Journal of Experimental Psychology*, 1973, **97**, 397–399.

Saer, D. J. The effect of bilingualism on intelligence. *British Journal of Psychology*, 1923, **14**, 25–38.

Saporta, S. Applied linguistics and generative grammar. In A. Valdman (Ed.), *Trends in language teaching*. New York: McGraw-Hill, 1966.

Saville, M., & Troike, R. *A handbook for bilingual education*. Washington, D.C.: TESOL, 1971.

Schank, R. C. Cognitive dependency: A theory of natural language understanding. *Cognitive Psychology*, 1972, **3**, 552–631.

Schlesinger, I. M. Production of utterances and language acquisition. In D. Slobin (Ed.), *The ontogenesis of grammar*. New York: Academic Press, 1971.

Schmidt-Rohr, G. *Muttersprache*. Jena: Amt der Sprache bei der Volkwerdung, 1933.

Schumann, J. H. The implications of pidginization and creolization for the study of adult second language acquisition. *TESOL Quarterly*, 1974, **8**, 145–152.

Schumann, J. H. Affective factors and the problem of age in second language acquisition. *Language Learning*, 1975, **25**, 209–235.

Scovel, T. Foreign accents, language acquisition, and cerebral dominance. *Language Learning*, 1969, **19**, 245–254.

Seelye, N. H., & Balasubramonian, K. *Evaluating cognitive growth in Illinois bilingual programs*. Chicago: Office of Public Instruction, 1973.

Seidl, J. C. G. *The effect of bilingualism on the measurement of intelligence*. Unpublished doctoral dissertation, Fordham University, 1937.

Selinker, L. Interlanguage. *International Review of Applied Linguistics*, 1972, **10**, 209–231.

Selinker, L., Swain, M., & Dumas, G. The interlanguage hypothesis extended to children. *Language Learning*, 1975, **25**, 139–152.

Senn, A. Einiges aus der Sprache. *Studi Baltici*, 1932, **2**, 35–58.

Seuren, P. A. M. *Semantic syntax*. Oxford: Oxford University Press, 1974.

Shipley, E., Smith, C. S., & Gleitman, L. A study in the acquisition of language: Free response to commands. *Language*, 1969, **45**, 322–342.

Sinclair-de Zwart, H. Language acquisition and cognitive development. In T. E. Moore (Ed.), *Cognitive development and the acquisition of language*. New York: Academic Press, 1973.

Singh, J. A. L., & Zingg, R. M. *Wolf-children and feral man*. Hamden, Conn.: Archon Books, 1966.

Skinner, B. F. *Verbal behavior*. Englewood Cliffs, N.J.: Prentice-Hall, 1957.

Slobin, D. I. The acquisition of Russian as a native language. In E. Smith & G. A. Miller (Eds.), *The genesis of language*. Cambridge, Mass.: MIT Press, 1966. (a)

Slobin, D. I. Grammatical transformations and sentence comprehension in childhood and adulthood. *Journal of Verbal Learning and Verbal Behavior*, 1966, **5**, 219–227. (b)

Slobin, D. I. Developmental psycholinguistics. In W. O. Dingwall (Ed.), *A survey of linguistic science*. College Park, Md.: University of Maryland Linguistic Program, 1971.

Slobin, D. I., & Welsh, C. A. Elicited imitation as a research tool in developmental psycholinguistics. In C. A. Ferguson & D. I. Slobin (Eds.), *Readings in child language acquisition*. New York: Holt, Rinehart & Winston, 1973.

Smith, M. E. A study of the speech of eight bilingual children of the same family. *Child Development*, 1935, **6**, 19–25.

Smith, M. E. Some light on the problem of bilingualism as found from a study of the progress in mastery of English among preschool children of non-American ancestry in Hawaii. *Genetic Psychology Monographs*, 1939, **21**, 121–284.

Snow, C. E., & Hoefnagel–Höhle, M. *Age differences in second language acquisition*. Paper presented at the Fourth Congress of the International Association of Applied Linguistics. Stuttgart, Germany, April 1975.

Snow, K. A comparative study of sound substitutions used by "normal" first grade children. *Speech Monographs*, 1964, **31**, 135–142.

Sperry, R., & Gazzaniga, M. S. Language after section of the cerebral commisures. *Brain*, 1967, 90, 131–148.

Sperry, R., Gazzaniga, M. S., & Bogen, J. E. Interhemispheric relationship: The neocortical commissures; syndromes of hemispheric disconnection. In. P. J. Vinken & G. W. Bruyn (Eds.), *Handbook of clinical neurology* (Vol 4). Amsterdam: North Holland Publishers, 1969.

Spoerl, D. T. The academic and verbal adjustment of college age bilingual students. *Journal of Genetic Psychology*, 1944, **64**, 139–157.

Spolsky, B. *Advances in Navajo bilingual education 1969–1972* (Vol. 2). Washington, D.C.: U.S. Bureau of Indian Affairs, 1973.

Staats, A. W. *Learning, language, and cognition*. New York: Holt, Rinehart & Winston, 1968.

Starr, S. Discrimination of syntactical errors in children under 2 and one-half years. *Developmental Psychology*, 1974, **10**, 381–386.

Stern, C., & Stern, W. *Die Kindersprache: Eine psychologische und sprachtheoretische Untersuchung*. Leipzig: Barth, 1907.

Stern, H. H. *Foreign languages in primary education*. London: Oxford University Press, 1967.

Stern, H. H. (Ed.). *Languages and the young school child*. London: Oxford University Press, 1969.

Stern, H. H. *Perspectives on 2nd language teaching*. Toronto: Ontario Institute for Studies in Education, 1970.

Stern, H. H. Bilingual education: A review of recent North American experience. *Modern Language*, 1973, **54**, 57–62.

Stewart, W. A. Facts and issues concerning Black dialect. *English Record*, 1971, 21 (4).

Stolz, W., & Tiffany, J. The production of "child-like" word association by adults to unfamiliar adjectives. *Journal of Verbal Learning and Verbal Behavior*, 1972, **11**, 38–46.

Swain, M. *Bilingualism, monolingualism, and code acquisition*. Paper presented at the Child Language Conference, Chicago, November 1971.

Swain, M. (Ed.). *Bilingual schooling: Some experiences in Canada and the United States*. Toronto: Ontario Institute for Studies in Education, 1972.

Swain, M. French immersion programs across Canada. *Canadian Modern Language Review*, 1974, **31**, 117–129.

Swanson, M. M. Bilingual education: The national perspective. In G. A. Jarvis (Ed.), *Responding to new realities*. Skokie, Ill.: National Textbook Co., 1974.

Sweet, H. *The practical study of languages*. Oxford: Oxford University Press, 1899.

Tabouret–Keller, A. L'acquisition du langage parlé chez un petit enfant en milieu bilingue. *Problemes de Psycholinguistique*, 1962, **8**, 205–219.

Taylor, B. P. Toward a theory of language acquisition. *Language Learning*, 1974, **24**, 23–35.

Taylor, B. P. The use of overgeneralization and transfer learning strategies by elementary and intermediate students in ESL. *Language Learning*, 1975, **25**, 73–108.

Teschner, R. V. Differing approaches to the study of bilingual schooling. *Modern Language Journal*, 1973, **57**, 415–421.

Thurstone, L. *The differential growth of mental abilities*. Chapel Hill, N.C.: University of North Carolina Press, 1955.

Ticknor, G. *Lecture on the best method of teaching the living languages*. Boston, Mass.: Carter, Hendee & Co., 1833.

Titone, R. *Teaching foreign languages*. Washington, D.C.: Georgetown University Press, 1968.

Titone, R. *Bilinguismo precoe e educazione bilingue*. Rome: Armando Armondo, 1972.

Titone, R. Some factors underlying second-language learning. *English Language Teaching*, 1973, **27**, 110–120.

Tits, D. *Le mécanisme de l'acquisition d'une langue se substituent à la langue maternelle chez une enfant espagnole âgée de six-ans*. Brussels: Veldeman, 1948.

Totten, G. O. Bringing up children bilingually. *American Scandinavian Review*, 1960, **48**, 42–50.

Treisman, A. M. The effect of redundance and familiarity on translating and repeating back a foreign and native language. *British Journal of Psychology*, 1965, **56**, 369–379.

Tucker, G. R., & d'Anglejan, A. Language learning processes. In D. L. Lange (Ed.), *Pluralism in foreign language education*. Skokie, Ill.: National Textbook Co., 1973.

Tulving, E., & Colotla, V. A. Free recall of trilingual lists. *Cognitive Psychology*, 1970, **1**, 86–98.

Tulving, E., & Madigan, S. A. Memory and verbal learning. *Annual Review of Psychology*, 1970, **21**, 437–484.

Turner, E. A., & Rommetveit, R. Experimental manipulation in the production of active and passive voice in children. *Language and Speech*, 1967, **10**, 169–180.

Ulibarri, H. Bilingualism. In E. M. Birkmaier (Ed.), *Foreign language education: An overview*. Skokie, Ill.: National Textbook Co., 1972.

Valdman, A. Criteria for the measurement of success in an individualized foreign language program. In H. B. Altman & R. L. Politzer (Eds.), *Individualizing foreign language instruction*. Rowley, Mass.: Newbury House, 1971.

Valette, R. M. Some reflections on second-language learning in young children. *Language Learning*, 1964, **14**, 91–98.

Valette, R. M. *Modern language testing: A handbook*. New York: Harcourt, Brace, & Jovanovich, 1967.

Velten, H. V. The growth of phonetic and lexical pattern in infant language, *Language*, 1943, **19**, 281–292.

Vey, M. Le vocabulaire tchèque en Grande-Bretagne pendant la guerre. *Revue des Études Slaves*, 1946, **22**, 117–127.

Vietor, W. *Der Sprachunterricht muss umkehren*. Leipzig: Barth, 1905.

Vildomec, V. *Multilingualism: General linguistics and psychology of speech*. Leyden: Sijthoff, 1963.

Vocolo, J. M. The effect of foreign language study in the elementary school upon achievement in the same language in high school. *Modern Language Journal*, 1967, **51**, 463–469.

Volterra, V., & Taeschner, T. *The acquisition and development of language by bilingual children*. Unpublished paper. Institute of Psychology, National Council of Research, Rome. December 1975.

Vygotsky, L. S. *Thought and language*. Cambridge, Mass.: MIT Press, 1962.

Wagner–Gough, J. Excerpts from *Comparative studies in second-language learning*. In E. Hatch (Ed.), *Second language acquisition*. In press.

Wagner–Gough, J., & Hatch, E. The importance of input data in second language acquisition studies. *Language Learning*, 1975, **25**, 297–308.

Weinreich, U. *Languages in contact*. The Hague: Mouton, 1953.

Weir, R. H. *Language in the crib*. The Hague: Mouton, 1962.

Weisgerber, L. *Deutsches Volk und deutsche Sprache*. Frankfurt: Main, 1935.

Werner, M., & Kaplan, B. *Symbol formation*. New York: Wiley, 1964.

Wilkins, D. G. *Linguistics in language teaching*. Cambridge, Mass.: MIT Press, 1972.

Wilkins, D. G. *Second-language learning and teaching*. London: Arnold, 1974.

Williams, J. *Monoglot or bilingual*. Inaugural Lecture, University College of Wales, Aberystwyth, 1962.

Winograd, T. Understanding natural languages. Edinburgh: University Press, 1972.

Wode, H. Developmental principles in naturalistic L1 acquisition. *Arbeitspapiere zum Spracherwerb,* No. 16, Department of English, Kiel University, 1976.

Yoshioka, J. G. A study of bilingualism. *Journal of Genetic Psychology,* 1929, **36,** 473–479.

Zaręba, A., Język polski w szwecji. *Jezyk Polski,* 1953, **33,** 29–31, 98–111.

Zedlitz, G. W. von. *The search for a country.* Wellington, New Zealand: Paul's Book Arcade, 1963.

Zirkel, P. A. Bilingual education programs at the elementary school level: Their identification and evaluation. *Bilingual Review,* 1975, **2,** 13–21.

Author Index

The numbers in *italics* refer to the pages on which the complete reference is cited.

231

Subject Index